The Writing Family of Stephen King

ALSO BY PATRICK MCALEER
AND FROM MCFARLAND

Inside the Dark Tower *Series: Art, Evil
and Intertextuality in the Stephen King Novels* (2009)

The Writing Family of Stephen King

A Critical Study of the Fiction of Tabitha King, Joe Hill and Owen King

PATRICK MCALEER

foreword by MATTHEW HOLMAN

McFarland & Company, Inc., Publishers
Jefferson, North Carolina, and London

LIBRARY OF CONGRESS CATALOGUING-IN-PUBLICATION DATA

McAleer, Patrick, 1980–
 The writing family of Stephen King : a critical study of the fiction of Tabitha King, Joe Hill and Owen King / Patrick McAleer ; foreword by Matthew Holman.
    p.   cm.
 Includes bibliographical references and index.

 ISBN 978-0-7864-4850-0
 softcover : 50# alkaline paper ∞

 1. King, Stephen, 1947– — Criticism and interpretation.
 2. King, Stephen, 1947– — Family. 3. King, Tabitha — Criticism and interpretation. 4. King, Owen — Criticism and interpretation. 5. Hill, Joe — Criticism and interpretation. 6. American fiction — History and criticism. I. Title.
 PS3561.I483Z7837   2011
 813'.54 — dc22   2010048341

British Library cataloguing data are available

© 2011 Patrick McAleer. All rights reserved

No part of this book may be reproduced or transmitted in any form or by any means, electronic or mechanical, including photocopying or recording, or by any information storage and retrieval system, without permission in writing from the publisher.

Cover photograph © 2011 Stock Exchange

Manufactured in the United States of America

McFarland & Company, Inc., Publishers
 Box 611, Jefferson, North Carolina 28640
  www.mcfarlandpub.com

for Kim

Acknowledgments

Repeating the sentiments of the dedication, I would like to thank Kim Socha — my friend, my partner, and my love — for all of her help and support with this book: I wholeheartedly believe that if it were not for you, I would not have been able to complete this volume at all.

Next, I would like to thank Matthew Holman for his foreword: your words and enthusiasm are more than just appreciated — they are a vital foundation for this text. I would like to thank the students from my English 2238: Contemporary Fiction course from the spring of 2010: your criticisms, both positive and negative, regarding the works of Owen King, Tabitha King and Joe Hill, as well as your insights and discussions on the contemporary fiction scene, are much appreciated. Last, thanks to Mom, Dad, Candace, Jen, Matt, Joel, Mary, Sandy, and Art: simply put, thanks for your support and interest in my work. It means more than you know.

Table of Contents

Acknowledgments	vii
Foreword (by Matthew Holman)	1
Preface	5
1. What's in a Name? Intersections and Collaborations Among the (Horror) Fiction of the King Family	9
2. Like Father, Like Son(s)? The Art of the Short Story, or, What About Mom?	22
3. In the Footsteps of Fame, or, Starting with the Youngest: The Fiction of Owen King	42
4. More Than a Matriarch: Tabitha King's Canon	72
5. Emerging from the Shadows: Joseph Hillstrom King Becomes Joe Hill	127
Conclusion	181
Works Cited	187
Index	193

Foreword

As I was reading the works of Tabitha King, Owen King, and Joe Hill, I noticed a theme. In my defense, though, I did not do it on purpose.

But how could I not start thinking about mind control after reading *Locke & Key: Head Games*, the graphic novel by Joe Hill and Gabriel Rodriguez? There is something visceral about watching the characters use the Head Key to pop off the top of their skulls so they can muck about in their own minds (or, more maliciously, in the minds of others), dropping in books, and pulling out memories and emotions that look like tiny monsters. It gives a delightful physical element to the idea of mind control.

Locke & Key is not the only place Hill uses the concept. Craddock McDermott in *Heart-Shaped Box* used his razor blade pendulum to hypnotize his victims. When he continued to control minds even after his death, it is unclear if it is still hypnosis or if convincing people to kill themselves is simply the province of malevolent spirits in that world, but perhaps that is a distinction without a difference to Judas Coyne. In *Horns*, Ig Perrish's newly grown demonic protuberances give him the ability to see people's dark sides and encourage them to act on those desires. This is also a rare case of the mind controlling powers being used by a protagonist. Although Ig sees this ability largely as a curse, it is a chance for the protagonist to control minds instead of having to fight off an outside influence.

In Owen King's "My Second Wife," there is the issue of Stanley's relationship with Jesse. One could argue that it was merely alcohol and desperation that led Stanley to face down a charging emu and marry a stranger all in one night, but Jesse's marriages to one hundred and one additional men seems more reasonable if one believes she had at least some sort of power over their minds. Finally, there is that titular piece of furniture in Tabitha King's "The Blue Chair." Innocuous inanimate object though it may be, one gets the feeling that it wants to hurt Beth and actually encourages her into the self-destructive tryst with Jay. Each of these are different approaches to the idea of mind control, some direct and others more subtle, but it is clearly a storytelling technique these authors have put to good effect.

When I said before that I did not notice this theme on purpose, I want to be clear that I was not reading these works to "myopically search for the links," as Patrick McAleer describes it in the preface to this book. It just happened when I was reading for my own enjoyment. It seems that literary critics have earned, fairly or not, a reputation for stressing the second half of their titles and seeking out any imperfection that might be seized upon in order to harshly criticize a text and then snidely dismiss it, or at least compare it unfavorably with something that came before. It sounds like a fairly joyless exercise to pick apart a story or a poem in order to examine and label its component parts before judging them, and anyone who has ever had to suffer through a literature course where doing just that was the primary activity can confirm that any possible pleasure that might have come from the reading is quickly snuffed out when it is approached with that attitude. Many students in such a class will ask, or at least mutter quietly, "Why do we have to read this?" More perceptive students may ask, "Why do we have to read this story *this way*? Why can't we just read it for fun?" Indeed.

There is joy to be had in reading, just as there is in television or movies, but it doesn't always manifest itself in the same way. A particularly good one-liner from a movie may be quoted for years and years until it has lost all sense of context or meaning, yet an equally good line from a book rarely gets that kind of universal recognition. Likewise, we may ask our friends if they saw the game last night and what they thought of that amazing diving catch in the fourth quarter, but it is far less likely that we would ask them what they thought of that amazing use of imagery in the fourth chapter. And that, let me suggest, is a shame.

Perhaps such an attitude can be remedied by a book like this, in which, while paying critical attention to Tabitha King, Owen King, and Joe Hill, the emphasis is placed on the attention and less on the negative sense of being "critical." While not shying away from pointing out potential flaws and foibles in their work, Patrick McAleer takes care to point out their successes as well, while also examining the ways these authors have been constrained, not only by their familial relation to Stephen King, but also in terms of public expectation and the potential pigeonholing of genre. This overview of these three authors can be a solid foundation for those interested in their respective canons, including their more obscure works not readily available to the reading public. This book can also serve as a catalyst to foster discussion where there has been little before, and to encourage the scholarly community to not simply mentally shelve these books under "King" or "Horror" or any other one-word label, but to give them the attention they deserve.

Instead of taking works of literature like these and placing them under the microscope, let us place them under the spotlight. This is not to say that we should replace all criticism with mindless fawning praise, but more that we should be willing to get excited and talk about it when we find a place where an author has done something creative, or clever, or interesting. When a writer has achieved the literary equivalent of catching that game-winning touchdown pass, I don't think there is anything wrong with cheering and asking your friends the next day if they saw it.

A great example of this is something Joe Hill did on Twitter. As a follower of his on that social networking site, I noticed that he mentioned another user, @TYME2WASTE, several times in late February 2010. Eventually, curious as to who this person was and what made her interesting enough for Joe Hill to keep mentioning her, I followed the link. I quickly realized that what I was seeing was Hill's short story "Twittering from the Circus of the Dead" playing itself out in real time. I immediately put my laptop down, drove to the nearest bookstore to pick up a copy of *The New Dead*, as edited by Christopher Golden, and read the entire story. Afterward, I stopped to think about what had just happened. I had known about both the anthology and the Twitter-based short story which it contained, but had made no effort to get my hands on a copy. After seeing the story slowly develop entry by entry on Twitter, I was so excited about it that I had no choice but to make reading that story the very next thing I did. The next day I told other people about it, and the more zombie-oriented among them went out to read the story for themselves. Had Hill not put a portion of the story on Twitter for all to see, I might not have read it and told my friends. Clearly this was a clever bit of marketing.

Or mind control.

Matthew Holman

Matthew Holman of Indiana University of Pennsylvania has presented for the Stephen King Area of the Popular Culture Association, and has researched and presented on various issues within the field of Gothic studies.

Preface

The literary phenomenon known as Stephen King has been in the spotlight of the reading public for over thirty years, and in this time frame he has experienced reception, rejection, and most everything in between. The critic, the academic, the scholar and the casual reader all have entered the scene surrounding Stephen King with select commentary and analysis for much of his career, both celebrating his ability to capture the imagination and attention of the reader, and also repudiating his popular appeal while questioning his choices in, among other things, content and technique. The results, while largely split along the divide of the critic and the Constant Reader, have established a constantly growing conversation regarding the fiction of the most popular novelist of the late twentieth and early twenty-first centuries. But while the discussion surrounding his fiction continues, one cannot help but notice that the conversation regarding his *family* is comprised of little more than hushed whispers. Stephen King may be the primary draw or catalyst for examinations of the King family, but there is much more than the fiction of Stephen King that comprises the literary composition of his household.

While the nod towards Stephen's wife, Tabitha, and three children — Naomi, Joseph and Owen — may appear to be a call for an invasion of Stephen's privacy, the search for context surrounding Stephen's personal life is not the aim of this volume. Though curiosity about Stephen King is understandable, especially for those who utilize particular biographical elements for reading and interpreting literature, Tabitha King notes that some questions regarding Stephen, or any other author, are not always crucial to the larger picture: "As to whether he [Stephen King] was warped as a child or just born that way, the answer is as obvious as it is ultimately insignificant" ("Bogeyman" 176). Although there are certainly numerous questions surrounding Stephen King himself that are worth exploring, the aim of this book, rather, is to investigate the other writers of the King family — namely, Owen King, Tabitha King, and Joseph King (a.k.a. Joe Hill) — and their accompanying fictions. Although these writers, in an admirable display of humility, have never demanded the attention that their names inarguably attract, their fictions present the argument that attention is overdue.

In short, the purpose of this text is to examine and analyze the fictions of King's family members not necessarily because of their relationship to Stephen, but because these individuals, as writers, are able to stand on their own and have produced fictions which warrant attention and analysis due to their own merits. Their writings, despite any recognition received based on their writing ability, remain largely hidden from the public and academic eye, as is witnessed by a dearth of coverage by way of scholarship or even journalistic investigation. While attention has shifted towards these authors in recent years due to interviews, public readings and various internet presences, there looks to be a pattern of rather fleeting or temporary interest in that sustained focus on these three writers. Therefore, the ultimate goal of this book is to survey and critique the fictional territories of these writers (most of which appear to be largely unfamiliar to the mass reading public) rather than function as a means of advertisement for the King family. Of course, initiating a conversation on the works of Owen, Tabitha and Joe necessarily promotes a certain level of awareness, but awareness is different from advertising or advocacy. To be sure, this volume does proceed with the underlying premise that their writings are rather exceptional, and that the contents of these fictions will speak for themselves as to their scope and profundity. However, please be assured that criticism in the mold of discussing the lesser qualities of the authors and their writings is also present.

As with many academic texts that examine particular authors rather than entire genres or lengthy periods of time, analysis and even interpretation is necessarily at the heart of this book. This allows for critical focus to remain on the fictions of the authors to be discussed, and subsequently aims to establish an initial scholarly foundation in that the lack of secondary works on these writers asks for extended commentary and criticism. Additionally, standard literary scholarship which takes into account questions of genre, themes, and structure, for example, are to be found. Yet, the goal of this volume is not to simply discuss literary devices, utilize or apply literary theories just for the sake of following standard scholarly guidelines, or myopically search for the links among the King family by way of their connection to fiction and imagination. Rather, the primary aim is to explore the published fictions of the King family, critically and extensively discussing each family member's contribution to the current literary scene. Although the focus on published writing necessarily eliminates Naomi King from the discussion, as she is not actively publishing, the lack of focus on Naomi should not be interpreted as a dismissal of her as an individual; her decision not to publish warrants respect and the distance that is implicit with her career outside the writing circle in which one finds her parents and brothers. Further, there will be no sustained focus on Stephen King, although the criticisms that have met Stephen will be of importance and used as springboards for the examinations to follow. Most importantly, the spotlight here is reserved for Owen King, Tabitha King, and Joe Hill — three adept and engaging writers who have given contemporary readers more than tales that are branched off the success of the individual that the mass public has unfortunately and somewhat erroneously dubbed the "master of horror."

Owen King, Tabitha King and Joe Hill have written tales ranging from the macabre to the everyday, and have forged their own literary paths not necessarily to escape the shadow of Stephen King, but perhaps to make the statement that they need not be eclipsed by his fiction or undeniable celebrity. But the attempt to emerge as an original and independent writer is rarely easy. Stephen King himself says, "I've never considered myself a blazingly original writer in the sense of conceiving totally new and fresh plot ideas. Of course, in both genre and mainstream fiction, there aren't really many of those left" ("Playboy Interview" 47). Still, Owen King, Tabitha King, and Joe Hill, regardless of any themes or concerns in their fiction that intersect with Stephen King or any other published writer, each approaches the art and craft of fiction from decidedly unique perspectives in the attempt to create fiction which approaches the generally accepted standards of good literature:

> Great literature does three crucial things. It, first, effectively deals with, or reveals, some significant aspect of the human condition. It, second, allows its reader to be emotionally or intellectually uplifted, to learn something new about life, to become thoroughly involved with the characters or with a story that subsequently has some important meaning for the reader. And it, finally, must survive the "test of time." It must not be overly topical in its appeal [Hoppenstand 174].

As the following pages will argue, Owen King, Tabitha King and Joe Hill each approaches fiction with the goal of not merely entertaining the reader but to compose fictions that are more than topical and subsequently engage the reader in critical social issues. But their efforts and fiction, again, have gone relatively unnoticed.

In many ways this text functions like an introductory work, one which is not entirely concerned with a sustained or excessive focus on particular themes or theoretical frameworks that can be found within the pages that each King family member writes. Such an undertaking is something to be hoped for after a foundation has been set. Therefore, the importance of this project, as is the case with my previous book, *Inside the Dark Tower Series*, stems from *need*, as very little in the way of attention or scholarship on the works of the King family has been written. With no secondary sources other than various newspapers, magazines and journals at hand to assist with the search for information and insight into these writers, this book seeks to begin filling the existing gaps of scholarship concerning the King family. Although Owen King and Joe Hill are only in the beginning stages of their careers, there is no time like the present to begin the conversation regarding their fiction. With Tabitha King, her writing career has spanned more than twenty-five years, and although she cannot be considered as relatively new to the literary scene, the minimal commentary and criticism on her fiction, like that of her sons, begs to be exposed and expanded. Criticism of Stephen King, though, serves as a comparable foundation for potential criticisms of his wife and sons, as they face similar scrutiny and concern from readers, critics and scholars; but the invocation of Stephen and the many critical commentaries on his work are used not to distract or detract from the writing of his family. Rather, the criticisms on Stephen are utilized as starting points, as the conversations focused on his family are minimal, scattered, and in need of exposure and expansion that is aided, in a catalytic manner, by the established and published criticisms of Stephen. And it is with this overview that the exploration of the writings of Tabitha King, Owen King and Joe Hill now commences.

1

What's in a Name? Intersections and Collaborations Among the (Horror) Fiction of the King Family

Within the literary world, few writing families are readily and easily foregrounded or recognized for any particular reason other than a shared profession of writing. Even among the most notable writing families of the last two-hundred years, including the storied (if not crafted and mythologized) romance of Robert and Elizabeth Browning, in addition to the Shelley and Brontë families being noted for their literary contributions, their stories all begin with a union through the written word and have developed into tales resembling little more than fairy tales masquerading as biographies. While there are examinations of writers related to one another by blood or marriage that do extend beyond overarching if not overbearing narratives, simple investigations into the lives of writers does not always provide needed context for understanding and appreciating their work. Indeed, one must question if extensive focus on the life of a writer and his or her relations begins to overshadow the actual *works* such writers produce. To that end, one of the largest (and simplest) questions that looms over discussions of literary relatives is the following: "What is in a name?"

From the end of the twentieth century and into the twenty-first century, one particular name has continued to highlight the best-seller lists and has become such a household name that references to this individual commonly permeate the American culture by way of television shows and even dinner conversation. And that name, of course, is Stephen King. But beyond Stephen's monumental success, readers, scholars, and critics have all been exposed to much more than just Stephen's fiction — they have been witness to the King family story, which consists of the content, context and reality beyond Stephen's fiction. Both the casual reader and fanatic of Stephen's writing are likely familiar with how, when Stephen was a child, Stephen's father left home one night for a pack of cigarettes, never to return; that Stephen battled various addictions up to and through the 1980s, and subsequently conquered these demons; and that Stephen is a die-hard Boston Red Sox fan. But there is more to the King family story than just the bespectacled patriarch—notably, that he has a wife and three children, all of whom have been recognized and included in King's writing in one way or another. For example, *Gerald's Game* is dedicated to the Spruce women of his wife's family; *The Eyes of the Dragon* was written for his daughter Naomi (and Ben Straub, son of fellow writer and collaborator Peter Straub); his son Joseph was cast as young Billy in the film *Creepshow*; and Stephen's youngest child, Owen, is noted in several places in King's canon (notably, in the plainly yet lovingly titled poem "For Owen"). Although the names Tabitha King, Joseph King, Naomi King and Owen King may not be as well-known as Stephen King, the King family is certainly more well known than many other families throughout the world. But despite the familiarity that the public has with the King family, it is a wonder why more attention has not been given to Stephen King's wife and children, especially when such attention is not simply a call to pry into the private lives of these individuals, but rather is a beckoning towards their voluntary link to the world at large: fiction.

The literary marketplace is inundated with new selections each year, making it nearly impossible for the casual reader, or the academic, to be fully aware of what is available and to be completely knowledgeable as to how the trends in fiction are developing. General theories of competition, economic or otherwise, suggest that the *best* stories will eventually become known, consumed, and appreciated. Yet, as Stephen King says, "Books themselves have become a niche market, short stories are an even smaller market, and so you want to make people as aware as possible that this stuff is out there" ("Stephen King: The Art of Fiction" 91). Here he provides the reminder that fiction, despite the high volume that is produced and published each year, needs some assistance finding its way into the hands of a given reader and into the public consciousness. While this may resemble nepotism, especially as Stephen King has edited and promoted numerous authors throughout his career (and even edited the annual *Best American Short Stories* collection in 2007), any exposure to or advocacy of selected fictions are often just gestures aimed at helping one sort through the numerous choices in fiction that have been made available. To that end, as the name "King" is nothing less than a boon of familiarity that helps promote awareness for the fictions of Tabitha King, Owen King and Joe Hill (especially as it has been revealed that Joe is Stephen King's son), the favorable name recognition is still only a catalyst and does not ensure any success for the fictions of the King family. Moreover, explorations into the actual writings of the King family suggest that the successes achieved by these writers can be attributed to the fiction in and of itself. To say it another way, the link to Stephen King that Tabitha, Owen and Joe have may not have hindered their careers, but it certainly did not propel them or their craft the way that their actual *writing* did.

A Family Affair?: Questions of Writing, Genre, and Success

Exploring literary bloodlines may be perceived as a superfluous practice which seeks to find some sort of evidence for the natural or genetic foundations of creativity. However, as Lucy Sussex notes, "Literary ability does not tend to be inherited and the exceptions are rare" (22). To be sure, if it is discovered that writers and other artists are born with predispositions and predilections to creativity, such deterministic allusions tarnish conceptions of art as spontaneous, original, or imaginative. But there is a sense of intrigue with the King family, as four of its five members are writers (in addition to Owen King's wife, Kelly Braffett, being a published writer as well). Yet beyond merely noting that Stephen, Tabitha, Owen and Joe King are all published authors, one must consider that while the King family name can function as a boon in terms of familiarity, it can also be seen as a burden by way of expectations, generic or otherwise. When considering Stephen King's family, one cannot help but notice a certain expectant positioning of King, his wife, and children as those ultimately and apparently meant to reside in creative circles, those whose careers and crafts are little more than fortunate or cosmic coincidences.

Another key consideration is that the question of genre is difficult to ignore when discussing the King family, as Stephen has been branded as both a horror writer and a contemporary Gothic writer; and that the expectations of the dark and dreary have extended to Tabitha, Owen and Joe. While there are selections from each writer's canon that might be classified under the horror or Gothic labels for certain traits, a holistic analysis of any single work by these authors suggests that singular genre classifications are inaccurate. Denying genre demarcations is not just an attempt to reconsider the misleading labels that have been attached to Stephen, even though "his work has changed the horror genre and blurred the lines between horror and literary fiction," but is, rather, an anticipatory response to expectations of the fiction penned by his family members (Dyson 5). Expecting fictions of horror or the Gothic from Tabitha, Owen and Joe may be fulfilled by parts of their fictions, but, as a whole, the writings of the King family cannot be fully understood or appreciated within categorical restraints.

Although literary scholars have a pattern of consistently labeling fictions according to elements of content or within temporal boundaries, there is something to be said for shedding such encumbrances, especially regarding the Gothic; Clara F. McIntyre states, "The term [Gothic] is simply a convenience of designation" (667). As Fred Botting concurs when he says that "the diffusion of Gothic forms and figures over more than two centuries makes the definition of a homogeneous generic category exceptionally difficult," one would do well to exercise caution when approaching the fictions of the King family solely through lenses of genre (14). Also, battling the limitations placed on the King family in terms of genre must be faced with regard to horror. In some instances, horror is accurately portrayed as "entertainment of shock and revulsion" (Wisker 3). Yet horror is concerned with more than visceral reactions, as "horror disturbs our sense of what is comforting and normal," which suggests that horror, like most any work of fiction, seeks to engage readers on more than just a reactionary level (Wisker 8). While the conflicted and conflated elements of genre and expectations that generic classification place on particular works severely limits and corners fiction, the imposition of genre is only part of the equation of misrepresentation and misguided interpretation that the King family, and their fiction, faces.

Aside from expectations that have been crafted concerning genre are those which tend to view any writing success of the King family, beyond just name recognition, as a mere result of Stephen's immense popularity. For example, Katheryn Shattuck attempts to portray the writing relationship of Tabitha and Stephen as one of symbiosis and interdependence when she says, "To talk about [Tabitha] King without mentioning her husband is to omit part of the equation. Theirs is a vital partnership, a mutual support system intertwined by independent writing careers and their three children" (61). However, the sense of dependence upon one another that Shattuck suggests is deceptive. While both Stephen and Tabitha have noted that each edits the other's work with a critical and discerning eye, to claim that their successes are dependent upon one another is certainly inaccurate. Tabitha may have infamously rescued Stephen's first published novel, *Carrie*, from the trash, and Stephen's eventual connection to the publishing world may have opened the door for Tabitha's writing career. But to consider Stephen and Tabitha as anything more than catalysts for each other's writing is to unfavorably present their relationship and writing. When Tabitha notes, "He's [Stephen King] one of the most interesting writers in America, but people put him in a box, and I get boxed, too, because I'm married to him," she reminds readers that any connection noted or forcibly forged between her fiction and her husband's fiction results in a drastic oversimplification of their craft (W. Davis B1). In sum, to look at Tabitha solely as the wife of Stephen King, or to look at Owen and Joe solely as Stephen's sons, is to re-write and counterfeit the King family story.

The King Children: Naomi King, Joseph Hillstrom King (Joe Hill), and Owen King

It should go without saying that there is much more to the King family than their leanings towards fiction, whether such leanings are fabricated or real. For the oldest child of the King family, Naomi, writing is not her chosen profession, and she has been afforded some sense of privacy that the spotlight of fame does not always allow her brothers and parents. Even though Naomi is not a writer, her place in the King family does not always allow for a separation from the celebrity of her last name or a distance from the realm of literature. Case in point: Bob Thompson depicts Stephen's daughter Naomi as a reluctant artist, despite her detachment from writing (in that she has no publications to her name), when he claims, "The Kings' oldest child, Naomi, is a Unitarian Universalist minister who channels her storytelling impulses into sermons" (C01). While Thompson's portrayal of Naomi's sermons is subjective regardless of either direct observation or speculation on his part, the arbitrary and forced correlation between Naomi's profession and storytelling is more than an implicit or accidental critique of her position as a minister. The claim that Naomi is adept at relaying fictions, and perhaps in creating fictions, reflects a parochial view of the King family, a common yet erroneous perception that depicts the individuals of the King family as nothing more than vessels of make-believe.

Whereas discussions concerning fiction and Naomi King are unwarranted and needless, even though she is credited with the short story "Children of Tomorrow" (which is held in the Stephen King Special Collection of the University of Maine-Orono's Raymond Fogler Library) and was given the Stewardship Sermon Award of 2005 for her sermon "Stand by This Faith," conversations regarding fiction and her brothers, Owen and Joe, are understandable if not in short supply. With Joe Hill, much of the existing conversation looks towards the secrecy surrounding his pen name and the subsequent popularity that followed once his identity became widely known. Perhaps the growing popularity surrounding Hill can be attributed to the clandestine origins of his writing career, but the noted success that he has achieved in America with his first novel, *Heart-Shaped Box*, and his graphic novel series *Locke and Key* cannot be reduced to just awareness of his bloodlines (just as the numerous awards he has earned cannot all be explained or justified by his genealogy). While Joe Hill's identity is now widely known (although his mother mentioned in her 1979 essay "Living with the Bogeyman" that Joseph Hillstrom King is known as Joe Hill within the King family), his early successes in the United Kingdom with his short-story collection *20th Century Ghosts* indicates that Hill's writing began to garner attention and praise because of the writing itself rather than Hill's relationship to Stephen King. When Hill notes, "I wanted to come in under the radar as long as I could.... I didn't want to be treated as some famous guy's kid," he reminds readers that the doors through which he and his fiction walked were not opened for him because of his lineage but because his craft garnered the opportunity to be published and found its own success among readers (Minzesheimer 1D). To that end, Hill has reached into a number of genres and has produced several tales of short fiction, has ventured into the realm of the graphic novel, and has also provided the reading public with a handful of novels; and he has done so on his own terms in the hope that any successes or failures are his and his alone. And among the growing canon of Joe Hill, the variety of fiction that he writes and embraces confirms his devotion to fiction itself instead of the fame associated with publication, reflecting a dedication to further establishing himself as a writer in his own right.

With Hill's brother Owen, no name change marks his publications, but he has also anticipated and faced the struggles of expectation while attempting to also forge his own path as a writer. Given the pressure to follow in the footsteps of his father, Owen makes clear that his writing, with respect to content and style, is something that he wishes to create as his own:

> My writing is very different from my dad's, and the last thing I want to do is to present something as "Stephen King, Part II," and have it be something that's a big disappointment. I made a decision a long time ago that I didn't want to write horror. There's already one Stephen King, and he's really good [Shoard 22].

Indeed, Owen King has positioned himself in the writing world as a writer that is not Stephen King and does not need to be. Although literary classifications are often impositions to understanding and accessing literature, in the case of Owen King the reference to genre is helpful in beginning to approach his writing because he does not adhere to a particular genre — especially that of the Gothic or horror. Owen's fiction tends to examine the everyday lives of people without the supernatural veneer of the Gothic or the often disturbing and discomforting elements of horror. He thus separates himself from his father and his brother Joe, who at times works within the general Gothic (or horror) frame. Yet the distance that Owen finds from his family in terms of his writing is not at all problematic. Rather, Owen's fiction, whether one finds it to be profound or in need of sharp criticism, truly sets the tone for the King family in terms of individualism, which is something that each writer strives for but is not always afforded, by both the reader and the critic.

Stephen's Spouse: Tabitha King

In 1984, Douglass Winter asserted that "King's wife, Tabitha, has also established herself convincingly as a novelist of the first rank," indicating that despite Tabitha's union to Stephen, her writing could and should be regarded on its own merits (151). Still, perhaps more so than Joe Hill and Owen King, Tabitha King has been cast into the shadow of her husband and has had her fiction forcibly connected to Stephen's, resulting in a certain deprecation of her fiction. As many of Tabitha's novels are set in Maine, which is the primary location for Stephen's fiction, some reviewers of Tabitha's fiction have been unable to set aside any similarities that Tabitha's fiction has to her husband's writing. In Elizabeth Hand's review of *Pearl*, she cannot help but link and unfairly compare Tabitha's writing to Stephen's, stating, "Like her husband Stephen, Tabitha King paints a portrait of the Maine countryside so clearly that you can smell the rich thawing earth in its fields and graveyards" (X8). Possibly more telling than the observations on Tabitha's descriptions is Hand's reference to graveyards in her review, further creating a questionable link between Tabitha's fiction and Stephen's, especially as the invocation of death tends to belittle the content of each writer's fiction in that it reduces the writing to gimmickry afforded by the taboos and spectacles associated with the dead. And although death populates both Tabitha and Stephen's stories, such a focus reflects, above all else, a failure in imagination and objectivity in that the Kings tend to be cornered as writers with excessive preoccupations with all things horror.

Among the obstacles that face the King family, one potential issue that is particular to Tabitha is that of gender. Although the question of gender may be viable and crucial to clear insights into Tabitha's fiction and her person as an author, to limit her writing, her identity and her *authorial* identity as solely female tends to bring burdens and limitations to one's reading of her fiction. This is not to dismiss any troubles that may have been imposed onto Tabitha because of her gender or to deny any purposely gendered elements of her writing, but viewing her fiction solely through the lens of gender, or feminist literary theory, closes more doors than it opens. When Mary Eagleton notes that "the dominant narrative of feminist cultural criticism has concerned women gaining access to the cultural sphere, being seen and heard and establishing some level of cultural authority," she implies that female authors constantly struggle with reception and must constantly maneuver themselves and their fictions in a manner to escape oppressions specific to female writers (13). And as it would be quite foolish to deny the tribulations that female authors do face, Tabitha King's fiction seems to be less concerned with focusing on feminism and empowerment and more concerned with *story*—that which is difficult to fully define but can be said to mainly concern itself with multidimensional characters and suspenseful plot progressions that ask the reader to find pleasure in the journey of the reading experience above all else. Tabitha may create strong and intriguing female characters all throughout her canon, but one is hard-pressed to consider her tales and characters as those which wholly adhere to and focus on a single philosophy, like the tenets of feminism, especially as most fictions rarely fulfill completely the formulas or expectations established by literary theories (or genres). Moreover, applying or forcing feminist readings onto Tabitha's fiction results in a myopia that tends to dismiss Tabitha's ability as a storyteller. Again, while Tabitha King may be female, and while females may heavily populate her fiction, to read her female characters through the clouded lenses of feminist theory is to miss the *story*—the plotting and pace rather than didactic or esoterically erudite symbols and references—that Tabitha painstakingly crafts in each of her novels.

Working Together: Familial Connections, Intersections and Collaborations

Exploring the connections and intersections among writers, whether such connections are real or imagined, is often done from a purely comparative standpoint and with two separate fictions being placed under the microscope. Collaborative projects, however, are not unheard of in the literary world, and neither are they within the King family. The result is a bridge of sorts which brings two writers together under a single title and generally allows for more illuminating investigations than those that may ultimately force two fictions side by side for the sake of unraveling the fortunate, and perhaps coincidental, similarities between two given authors. While certain connections among authors are rather difficult to ignore or dismiss, the collaborative projects among the members of the King family are rather interesting and revealing— in that the cooperative efforts which comprise their respective collaborative works inherently ask that each writer's efforts be examined.

As Stephen King has teamed with Peter Straub to pen the adventures of Jack Sawyer in *The Talisman* and *Black House*, and as Tabitha King finished writing *Candles Burning* after the original author, Michael McDowell, passed away before the book was finished, these collaborations reveal much about each author. But more interesting is the collaboration and cooperation that has occurred solely within the King family, adding yet another layer to the deep story of the King family that complicates the forming picture of individual and independent writers, each approaching the art of fiction from different angles and perspectives. Some collaborations are not widely known or available, such as the cooperative project between Joe and Stephen, titled "But Only Darkness Loves Me," that is held in the Special Collections of the Raymond Fogler Library at the University of Maine in Orono. Additionally, it was reported in 2005 that Owen and Joe were "working on a screenplay of *Fadeaway*, a basketball murder mystery" (McGee 22). Although *Fadeaway* remains unfinished, or at least unavailable to the public, one collaboration among the members of the King family has been written and has begun circulating among the masses for reading pleasure (or consumption, depending on one's view): "Throttle." This story, written in homage to Richard Matheson's short story "Duel," comes from the pens and minds of Stephen King and Joe Hill, and together they create a tale that reads as a genuine collaboration, with neither writer's voice or style dominating the tale. The end result is a story that simply explores the human condition when faced with extraordinary circumstances and coincidences, which serves as an appropriate reflection of the King family fiction—that which may be considered horrific but ultimately functions as more than entertainment without arrogantly insisting upon a greater truth to be found in the text.

"Throttle" can be summed up as a story in which a drug deal simply goes bad for a band of bikers dubbed the Tribe, a collection of former military soldiers who have come together and become linked with methamphetamine—as sellers rather than users, simply to make money. With the early focus of the story looking at how the Tribe "got fucked out of sixty grand," there hides an implicit criticism of veteran treatment in America (King and Hill 19). "Throttle" intimates that the Tribe's involvement in the drug trade is more embarrassing than shameful and illegal, in that it is assumed these veterans have to resort to illegal activity as a means of sustenance. Additionally, with the references to the military, "Throttle" reveals the first indication of collaboration between Stephen and Joe, as both the Vietnam War and the Iraq War are included as backstory for the members of the Tribe. With Vietnam being a prevalent aspect of Stephen's early adult life, and as Iraq is in the forefront of Joe's adult life, the memories and images of each war within the story function as a bridge between generations—those that separate the authors and characters in the story—and also serves as a critical reminder of the near-constant presence that war has had in American history. Although the military references in "Throttle" mainly function as peripheral elements of the story, the inherent criticism of war in this story cannot go unnoticed, especially when recalling numerous instances in which Stephen has made his opposition to the war in Vietnam and Iraq fairly well known. But "Throttle" is by no means a fictional soapbox for Stephen and Joe, as their use of war, whether through allusion or otherwise, primarily propels the story towards a conclusion reflective of a war-like mentality: anything short of victory results in death.

With the drug deal gone awry, the leader of the Tribe, Vince Adamson, and the rest of the bikers that make up this group end up facing more than just the prospect of lost money when death enters into the story. Mistrust and miscommunication arise among the Tribe and their dealer, Dean Clarke, and the story then takes readers into the realm of the grotesque with two brutal murders—one by machete (Dean Clarke's girlfriend, Jackie Laughlin) and another by shovel (Dean Clarke). At this juncture, "Throttle" underscores the questionable and detestable elements of the drug world, as the murders of Clarke and Laughlin are performed in such a manner that the lost money, which is the initial focus of the Tribe, becomes rather unimportant. Not only is there the prospect of legal ramifications when the bodies of Clarke and Laughlin are eventually discovered, but the mental and moral anguish stemming from the brutality of taking a life by brutal, savage means that are largely unimaginable prompts several members of the Tribe to reconsider their current life paths: "Most of these guys have never seen anything that heavy and

I think a bunch — the smart ones — are going to scatter to the four corners of the earth, as soon as they can. Find a new purpose for being" (King and Hill 26). Here the focus on survival in "Throttle" shifts from that of the economic to actual physical survival, as the Tribe must face their ruined drug deal and a clouded future as a result. But more than uncertainty, the Tribe is subjected to revenge for the deaths that they caused.

As chance and plotting would have it, the murdered Jackie Laughlin is the daughter of a trucker who not only learns of his daughter's death in a quick and timely fashion, but also, as serendipity would have it, discovers the identity of her killers. As the story progresses, this trucker follows the Tribe and begins to take their lives by running them down with his truck. The man in the truck is eventually killed when the Tribe force him and his truck off the road with the help of a homemade flash bomb; but beyond the chase for retribution and the pursuit of survival, "Throttle" takes its most interesting turn in the end with the exploration of the father-son relationship between the leader of the Tribe, Vince Adamson, and his son, John "Race" Adamson. Early in the tale, Vince tells his son, "You know just because I'm your father doesn't mean I got to like you," which effectively foreshadows the ultimate conclusion of "Throttle," with Vince and Race parting ways as two people with little in common other than their last name (King and Hill 31). The strained father-son relationship woven into "Throttle" has the potential to be given inflated significance due to the fact that the story itself is crafted by a father-son tandem. And while it would be hard to resist a reading of "Throttle" and its treatment of turbulent family life as a possible insight into the King family, such is assuredly not at the center of the story or the King family.

In assuming that a strained father-son relationship on behalf of the authors could not have resulted in the successful completion of "Throttle," it can be reasonably concluded that the story is not reflective or indicative of some dark and hidden aspect of the relationship between Stephen King and his son Joseph. However, with numerous potential entry points into the minds and lives of the King family that the collaborative project "Throttle" provides (since each and every fiction written by any member of the King family can serve as a roadway into the personal), some investigations are rather needless if not presumptuous, as is also the case with symbolism in fiction. Although Joseph Reino claims that "symbolism is often more poetic and provocative than the plot," speculative searches for meaning and the symbolic in fiction tend to lead towards nothing more than dead ends (72). When Stephen King states, "The blood imagery in *Carrie* doesn't make it a great book," he suggests that while symbolism may be a conscious effort on the part of a given author, an uncanny or unnecessary emphasis on the parts of the whole do not always allow for a clear conception of what is being presented ("Typhoid Stevie" 15). And in the case of the King family fiction, as with any fiction, the prospect of investigative dead ends should not function as deterrents but should serve as reminders that stretching particular readings to fit certain agendas (or theories) strains more than just credibility, it also wears upon the promise of pleasure that a given story may be aimed towards. Dedication to plot and pleasure marks the King family canon in a brave and brilliant opposition to the often artificial or inflated attempts at fabricating sophistication that other creators and purveyors of "high" art tend to promote as being the only element of any consequence to be found in a genuine work of art. As Harriet Hawkins states, "It is not the artistic tradition but the academic tradition that has erected barriers between 'high art' and popular genre"; consequently, readers would do well to consider that any potential criticisms that an author must face has likely already been anticipated and purposely ignored instead of altered so that external standards and expectations are realized (113). And with the King family, one would also do well to approach their writings as work which is not necessarily deficient or flawed if it does not fulfill certain expectations—especially expectations that the fiction of the King family is simply a semi-murky window that exposes its secrets and mysteries.

The audacious supposition that stories by members of the King family reveal particular secrets and truths about the family is dangerous and results in much superfluous conjecture. For instance, an analysis of the descriptive language in "Throttle," perhaps when compared to the writings of Tabitha and Owen King, does not reveal much besides a common usage of writing convention that is fairly standard among fiction writers. As a case in point, the scene in "Throttle" when the Tribe first faces impending death from Jackie Laughlin's father includes a description that simply functions as a comparative simile: "Vince heard the grinding thunder of a big engine behind him and took a long lazy look back over his shoulder just in time to see the truck come bearing down on them. Like a lion breaking cover at a watering hole where a bunch of gazelles were loafing" (King and Hill 32). While the allusion to stalking and hunting is appropriate for the scene Stephen and Joe create, it could also be construed as a continuation of simile usage in the fiction of the King family. For example, one could reference the opening paragraph of Tabitha King's *Small World* and note her use of religious similes as perhaps an indication that she, her husband, and her sons all exhibit a predilection towards descriptive language, as aided by basic literary devices:

> Bells chimed a soft release. Roger Tinker was alone in a three-sided cell, one element in a honeycomb maze of partitions that displayed the museum's collection. The light falling from the skylights had the honeyed richness of late afternoon. Dust motes swam through diffuse golden streams and vanished into the angled shadows of the walls. The whisperings of departing visitors and the "good-days" of the staff intruded on the ecclesiastical silence like muffled prayers [3].

Further, if one were to look at Owen King's short story "My Second Wife" and note that he, too, uses similes in his writing—"The book covers showed elaborately painted action scenes: Jesus smashing the moneychangers' table with a kung fu kick, and David taking a chainsaw to Goliath's spewing jugular, and 'THE BIBLE' in bullet print above the pictures, like it was a Steve McQueen movie"—readers, scholars and critics might turn their attention away from the fiction itself and deconstruct or even destroy the fiction of the King family in the search for patterns and coincidences (such as religious references) regardless of their minimal purpose or effect (207). Additionally, while it may be interesting to note that Owen King's reference to Steve McQueen creates a link, albeit a weak one, to his father's *The Dark Tower* series (as the fifth book in this cycle, *The Wolves of the Calla*, is based upon a movie starring Steve McQueen titled *The Magnificent Seven*), the downward spiral that is created when dismissing the actual fiction of the King family in favor of imagined symbolism, thematic coincidences or other faint commonalities asks that frivolous searches for certain answers and revelations be halted. Shared references, similar interests, mirrored concerns for the larger social scene and parallel elements of fiction among the King family may possess the potential for shining light into the dark corners of the King family's literature. But, more likely than not, the doorways into the literary realm that these authors provide through their literature are simply entrances into their imaginations. Although the fictions of the King family may be more than purely imaginative or entertaining tales, they are not infallible keys that unlock purported secrets and mysteries that surround these authors.

Conclusion

Exploring the collaborative efforts of Stephen King and Joe Hill in "Throttle" certainly asks that speculation and interpretation take place, as is the case with most fictions, but, as suggested, particular paths of reading are less than fruitful. If one reads "Throttle" with limited forethought given to the authors, or to whom they are related, the larger issues of the story surface, including themes of weakened familial bonding, revenge, and greed. More importantly, however, a purposeful indifference to the bloodlines behind the composition of "Throttle" (or any writing by any member of the King family for that matter) allows readers to enjoy the heart of the fiction — the actual *story*. With "Throttle," much of the pleasure is derived from the harrowing chase and threat of imminent death which pulls readers into the story and onto the dusty, deserted and unforgiving roads that the Tribe rides in its pursuit of money and, ultimately, their very lives. And it is with this reminder that *story*, regardless of its position as a nexus of sorts for the King family, becomes the focal point of the ensuing discussion: It is *story*, as a whole, that marks and distinguishes the fictions of Tabitha King, Owen King, and Joe Hill as exemplary works by writers who simply are related to one of the more popular storytellers of the twenty-first century. While these authors are exceptional writers, they are nonetheless ordinary people, and need not have their fiction and writing tarnished by fabricated images and outlandish expectations. When Tabitha King bluntly and humbly says that "the extraordinary does erupt now and then in our lives, but so far as I know it does in everybody's," she reminds readers that the King family, and their fictions, are just another piece of the global mosaic ("Bogeyman" 176). Then again, there is a noticeable shine to the King family's contribution to the worldwide spectrum of family portraits; and with this family, especially by way of their fiction, there is plenty of substance behind the luster.

2

Like Father, Like Son(s)? The Art of the Short Story, or, What About Mom?

Among the numerous intersections that link the fictions of Stephen King, Tabitha King, Owen King and Joe Hill, one key thread which ties these writers together beyond blood is the form of the short story. With the short story itself, its consistent presence in the King family canon is not necessarily reflective or indicative of some grandiose revelation about these writers—it is simply a form of fiction, with a noted flexibility and purposely limited word count, which has offered each of these writers a form and forum for experimenting with their craft. But the focus on the short story form in this chapter is not one which examines theories and expectations of the short story, especially as renowned writer Joyce Carol Oates suggests that categorical or definitive studies of writing and the short story are problematic: "Formal definitions of the short story are commonplace, yet there is none quite democratic enough to accommodate an art that includes so much variety and an art that so readily lends itself to experimentation and idiosyncratic voices" (47). To wit, "Throttle," as a short story, reveals little in the way of the preferences and patterns of its authors, even though there are basic elements of the grotesque and horrific in the story, which are common to the writings of both Stephen King and Joe Hill. Yet, aside from possible interpretations of "Throttle" and how the text potentially reflects the separation among Stephen and Joe in terms of age, experiences, and writing styles, attempting to find a singular, distinctive voice among writers, whether considering collaborations or fictions stemming from a single author, is difficult if not quixotic, and not entirely enlightening.

Isolating particulars within fiction is rather parochial in its scope and subsequent treatment of a given writer, although theorists and critics tend to find numerous ways to speak about singular elements in fiction to the point of becoming wearisome. Still, focused examinations of the writers in the King family are helpful concerning not just comparisons but also establishing a foundation for approaching the lengthier writings of Tabitha, Owen and Joe. And although each writer in the King family utilizes the short story form, there are clear differences in how each uses the form; and there is a noticeable variation in content. Of course, there are critics who do not find any value in literature which is not blatantly or directly concerned with the purported standards of aesthetics or sophistication. One such critic is S. T. Joshi, who asks, "Can one really believe that [Stephen] King's comic book plots, TV movie dialogue, and soap opera sentimentality have any value as social commentary?" (93). On the other hand, there are those critics and scholars, such as Tony Magistrale, who dismiss the sharp and scathing criticisms of Stephen King: "King must be viewed as a serious social critic whose work reflects some of the core concerns treated throughout the American literary tradition" (157). Beyond simple comparisons and observing similarities between King's writing and that of, say, Herman Melville, Flannery O'Connor or even Toni Morrison (authors whose writing tends to be viewed as an insight into the flaws of humankind through a purely artistic and literary means of conveyance), Stephen King's writing should need no such backdrop to tout its merits and qualities as a keen look into the American psyche. And with regard to Tabitha King, Owen King and Joe Hill, their fictions also need not be attacked for their varied approaches towards similar ends: entertainment and illumination without the domineering sway of the didactic or the arrogant severely affecting and directing how one reads.

In terms of form, Joe Hill's short fiction best reflects the experimentation offered by the short story, as his writing is not limited to just words (as seen in his forays into comics). And in terms of content, the short stories of the King family are comprised of a wide range of topics and themes which ultimately displays an overarching *absence* of horror, at least in terms of standard definitions and expectations of horror (which includes monsters and monstrosities, coupled with disturbing and grotesque locations and occurrences). Yet, as noted previously, horror is a genre that encompasses much more than the mainstream conceptions depicting horror as that which is primarily concerned with revulsion. Horror, like the short story, is flexible enough to encompass questions and issues pertaining to race, family, and other common locales of everyday life that are rarely depicted as horrific, despite the dark and troubling occurrences that tend to constantly occur within such circles. Further, when Stephen King suggests in his cornerstone contribution to the study of horror as a genre within fiction and film, *Danse Macabre*, that "we make up horror to help us cope with the real ones," he implies that fiction is a vehicle for facing and confronting particular elements of life, although sometimes rare, which warrant attention if not also action (27). However, Owen King and John McNally suggest that some fictions, whether they are indirectly horrific or otherwise, are not as profound or powerful as other fictions, which are more forceful and candid in their examinations of the human condition and the world at large: "What use is all this fancy in the face of so much real darkness? If we're honest, we have to concede that it's probably no use at all" (xiii).

But somewhere in the middle of the spectrum of fiction that can be derived from the commentary of Stephen King, Owen King and John McNally is a range which positions fiction as a key to understanding the self and perhaps altering the world, because "works of popular culture often provide a quiet forum in which the viewers and readers of America symbolically address serious concerns of the day" (Gallagher 48). And within the short fiction of the King family, even though Stephen claims that with the short story, "current conditions [are] stable, but apt to deteriorate in the years ahead," one finds that their stories run the gamut of approaches and concerns, providing not just additional doorways into the rest of their fiction but also instances of the world at large captured in fiction for the purpose of instigating introspection, discussion, and even change ("Introduction" xviii). The suggestion, or hopeful implication, resulting from this broad starting point concerning the fictions of the King family is that perhaps fiction has developed into that which is more than mere entertainment with little use value, and that fiction is crafted in the hope that it is accepted as something both useful *and* enjoyable, and that will endure past the current market flooding and pressures.

From the Horrific to the Mundane: The Example of Stephen King's Short Fiction

Stephen King has composed well over two hundred short stories, and each story is distinct and unique from one another. Of course, there is a noted tendency in Stephen's fiction to connect to other stories by way of shared characters or shared locations; but among the universe that he has created, each tale, connected or isolated, only provides the smallest glimpse into his expansive body of work. Beyond breadth and intertextuality, as critics have constantly attacked Stephen's corpus of novels for a variety of subjective and sometimes elitist reasons, his short stories are considered by some to be a rather poor representation of his writing: "King's short stories sometimes conclude with O. Henry–like endings, which, though momentarily pleasurable to millions of unsophisticated readers (who are only concerned with what horror 'finally happens'), have been justly censured by perceptive reviewers" (Reino 102). Although such criticisms of Stephen King and his writing are aimed directly at him, these criticisms, along with comparisons of Stephen King's fiction to his wife and sons, are actually useful tools for moving into the discussions on Tabitha King, Owen King and Joe Hill. With that said, among the multitude of short stories that Stephen has penned, the three tales to be discussed here are "Man with a Belly," "Morality" and "The Man in the Black Suit." These tales provide not just a representative temporal range of Stephen's publication history, but also differ to a degree that one is able to observe several concerns treated in vastly different ways. Moreover, the range that Stephen King has shown his Constant Reader throughout his career is something that most definitely runs in the family, as each author displays a sharp eye regarding their peers and society while also foregrounding their abilities as writers to construct and craft engaging and entertaining stories. And as a doorway into the fictions of the King family, Stephen King enters into the discussion only briefly as a backdrop and means of comparison for the pointed and pleasurable stories written by his wife and sons.

The first of the stories to be discussed, "Man with a Belly," is crafted in the mold of Stephen's attempts to capture elements of the Mafia culture, such as "Quitters, Inc." and, to a lesser extent, *Thinner* or *The Drawing of the Three*. "Man with a Belly" is a tale about a hit-man who accepts an assignment that does not include murder but rather rape. Vito Correzente, a noted mobster who is shamed by his wife's extravagant lifestyle (as her frivolous spending reflects poorly upon Vito), tells his "hit-man" Bracken, "It's my wife. I want you to rape her…. I want you to hurt her" (S. King, "Man with a Belly" 22). Incidentally, and perhaps due to the nature of this story, it has only been published twice—first in 1978 in the December issue of *Cavalier* and again in 1979 in another "gentlemen's" magazine, *Gent*—and the story is not well-circulated among Stephen King's readers even though the description of the rape itself gives way to a focus on the preceding struggle involved in Bracken's hit as he ultimately batters Vito's wife so that he can complete the rape. However, with the tried and tested elements of pride, shame, money, power, influence, greed and fidelity all surfacing in "Man with a Belly," this story becomes more than an attempt to disgust readers with the inclusion of rape and seeks to do more than capitalize on the success of, say, Mario Puzo's *The Godfather*, especially as Vito Correzente's justification for wanting to see his wife raped reflects outdated ideals which still find their way in American society. To clarify, after Bracken rapes Vito's wife Norma, he says to her, "I am told to tell you that this is how your husband pays a debt to his honor," which can certainly be read as a criticism of the fascination and obsession that people have with the arbitrary and often pointless value of honor (S. King, "Man with a Belly" 23). The story then takes a rather unbelievable turn, as if the original premise were believable enough, as Norma hires Bracken to impregnate her as a form of revenge against Vito Correzente. Illegitimacy and inserting one's bloodline into another family has a medieval feel, in the mold of Tristan and Iseult, but Stephen's imagination regarding the baseless and overpowering notion of honor provides "Man with a Belly" a key underlying theme that holds much importance for the story and serves as an example of Stephen's critical eye on social and cultural norms, especially when focus is shifted slightly to consider that Bracken not only accepts an assignment to commit rape, but also takes payment for the act.

As "Man with a Belly" and its 1978/9 publication date might suggest a certain timeliness in its content and criticisms, any reader of Stephen King's fiction would do well to consider that at the heart of most of his stories are ideas which transcend temporal limitations, though his fictions cannot be considered entirely universal either. Although one of Stephen's more recent fictions, "Morality," looks to provide a darkly humorous presentation of the American economic woes that mark the end of the first decade of the new millennium, the inherent question of this story — what would a given individual do for a sizeable sum of money? — extends far beyond the specific time in which it was published, especially considering "Man with a Belly" visits the very same question. In "Morality," however, a young couple, Chad and Nora Callahan, face financial difficulties partly due to the economic environment and partly because of Chad's profession as a teacher: "With the hiring freeze in effect in the city schools, subbing was the best Chad could do.... As a sub, he sometimes spent weeks on the bench" (S. King, "Morality" 58). As to whether or not Stephen's experience as a teacher in the early 1970s influenced this particular element of the story, or if the constant outcry regarding underpaid teachers is the inspiration for making Chad a teacher, is up for debate. Yet an interesting twist to "Morality" is that Chad, like Stephen at the beginning of his teaching career, is attempting to break into the publishing world; he is composing a book based on his teaching. Although the early reviews by Chad's agent are promising, there are no guarantees, which may further place "Morality" in the category of a thinly-veiled autobiography, as Stephen, too, hardly had any guarantees that his desire to write fiction for a living would actually materialize. However, despite the similarities between the author and the characters in "Morality," resisting the urge to connect Stephen's writing to his personal life is just as warranted as ignoring some of the intertextual elements of his writing (in that the surname of the main characters, Callahan, is little more than a shared and recycled name of the priest Donald Callahan from '*Salem's Lot*). Indeed, the primary concern of this tale is money and its dubious yet prosperous union with, as the title suggests, morality.

Aside from the struggling Callahan couple, "Morality" features the Reverend George Winston, a retired preacher who suffers a stroke and eventually ends up in Nora's care. Winston comes from a wealthy family, and in conjunction with the various perks offered by his position within the church, Winston remains well-to-do. Yet the Reverend holds an uncanny secret desire: "I have only one regret: In all my years, I've never committed one of the sins I've spent a lifetime warning my various flocks about" (S. King, "Morality" 60). But as the Reverend has suffered a stroke, his ability to commit a sin is limited; and he anticipates that his desire for sin can be accomplished vicariously through Nora, and that this act can be bought from her for $200,000 cash. Of course, Nora ultimately injures a child at a public playground while the child's mother is not paying attention, striking the child with her fist, and capturing the moment on video for the Reverend to witness and replay at his leisure. And while Nora fulfills the terms of the deal (in which the Reverend clearly and sickeningly states that for his sin, "I expect to see blood flow. Let *me* be clear about *that*"), Stephen King's "Morality" comes to function as more than just a glimpse into the unexpected or even the unbelievable in terms of a priest that wishes to see harm come to another person (S. King, "Morality" 63). Assuredly, "Morality" is an example of fiction within the Stephen King canon that does not fear to ask frightening or unheard of questions, which includes pondering as to what can be bartered in exchange for one's morals or ethics. And while money is highlighted as a root of evil, or at least of mischief, in "Morality" the lure of the unknown or forbidden, despite better judgment, offers a strangeness and excitement to most anyone. And while the Reverend serves as an example of one who would otherwise seem incorruptible yet shows a desire for that which he knows he should have no yearning, "Morality" is anything but an attack on the clergy, despite Stephen's noted distance from organized religion ("Everything I see about organized religion appalls me" ["*Penthouse* Interview" 187]). If anything, "Morality" is an attack on the capitalist regime and ideologies that have run rampant and, ultimately, pushed Chad and Nora to the financial brink. But "Morality," like many of Stephen's other tales, cannot be reduced to one major purported theme or read solely through a particular lens, such as a Marxist reading.

More than money alone, "Morality" asks readers to consider the costs, especially imagined or intangible costs, of acting in a manner that contradicts decency and common sense. For Nora, the hidden cost of her agreement with Reverend Winston is a sense of guilt that manifests in itself a newfound desire for a sadomasochistic sex life, which comes to include excessive physicality as she forcibly asks to be slapped and hit by Chad. As Chad grows leery and tired of Nora's altered sexual appetites, and later refuses to be rough with Nora, "Morality" moves to its expected ending; Nora and Chad split, leaving Nora with the looming burdens and consequences of amenable and negotiable morality which costs her more than just her marriage.

Stephen King, just like Tabitha King, Owen King and Joe Hill, constantly faces the burden of expectation, and typically the reading public desires from him tales of the horrific and the macabre, or rather near-cliché stories that tend to resemble one another. With "Man with a Belly," one could argue that the horrors of rape portrayed in this story is an instance in which King has crossed some sort of imaginary line separating good taste from good storytelling. And with "Morality," the prospect of hiring an individual to harm a child, even among the larger picture of financial strain and extreme manifestations of guilt, could be perceived by some readers as Stephen blatantly and brazenly moving into a zone of discomfort into which not even his most loyal readers would dare follow. But for every example of Stephen King "crossing the line" or simply adhering to the demands of his audience, there is another example of a story that does not necessarily seek to be anything more than just an enjoyable *story*, which is the case with "The Man in the Black Suit."

As Stephen opens the story with the narrator providing a disclaimer of sorts—"I've never told anyone about what happened at the fork in the stream that day, and I never will ... at least not with my mouth"—the tale begins not only with a sense of mystery and secrecy but that of tension, with which the reader becomes engaged and enraptured (S. King, "The Man in the Black Suit" 35). Although such an opening could be considered a gimmick, Stephen dispels this potential criticism when he clarifies the narrator's position within the story as one who is relaying one of his own experiences, one that has haunted him for decades. As the narrator states that "a man in his nineties should be well past the terrors of his childhood," "The Man in the Black Suit" completes its initial climb towards a sort of primary climax which reveals the purpose for telling the rest of the story—that the narrator is not only telling a story but is, rather, relaying the horrors of his childhood for catharsis (S. King, "The Man in the Black Suit" 36). With the relief that the narrator finds in telling his story, and with no real audience imagined, "The Man in the Black Suit" is therefore hardly a story dedicated to horror and atrocity, which many readers incorrectly perceive to be the core of Stephen King's canon. Rather, most of the horror connected to this story comes from the author's experience in writing it.

Moving from the fictional elements of writing within "The Man in the Black Suit," Stephen King admits his own real frustrations with the tale itself and describes it as *"a rather humdrum folktale told in pedestrian language"* ("The Man in the Black Suit" 68). Stephen also describes the process of writing "The Man in the Black Suit" as rather painful and that he simply finished the story because *"sometimes stories cry out to be told in such loud voices that you write them just to shut them up"* ("The Man in the Black Suit" 68). Regardless of Stephen's harsh criticism of his writing and his story, "The Man in the Black Suit" won the O. Henry Best Short Story competition for 1996. But more important than the author's criticisms of his fiction and the accolades received from the outside world is that this story does not seek to be anything more than just a story, which poses problems for literary critics who are unsatisfied with purportedly simple yarns. To that end, although the foundation for this fiction in which the narrator recounts a meeting with the Devil is similar to Nathaniel Hawthorne's celebrated "Young Goodman Brown," readers and scholars of Stephen King know that his links to other earlier writers (namely, Poe and Lovecraft) are bonds of genre and content rather than plot and intent.

Although most any writer of horror or the Gothic might approach a description of the Devil in the same manner that Stephen does ("I recognized the aroma baking up from the skin under the suit—the smell of burnt matches. The smell of sulfur. The man in the black suit was the Devil"), Stephen breaks from his literary predecessors, especially Hawthorne, and ensures that his story takes on an identity of its own (S. King, "The Man in the Black Suit" 47). True to the juvenile yet entertaining elements of his early fictions, Stephen writes of the Devil in "The Man in the Black Suit" as more than just a purely evil character, and he portrays the Devil as an individual akin to his comedic yet frightening Randall Flagg (*The Stand, The Eyes of the Dragon, The Dark Tower*) when the Devil sarcastically makes note of how the narrator, Gary, has expressed his fear by urinating in his pants: "Opal! Diamond! Sapphire! Jade! I smell Gary's lemonade!" (S. King, "The Man in the Black Suit" 48). Although critics have noted, perhaps with disgust or arrogance, that Stephen "writes about the less commonly mentioned aspects of human life: shitting, farting, pants-wetting, nose-picking," his willingness to write fiction that shuns elitism and the fabrications of the human condition that "high" art often seeks and creates speaks volumes of his craft and his overall believability as a writer (Labrie 54). If truth be told, what is more real than vulgar language and bowel movements? Additionally, "The Man in the Black Suit" extends its veracity from the commonality of natural bodily functions, especially when one is frightened, to the conclusion of the story, which simply reflects the narrator's opinions on his meeting with the Devil. He realistically concludes, "I feel more and more strongly that escaping him was my luck—*just* luck, and not the intercession of the God I have worshipped and sung hymns to all my life" (S. King, "The Man in the Black Suit" 67). In short, the range that Stephen King weaves into his fiction, in the attempt to capture the real from as many angles as possible, reflects a resistance to generic classification and a turning away from the classification of "high" art. The accessible and popular writing that Stephen and his family creates is more genuine in its probing of the world at large than a work of art that is purposely obscure and even incomprehensible. Even though Stephen may venture into science fiction or the mystical in his writings from time to time, suggesting that any reality in his fiction may give way to the unbelievable or the inconceivable, he is always careful to ensure that *story* is not lost, which is a foundation of fiction not only observed in his sons' fictions, but which is also observed in the writings of Tabitha King.

Tabitha King's "Lost" Stories:
"The Blue Chair" and "Djinn and Tonic"

While much of the writings by Owen King and Joe Hill consist of shorter fictions, Tabitha King is primarily considered to be a novelist. However, unbeknownst to many, Tabitha has also dabbled in the short story form and has written a small selection of short tales that have been unceremoniously buried by the years and by the obscure publications in which these tales appeared. Nonetheless, with two examples of short stories composed by Tabitha, "The

Blue Chair" and "Djinn and Tonic," one notices that she tends to be rather sharp and witty in her writing, as well as crafting fiction that has moments of ambiguity, both purposeful and burdensome (although Jack M. Bickham suggests that writers should, "Leave nothing to the reader's imagination" [74]). Upon reading the short fiction and novels of Tabitha King, one concludes that she is a writer who does not always create tales that are direct or completely transparent, which may be frustrating at times but nonetheless asks for readers to be more than passive participants in the storytelling experience. Vague and elusive tales are not uncommon and are often celebrated for the seemingly inherent integrity that these elements of writing are reported to possess, but mystery and the subsequent necessity for the reader to actively engage with a text to discover its secrets may sometimes result in imposed and inaccurate readings. However, despite any potential for misreading and reader uncertainty, Tabitha's willingness and dedication to keep some things hidden in her fiction should be seen as one of her strengths as an author rather than a weakness, especially as imagination is certainly conducive to reader immersion and pleasure.

"The Blue Chair" (1985) reflects the assertion that Tabitha King is a writer who tends to compose fiction with certain ambiguities; and as to whether or not such an approach is simply a device or a carefully conceived tactic is up for debate. With "The Blue Chair," the ambiguity that mainly marks this story concerns the focus of the title itself — a blue chair which appears to pose a threat to the main character, Beth, who notes the looming presence of this chair and that it eats "bits and pieces of me, when I get too close" (T. King, "The Blue Chair" 105). The blue chair, presumably, adds an element of the supernatural as well as the horrific to the tale with its presumed sentience, liveliness and malevolence, as reflected in the ghastly images of sacrifice that Tabitha writes into the story:

> The blue chair sat in its place, a few of her papers drifted on its seat and arms. There was something unnerving about its hideous indifference, the idiot serenity of a pagan idol, with the pale, bloodless bodies of its sacrificial victims cradled in its dark arms. And she didn't remember moving it back into its place at all [T. King, "The Blue Chair" 97].

And even though the conclusion of the tale has Beth falling backwards into the chair as "the blue arms embraced her," redirecting focus to the uncertain possibility that the main element of the story is a purportedly evil piece of furniture, "The Blue Chair" looks to otherwise focus on sexual frustrations and taboos associated with failed relationships and elements of fantasy (T. King, "The Blue Chair" 111). In short, one way of reading "The Blue Chair" is to ignore the chair altogether.

In purposely setting aside any potential significance that the blue chair possesses, the story itself primarily focuses on the relationship between Beth and her cousin, Jay, each of whom happens to be in Washington D.C. and, coincidentally, available to meet for dinner and conversation. Admittedly, with the slightly drawn out yet adeptly detailed look at Beth's back story and her familial relationship with cousin Jay, their family network suggests that the primary players in this story are the *people* that populate the tale rather than the object from which the title is derived. To that end, "The Blue Chair" initially comes across as a slice-of-life story which simply looks into a single moment in the life of the main character; but like the blue chair itself, the larger life picture of Beth is set to the side as a seemingly innocent dinner with her cousin takes a turn towards the uncanny and unexpected. From here to the conclusion of the story, "The Blue Chair" transforms into a tale which appears to be a modern incarnation of the Gothic as Beth and her cousin Jay ultimately consummate a brief sexual union based on an innocent yet incestuous childhood attraction that is aided by alcohol and the opportunity to actually have sex (as Beth is recently divorced and Jay is reported to be in a loveless marriage). But as Beth and Jay engage in their sexual congress, Tabitha, as the author, appears to display a mild inability, or unwillingness, to write of the carnal details of their encounter. Although Tabitha notes the roughness of the sex—"He [Jay] bruised her deliberately; he kept going until she was almost in tears"—there is little to no detail about the foreplay or the actual sex— which is not exactly a call for Tabitha to create an invading or near-pornographic scene but is rather a point of concern in that her later novels do not possess the same apparent shyness that "The Blue Chair" presents ("The Blue Chair" 109). However, the sex between Beth and Jay is not the most important or even disturbing aspect of "The Blue Chair."

Past the taboos of incest and infidelity, Tabitha adds a rather surprising and troubling element to her story when she reveals that the encounter between Beth and Jay is neither completely spontaneous nor the somewhat understandable if not acceptable fulfillment of misplaced and socially abhorrent childhood desire. Amidst the rough sex and the consideration that Jay seeks to belittle Beth through his dominance, Beth attempts to enact a semblance of retribution or turnabout when she reminds Jay that his infidelity will be hard to disguise, saying, "I hope your wife likes your war wounds," and noting the scratches she left on his body as a result of both passion and pain (T. King, "The Blue Chair" 110). In response, Jay bluntly asks Beth, "What wife?" indicating that he has sex with Beth not as a cathartic release from a loveless marriage or because he gives no mind to the social norms that prohibit incest in any form, but because he simply wishes to exercise power (T. King, "The Blue Chair" 110). With the revelation that Jay is not married and simply has sex with his cousin because he surmises he will be able to perform any sexual acts he desires, the core of "The Blue Chair" is unveiled as a concern regarding how people unethically and immorally utilize the ability and desire to exercise domination and control over another individual. Questions of motivation purposely set aside, Tabitha King's first published short story plainly and bluntly asks, rather, that attention be given to situations and conditions of imbalance and disempowerment, sexual or otherwise, which are dispersed throughout the society from which Tabitha draws upon for her craft (and which also receives treatment in another of her short stories, "Djinn & Tonic").

"Djinn & Tonic" (1998) features a rather unhappy couple, Scott and Heidi Kravitz, who happen to discover a magic lamp, complete with a genie — or, rather, a djinn — that fulfills wishes. With the premise and subsequent content of "Djinn & Tonic" coming across as a loose fictional ambiance for her light story, which, like Stephen's "The Man in the Black Suit," is purely meant for entertainment, Tabitha establishes a certain lack of pretension and arrogance by opening the story with a bit of sarcasm and wit: "Once upon a time — well, it was last Tuesday, or *next* Tuesday — a Tuesday, certainly a Tuesday" (213). Tabitha further establishes the lighthearted nature of the story by setting the opening scene at the beach, thereby creating a sense of relaxation for the reader and her fictional Kravitz couple, and noting that each is engaged in pleasure reading consisting of "fat paperback novels (Stephen King for him, John Grisham for her)" ("Djinn & Tonic" 215). But beyond the amusing advertisement for her husband's fiction, and opening the story with a pleasurable sense of ease (along with later implications of fantasy as the jovial and smarmy djinn enters the tale), Tabitha creates a story focused on a sharp and biting commentary as to the materialistic and superficial desires of the general populace — but without a sense of force or superiority, which allows the reader to read what he or she wants without the imposition of instruction or admonishment.

The first wish that the Kravitz couple makes comes from Scott, who wishes, of course, for money. But with no immediate proof of this wish coming true, a frustrated Heidi utters, "Goddamn it, I wish he was dead" (T. King, "Djinn & Tonic" 219). Of course, Scott dies at the hands of the obedient and literal djinn; and evidence of his fortuitously acquired wealth is discovered only after he dies, ultimately "making her [Heidi] a very wealthy widow" (T. King, "Djinn & Tonic" 219). Humor and marital commentary noted (yet set aside), the crux of "Djinn & Tonic" is found in the numerous additional wishes that Heidi acquires with her final wish, as she obtains a pair of magical shoes, which resembles the ages-old wish for more wishes. With the world, essentially, in the palm of her hands, Heidi Kravitz wishes for, above all else, changes to her appearance and status in the hope of securing an ideal(istic) position for herself in the society and world surrounding her:

> Rapidly she ran through a list of physical attributes, eliminating the softness under her chin, the bags under her eyes, the sagging of fanny and boobs and belly, the stretch marks, making herself a natural blonde with hazel eyes with perfect vision and perfect teeth. She wished herself seventeen, with a courtesan's skills, if courtesans really had any. Later, she promised herself, she would wish herself Kevin Bacon to try them out on [T. King, "Djinn & Tonic" 224].

Although Heidi appears to be happy at first with her complete physical make-over, it does not take Heidi long to realize that her wishes come with major consequences. While the basic message in "Djinn & Tonic" comes down to the misery that Heidi later endures—"Suddenly she was lonely. 'I wish Scott was here,' she said, 'I'd like to tell him I'm sorry. I wish I could take it all back'"—Tabitha is careful to avoid stopping her story with a seemingly cliché moral that suggests that money and fame do not lead to happiness (T. King, "Djinn & Tonic" 226). Taking Heidi's suffering beyond the familiar territory of unhappiness even in the presence of affluence, Tabitha further explores the costs of greed and unbridled desire when she reviews the physical and tangible results of Heidi's wishes.

In conjunction with a fragile emotional state that is created through typical yet undeterred greed, Heidi is forced to confront the prospect that her psyche is not the only thing that has gone through a radical transformation; she realizes that her body is really no longer hers and that her wishes have effectively restricted the freedoms of the rest of the world, including her children:

> She looked into the mirror and saw that the size-six body was not her, but only an approximation of a strung-out boy with implanted boobs, the ideal of a decadent fashion industry. She realized that what she had wished for her children would take away their own free will, and their own random luck, the very process of life she had given them. She had no right [T. King, "Djinn & Tonic" 225].

Faced with the daunting reality of the fantastical opportunities that chance and greed have afforded her, Heidi eventually realizes that everything she has ever wanted has all but eliminated any possibility for any another person to exercise free will or even enjoy the pleasures of the mundane. As Heidi realizes that "I'm going to have to live with this," Tabitha's story reaches its conclusion and leaves readers with a new and powerful incarnation of an old tale in that Heidi is not offered any ready or easy release from the guilt of her indulgences, as might be expected from a similar tale (T. King, "Djinn & Tonic" 226). Therefore, to consider "Djinn & Tonic" as a merely recycled tale is a mistake; but while Tabitha does borrow the general plotline of an individual who is given an opportunity to see dreams realized, only to have them dissipate as catastrophic consequences materialize, she nonetheless paves her own literary pathway, one that asks readers to confront the pressures of modern ideologies in an innovative, straightforward, and entertaining manner. Moreover, Tabitha King establishes a certain flair for unnerving her readers by way of challenging their perceptions of what will be attained if one truly desires to have his or her dreams realized without consideration as to what those dreams may entail if given a chance to become reality.

Sampling Owen King: "The Cure"

Conflict tends to mark most fictions, and these conflicts are generally described as they manifest among relationships, such as the literary motifs of man or woman versus nature, and man or woman versus the supernatural. Within the fiction of Owen King, relationships among people dominate his canon and thereby position his writing as that which is primarily concerned with the real-life and everyday issues which face and plague the world population. "The Cure," for the first glimpse at the writings of Owen King, concerns itself with characters and situations which are familiar and sympathetic: namely, failed relationships and the struggle to regain the confidence and willingness to become immersed in the surrounding social-scape—for better or worse. Although such material for fiction is usually familiar to readers and seemingly recycled among authors, Owen's constant and consistent ventures into everyday relationships and the repetitive struggles found therein suggests that despite the recognizable and common elements of his fiction, the lack of any noticeable correction among the reading population thus far warrants continued fictional treatment and representation.

"The Cure" features a man, Abe, and his awkward interactions with the individuals who come in and out of his life. As Abe admits later in the story, "*Mostly I think I'm just lonely and out-of-practice with people*," readers witness Abe's self-imposed sufferings and distorted views of the world and people in his life via the relationship he has with his mother (O. King, "The Cure" 32). It is made known early on that Abe's father has passed away and that his mother lives alone and would warmly welcome Abe home (as he is recently separated). Readers are then offered a rather unsympathetic portrait of Abe as he contemplates living with his mother:

> Put plainly, Abe didn't want to see his mother every day until she died. There was a certain way Abe liked to live. He worked in construction; he liked things neat, put together; he liked to sit at night and read a book and sip a glass of wine in peace. His mother would obviously fuck all that up" [O. King, "The Cure" 2].

The majority of "The Cure" follows the lead of the early pages of the story, which set up Abe's inadequacies and ineptitudes with the women in Abe's life, notably his mother and her eccentric boarder Dorothy Ernst (who claims that her cat, named after the lead singer of the band the Cure, is her lover), establishing more than just his inability to compromise but rather his inability to embrace change (potential or otherwise). To wit, Abe's mother observes a stubborn streak in Abe as she tells him, "I don't mean to pick, Abe, it's just you're so slow to adapt to the times. Not that your father wasn't the same way. Spent half of his life saying it was too late to change. Went to his grave without ever laying his hand on an automatic shift" (O. King, "The Cure" 19). Additionally, Dorothy bluntly asks Abe, "Are you going to snap? Or are you going to manage to keep on going the way you are now? Honestly, neither options sounds that great to me" (O. King, "'The Cure" 25).

Through the brutal self-analysis prompted by the critical commentary offered by his mother and Dorothy, Abe eventually takes a turn for the better, as it is implied that Abe accepts the young and strange Dorothy as his new lover, and that her involvement in his life is a catalyst for the change he needs. But aside from Owen King's honest depiction of a man struggling to look inside himself and alter years of negative conditioning and patterns in "The Cure," one notices various elements in his writing that appear to be tangential but still offer humorous and keen insights into aspects of the contemporary world, regardless of being seemingly out of place. And it is with these probing and straying perspectives that Owen's writing gains its distinction.

As a gateway to Owen King's other fiction, a brief examination of purportedly digressive material in his work establishes not just a pattern in his work, but also asks that attention be given to the points in his writing that he feels the need to highlight in one way or the other. With "The Cure," web pages and other computer-age technologies are a noted presence in the story, which expounds upon the growth of technology and society's subsequent utter captivation with the possibilities and opportunities for, among other things, the self-indulgence of the personal homepage. As "The Cure" has Abe and Dorothy cross paths and lives, Abe's investigations into Dorothy's person and persona leads to her own website, about which she comments, "*I just made this page because I was bored and wanted to feel important. I think we should all get to feel important sometime*" (O. King, "The Cure" 22). Of course, Dorothy's musings as to the nature of her own homepage not only serves Abe as a catalyst towards seeking and achieving a sense of self-worth, but also subtly reminds readers of the mildly self-indulgent nature of the internet. Although it might be difficult to accept that "The Cure" mildly mocks the personal homepage, especially as Owen and the rest of the King family writers have their own websites dedicated to their fiction, Owen King's writing often crosses particular boundaries that one might not expect, especially when such tangents appear to be rather critical or out of place. But Owen does not employ the side-note as mere happenstance or as an exercise in authorial power, which seeks to use the medium of fiction as a didactic podium. Instead, Owen weaves extra threads of story and observation into his fiction to simply add even more critical commentary to a medium that is generally conceived as that which seeks to initiate change, or contemplation, within the reader.

Perhaps the most revealing example of Owen's purposefully digressive writing, similar to the overt political explorations of his novella "We're All in This Together," is the treatment of Thomas Pynchon's *Gravity's Rainbow* in "The Cure." Owen tells the reader that Abe had, time after time, tried to complete a reading of Pynchon's text — to no avail. The ensuing discussion of Abe's largely unsuccessful attempts allows Owen to write about one of the main impositions to art and fiction in his suggestion that conceptions of high art are often found wanting:

> Once, Abe managed to get over two hundred pages in, only to find himself in the midst of a scene where a woman was feeding a man her feces, and realized that he not only lacked any earthly idea how the narrative had reached this stage and

would therefore have to start back at the beginning (yet again) to figure it out, but that he would — no matter how many times he began again, no matter how hard he concentrated — never finish the book, let alone understand it [O. King, "The Cure" 13].

Quite possibly the commentary on Pynchon's text, which is both a contemporary "classic" as well as an exceptionally difficult book, serves as a metaphor for Abe's own personal mysteries or his inability to understand women. Perhaps this particular digression serves Owen himself by attempting to break down barriers that may serve as obstacles to his craft. But aside from any connections that Abe's frustrations with *Gravity's Rainbow* may represent, Owen's implicit criticism of the book as something which is considered great because of — not in spite of — its overwhelming elusiveness suggests that conceptions and standards of art and writing should be reconsidered. While the insights into the academy are only a peripheral element to "The Cure," its inclusion shows that Owen King is certainly not afraid to touch on any topic. And in doing so, Owen King effectively creates fictions for his larger, primary audience — the eager *reader* of fiction — rather than creating texts that tend to be crafted for and with the *critic* or *scholar* in the forefront of his mind and imagination, losing little more than elitist condescension that finds no value or solace in a good *story*.

Joe Hill: Running with and Away from the Short Story

Joe Hill, one could argue, has become a writer more known for his attempt to mask his identity as Stephen King's son than he is known for being a writer. Although "Hill's British publisher, Peter Crowther, says 'the least significant or important thing about Joe is his parentage,'" most any exposure to Hill's fiction entails a knowledge of his lineage and his fight to keep his identity hidden (Minzesheimer 1D). Even with his parentage exposed, Hill continues to write under his pen name, which is quite laudable. Although Hill has been referred to by his pen name by his parents in published media well before his identity became mainstream news (just prior to the publication of his first novel, *Heart-Shaped Box*), the secret is out and fairly well dispersed, ultimately allowing the focus to shift to Hill's actual writing.

With the gateway to the King family in this chapter being the short story, a look at Hill's shorter fiction shows a bit of a break from the standard prose piece with a limited word count. For example, Hill's "Fanboyz" (2005) is a short comic story that invokes images of the popular MTV show *Jackass*, in which outrageous stunts that typically entail physical harm and damage are commonplace. This particular story opens with an amusing disclaimer which reflects and somewhat mocks its foundation found in *Jackass*: "WARNING:

The stunts in the following program were performed by two-dimensional comic-book characters. Unless you bleed ink, do not attempt to recreate at home" (Hill, et al., 2/1). More to the point, "Fanboyz" is purposely over-the-top with its representation of dim-witted individuals attempting to scale buildings and swing from ropes in mimicry of the comic-book legend Spiderman. From broken glass and a helicopter crash caused by the dangerously moronic fan boy, a biting yet softly delivered critique of the *Jackass*-style stunts is present, with Spiderman making an appearance at the end to save the day. The tale does take itself lightly via a few crude jokes and images, including the typical yet juvenile physical comedy which depicts trauma to the testicles when the fan boy Duff Memphis swings open-legged into a streetlight. Much like Stephen King's minor projects that do not always portray the writer's best, or more profound, work, "Fanboyz" is difficult to negotiate and critique in that it is not entirely serious in its scope and therefore not necessarily meant for literary status. Although the debate as to the literary nature of comics/graphic novels will frame some of the later discussion surrounding Hill's *Locke and Key* series, "Fanboyz" does provide readers with not only a glimpse into the lighter side of Joe Hill's fiction but also reminds readers of the range of mediums and content with which Hill is more than willing to experiment.

Further investigations into Joe Hill's short fiction reveal not only additional ventures into the realm of the graphic novel but also a selection of obscure stories which are nearly impossible to acquire. The low print numbers of the original issues in which Hill's first two publications appeared—*Palace Corbie* 7 ("The Lady Rests," 1997) and *Implosion* 8 ("The Collaborators," 1998)—account for the absence of these stories from the reading public, even though one could assume that Hill could return these tales to the public forum if he so desired. What Hill has provided in lieu of his early writings are additional tales in the comic vein, "Freddie Wertham Goes to Hell" (a thinly-veiled critique on the anti–comic writings of Frederic Wertham found in *Seduction of the Innocent*) and "Rustle" (which is an adaptation of a story by the same name written by Hill's publisher in the United Kingdom, Peter Crowther), as well as "Jude Confronts Global Warming," a story only available online through Subterranean Press. All of these short fictions, like "Fanboyz," reveal the numerous angles and perspectives behind Hill's writing, ranging from the humorous to the horrific. However, there is little in these tales that gives them any notable distinction, in that they are short pieces with abbreviated content and scope. But perhaps more important than the tales in and of themselves is the publisher of these stories—Cemetery Dance Publications ("Freddie Wertham" and "Rustle") and Subterranean Press ("Jude").

On the one hand, Hill's increasing popularity, whether such is attributed to his fiction or his bloodline, could be seen as something which he has generously provided to these two smaller presses in the hope of increasing awareness for the numerous other titles each publisher produces, which is almost a necessity considering the vast number of works that the marketplace provides, oftentimes obscurely, each year. On the other hand, with Hill and his fiction beginning to find stable footing in the publishing world and with the reading public, one could also surmise that Hill's involvement with these presses is fueled by motives restricted solely to sales. Any casual navigation of the Cemetery Dance website, which boasts a number of original and reprint publications by Stephen King and Joe Hill, reveals that this publisher leans toward the production of special editions, ranging from autographed books to limited "deluxe" editions that often sell for hundreds of dollars. This reflects Darrell Schweitzer's 1987 criticism of Hill's father, which notes, "Stephen King is not only one of the most popular fiction writers of all time, but one of the most collectible" (153). As is the case with many of Joe Hill's recent fictions, Schweitzer also notes that the turn towards commercial publication adds a dubious distinction to fiction in general, as he says, "The limited, deluxe editions of [Stephen] King are artificial collector's items, priced originally far higher than they would be if published as ordinary books" (163). This raises questions as to the nature and purpose of Joe Hill following suit by selectively publishing many of his works with specialty presses that print his fiction in such short numbers that the rarity affects access in more ways than elevated price. Although speculations and criticisms of the financial aspects of the Cemetery Dance catalogue function as a detour to the writings of Hill, such musings and investigations should not be forgotten or readily dismissed.

With only a cursory examination of Joe Hill's fiction occurring thus far, a look at his 2007 short story "Thumbprint" (which has since been anthologized in *The Mammoth Book of Best New Horror, Volume Nineteen* [2008], edited by Stephen Jones) provides a clearer look into his fiction and ability as a writer. First and foremost, "Thumbprint" is a timely piece in that the main character, Mallory Grennan, is a former *female* soldier who served at the infamous Abu Ghraib prison in Iraq and must face the prospect of civilian life with the ghosts of torture and dishonor haunting her. Although Hill is careful yet deliberate in his choice of gender for Mallory, he, as the author, does not place an excessive amount of emphasis on her sex. However, his seemingly dismissive treatment of Mallory's gender is rather fascinating, even if he did not necessarily wish to draw too much attention to his main character's chromosomal makeup. From the standpoint of the reader, however, some might expect the treatment of a female soldier in a story about war to focus on her potential struggles, especially as readers tend to expect fictions concerning war to be concerned with the masculine, as "war provides society with definitions of manhood" (Adams 2). Mallory is instead positioned, or rather treated by other characters in the story, as a bit of a "demented bitch" (Hill, "Thumbprint" 226). Although such a label for Mallory might appear to be troublesome if not disparaging, she embraces this role not as a caricature of a strong female simply resisting male dominance or embracing masculinity, but rather as a reflection of her developed personality as prompted by her career and time in Iraq. She is, simply put, a soldier, or an individual hired and trained to perform a job in a specifically prescribed manner. And for Mallory, her job entails the acquisition of information by any means necessary.

Perhaps the most telling scene involving Mallory's gender, in conjunction with her job as a soldier, is one in which she takes part in torturing an Arabic prisoner dubbed the Professor and uses her gender to torture this prisoner by way of challenging his manhood (as informed by the value his culture places on masculinity). Mallory's torture comes down to her telling the Professor that he is sexually inadequate, as she places her fingers under his nose and says, "Smell that? That is the cunt of your wife. I fuck her myself like a lesbian and she said it was better than your cock" (Hill, "Thumbprint" 237). Here Mallory utilizes her gender and expectations of her femininity as tools, rather than as essential elements of her person, to accomplish her job, suggesting that the focus of "Thumbprint" is not necessarily the exploration of the *female* mind but that of a soldier. Although Mallory Grennan is far from androgynous, she is nonetheless a character that is not bound or limited by her gender, resulting in an overall lack of emphasis on her gender which allows "Thumbprint" to proceed as a story that is not burdened with excessive focus on the discussion, or deconstruction, of sex and gender.

Shifting from a focus on genetics to that of war, despite the inherent criticisms of the tortures at Abu Ghraib that Hill's story presents, "Thumbprint" is not a tale that chastises American soldiers or even the government which has deployed these men and women. Rather, the story embraces a sense of empathy by attempting to reveal and underscore the psychological complexities and horrors of war. While Hill is rather detailed in his recreation of the tortures that took place in Iraq, noting that his fictional accounts of torture do have a basis in reality, he stresses that his source material is rather specific and somewhat anomalous. He gives the following note before the opening of the story: "*It should be noted that hundreds of soldiers have served at the prison in the desert with honor and decency*" ("Thumbprint" 225). However, one of the underlying axioms of "Thumbprint" is that "People will tell you anything if you hurt them badly enough" (Hill, "Thumbprint" 243). As "Thumbprint" moves from its focus on Mallory and her role at Abu Ghraib to shift attention to another soldier at the prison, Carmody, who also witnessed and participated in the atrocities, Hill effectively and efficiently captures the mental and moral trappings of war.

Carmody, who is both mentally hardened and also mentally crippled by his time at Abu Ghraib, gives "Thumbprint" an exclamation point when he tracks Mallory down, under the impression that she is in on a conspiracy to capture and even kill him. From his time in Iraq, Carmody learns that despite any reservations one may have against torture, regardless of the degree, "You'd be surprised what you can do to people" (Hill, "Thumbprint" 239). And with

Carmody's fragile mental state insisting that Mallory knows something of importance with respect to the conspiracy he has constructed in his mind, he begins to torture Mallory as the story closes. The details of Mallory's torture are insignificant in that the aim of "Thumbprint" is not to disturb and disgust readers with details of torture; however, Hill does ask that his readers carefully consider the conditions which may lead an individual to abandon all good judgment and any semblance of sanity, ethics or morality, which makes for fascinating and what might be considered delicately didactic fiction. Literature, after all, is not just a form of entertainment, and in many cases Joe Hill's writing displays the insights into the world at large and the human condition that need critical observation and contemplation. But this is not to say that Hill's fictions are devoid of enjoyment and pleasure for the reader. To the contrary, like his father, mother and brother, Hill displays an uncanny ability to create a sense of balance within his writing in that he, like the rest of his family, is not just able to engage the reader by way of examining the human condition, but is able to so without many of the pretensions that are to be found in numerous other fictions, which, unlike the *stories* from the King family, tend to dismiss the importance of establishing a journey in terms of the actual reading experience.

Conclusion

As Stephen King has received the most attention compared to his wife and sons, it is time to shift attention to the fictions of Tabitha, Owen and Joe, especially as their fiction tends to follow the lead of Stephen King, who says, "The story is the only thing that's important. Everything else will take care of itself" ("Interview" 116). Additionally, while the criticisms and issues are similar among each author from the King family, investigation into Stephen's writing provides ample and appropriate gateways into the writings of Owen, Tabitha and Joe. When Jonathan Davis suggests that "literary content is often separated only by its varying surfaces; the concerns beneath are universally the same," he attempts to establish a standard for effective and careful literary criticism that may not be readily accepted by many critics, scholars and academics, but nonetheless sets the tone for this volume (110). Although it may seem rather reductive, and early, to conclude that the writing of the King family all points towards the same ultimate, or general, conclusion — that which seeks to better society through distorted yet accurate and mockingly condemnatory reflections captured in fiction and through a developed series of engaging and curious events — the template that this declaration provides primarily asks that those who read the fictions of the King family shed the excess baggage of generic expectation as well as other ways of reading which distracts from the story and its investigations. Jonathan Davis notes that Stephen King uses various literary vehicles to arrive at very similar destinations, pointing out that Stephen "utilizes popular culture appeal to make his books fun for us to read, but if people take the time to read into the subtexts of his fiction, they will find that he is trying to tell us much, much more" (4). Indeed, Davis reminds readers that lenses of reading are those which are hardly definitive and can be removed. With the King family, the lenses of reading which are to be used here, including those which look towards Stephen King for a catalytic starting point, are simply tools that open the many doors writers place into their fiction. And in the case of the King family, Tabitha, Owen and Joe have created numerous doorways into their writings, none of which are definitive or absolute, but all of which provide engaging and provocative insights into the writers and their concerns with their craft and the worldly sources for their fiction.

3

In the Footsteps of Fame, or, Starting with the Youngest: The Fiction of Owen King

With the fictions of the King family members, scholarship and criticism is all but absent. As a result, one must wonder what can be accomplished if the conversation surrounding Owen King, Tabitha King and Joe Hill has hardly begun. Assuredly, exploring the texts of these authors is just a single part of the foundation to be laid here, but merely exploring a given piece of fiction is hardly noteworthy. But beyond exploration, what is there with regard to analysis and critical commentary for fiction? Common practice within academic circles of literary studies is the rather liberal integration of criticism or literary theory when analyzing fiction, which can be just as dangerous as excessive summary and overly general commentary. As Ben Siegel claims, "[Scholars] are obsessed with meaning, especially hidden meaning. They are convinced fiction is not to be taken literally" (23). Additionally, Siegel claims that with such scholarship aimed at unveiling hidden meaning by way of writing criticisms that tend to include more content from outside sources than the authors themselves, "[Scholars] want to wrench literature from writers and keep it for themselves" (23). However, as has been noted, this study seeks to open the doors of conversation surrounding the fictions of the King family rather than create a jargon-filled tome of theory-speak that is largely inaccessible. Additionally, this study seeks to do more than just review or summarize the fictions of the King family. And it is within this middle ground that the conversation specifically focused on the fiction of the King family begins, with Owen King's fiction as the focal point.

Although clichés tend to be ineffective both within and outside of pure fiction, the claim that "stories are a dime a dozen" serves as an appropriate springboard for the analysis of Owen King's fiction. This is not to say or imply that Owen's writing is lacking or indistinctive, but rather that he attempts to avoid creating stories that can be easily cast aside. While writers tend to seek new routes onto bookshelves or into the psyches of their readers, experimentation and attempts at writing a wholly unique story is difficult yet desirable for a storyteller. As Robert Bloch asserts, "If we develop a knack for storytelling we find that people are willing to listen or even to read our efforts," he, perhaps purposefully, avoids discussing exactly what constitutes a notable ability to tell a story (25). Then again, merely having the ability to tell a story is hardly notable; telling a story in a way that engages and even enlightens the reader to some degree is certainly noteworthy. And Owen King's ability to tell a story by providing constant instances of humor, insight and pleasure shows a promise as a writer that asks readers to pay attention to his publications. He is a writer who, at times, is able to effectively manage the elements of story with the critical content that makes a story more than just an exercise in entertaining oneself for a brief period of time.

Among the general marks of Owen King's fiction are timely cultural references, such as the 2000 Bush/Gore election, and bawdy humor, including one instance in which a letter is composed claiming to hold a vagina hostage. Still, providing the reader with a tale that is somewhat familiar or even humorous, if not offensive (depending on the reader), begs the question as to what such a story seeks to accomplish. When it comes to Owen King's fiction, as well as the fiction written by his mother and brother, a key question to ask is why might a particular story by any one of these authors be remembered while thousands upon thousands of other stories that are written, and even published, each year are forgotten and left to fade away? Although questions and considerations of race, gender, and even technique make for innovative and even profound literature, the mere presence of purportedly sophisticated elements of fiction do not necessarily result in exceptional or lasting literature. Or, as Ben Siegel comments on the state of literature, especially outside of the academy, "Novelists and poets are not clear of what their cultural obligations are. A few writers may believe their efforts belong to society, but most simply do not care" (2). Faced with the question of purpose and direction, Owen King forwards a belief that writing is more than entertainment, even if it is not often received as more than fiction, or fabrication, and that one responsibility of the writer is to engage readers on a political level. As Owen says, "I think writers have a political responsibility.... The world has shifted so quickly and it needs addressing. But politics is not seen as where literature is at. It's not seen as artistic. And people are wary of doing it because those novels don't age well" (Shoard 21). With the awareness that writing, regardless of any political aims or responsibilities, is expected to carry a sense of artistic scope or literary aesthetic, Owen's writing seems to become caught in a perpetual struggle that is not uncommon for any writer — to focus on message at the cost of artistic value, or to focus on craft while neglecting the content.

If one had to gauge where in the writing spectrum Owen King resides, an accurate projection would place him towards the side of the popular novelist who seeks to engage with the audience rather than burden the reader or the story with an overwhelming overflow of didacticism or seriousness. As *New*

York Times critic Jon Zobenica notes of Owen, "Despite his penchant for elaborate homilies and quaint plotting, King also shows signs that he knows how lovely a simple image can be" (F19). The implication is made that Owen tends to be a microcosmic writer, or one who polishes minor elements of his writing rather than sustain a focus on crafting a polished story in its entirety. While such a criticism seems to be harsh, if not foreboding, for the youngest member of the King family, this element of his writing, which becomes foregrounded when reading his fiction, is actually one of the more enjoyable elements of his craft. Indeed, one sees that Owen seems to constantly attempt to weave into his fictions too much material that is ultimately poorly managed, and that his writing, while often unified under a main plot, tends to consist of numerous minor elements, scenes, characters or images that, while distracting and often disconnected from the story at times, results in as much criticism and cynicism as it does engagement.

While critics have noted the very same issue within the fiction of Owen's father — "One of [Stephen] King's problems as a writer is that his subplots often do not integrate effectively with the main story or theme; these asides are fascinating and amusing, but stubbornly refuse to reflect or comment on the spine of the work" — one must consider that Owen is actually displaying rather controlled writing instead of creating loose fictions comprised of numerous elements that are barely joined together by the umbrella of a story title (Warren 132). Perhaps the numerous loose threads that Owen weaves into his fiction are simply the result of the recent developments literature has undergone, whether in the short story form that marks Owen's budding oeuvre or in novel form. As Jago Morrison claims, "In the face of the transitions and challenges of the contemporary period, we might say that it has been necessary for the novel, too, to divide and evolve" (64). And while Owen has yet to pen a novel-length fiction, the assertion that novels, or fiction, have been asked to develop beyond tightly-woven stories in which all elements clearly and purposefully relate, is not an unreasonable statement.

While Owen may just be following suit regarding his post–modern predecessors by challenging and perhaps attempting to redefine the forms and expectations of fiction, confirming or rejecting such a premise is quite difficult. Further complicating a strong grasp of Owen's fiction and his intents as an author is his sense of humor. Rarely does an Owen King story escape some sort of juvenile jab or other attempt at producing grins or giggles in his readers. In his non–fiction piece "Sports," for example, Owen begins his article, which examines athletic elements of high school life, with the following statement: "The nagging suspicion that I was a shithead followed me through most of my high school years" (O. King, "Sports" 182). While Owen's honesty is much appreciated here, the immediate movement into comedic undertones is as enjoyable as it is frustrating when one considers or comes to anticipate such colorful peppering in his other writings.

Despite any perceived faults with Owen King's humorous threads and his desire to entertain his audience through experimentation and examination of the tried-and-tested thematic of the human condition, one would do well to note that Owen does have an exceptional ability to capture critical insights and truisms and effectively relay such thoughts to his reader. Returning briefly to Owen's article "Sports," it should not go unnoticed that among his musings on his own particular developments as a "shithead," such mildly despicable personality developments among teenagers are not uncommon, and he gracefully reminds his reader of this notion when he says, "Our teenage years are nothing if not a process of reduction, the time when we either sand away our quirks or learn well to conceal them" (O. King, "Sports" 199). With this seeming back-and-forth marking Owen King's fiction, however, one is left with the question as to what purpose Owen is attempting to achieve through such an apparently muddled approach to literature. Perhaps if one had to make a leap of literary faith and take a stand as to the purposes and intents behind Owen King's fiction, especially concerning its *form* (which accounts for many of the elements discussed), an acquaintance with and analysis of Owen's writing would push one to claim that his consistency in weaving loose plots and plot elements suggests a genuine attempt to aid in the *growth* of fiction. There are worse speculations than one which implies that Owen King sees a particular stagnation with fiction that needs an injection of purposeful playfulness to accompany elements of expected seriousness.

The Uncollected Stories of Owen King: "I Swear I'll Jump" and "Nothing Is in Bad Taste"

When Owen King entered the larger publishing scene with the publication of his 2005 collection of short stories titled *We're All in This Together*, he entered a literary landscape that saw the *Harry Potter* series coming to a close (with *Harry Potter and the Half-Blood Prince*) and the onset of Stephenie Meyer's *Twilight* series. With a rather extensive focus on and desire for young-adult literature, and perhaps a penchant for childish fantasies by way of magic or forbidden love of monstrous figures, dominating the early years of the twenty-first century, Owen's fiction often comes across as a bit of an anomaly, especially if one speculates that popularity drives the market of published fiction. When Mary Talbot asserts that "fiction production is highly professionalized," she pushes readers to consider exactly how and why Owen King pursued a career in fiction when it is noted that he hardly banked on his surname for exposure, and that his fiction is largely comprised of the every-day or the "slice-of-life" content that marks a considerable portion of the fiction produced over the last several decades (163). Although considerations of fiction production and reception tend to suggest that success within the field is dependent upon the waves of mass-public demands and the market's attempt to meet (or even create) such needs, it must be noted that there are other pathways into fiction writing than name recognition or shameless pandering.

With respect to the start of Owen King's publishing career, several of his short stories had been published in small magazines or journals prior to their inclusion in *We're All in This Together*, including "My Second Wife" (*The Bellingham Review*, 2001), "Wonders" (*Book Magazine*, 2002), and "Frozen Animals" (*Harpur Palate*, 2003). Additionally, "Wonders" has been anthologized in John McNally's *Bottom of the Ninth: Great Contemporary Baseball Stories* (2003), and Owen also provided McNally a non–fiction piece titled "Sports" for the anthology titled *When I Was a Loser* (2007). *When I Was a Loser* which also includes the short work "Fuck High School" by Owen's wife Kelly Braffet, author of the novels *Josie and Jack* (2005) and *Last Seen Leaving* (2006), and who, incidentally, published her short story "Bad Karma Girl Wins at Bingo" in the volume *Who Can Save Us Now?* which was edited by John McNally and Owen King. Although one can see some networking at hand when considering Owen's work with John McNally, as well as the profession of Owen's wife, publication and networking are not always an effective means of success, whether measured in terms of readership, money earned, or some other category of success, such as simple exposure to the masses. Success, to be sure, is quite the subjective measure of a writer's ability, scope, and intention. Regardless of how one measures the success of Owen King, the simple fact remains that he has published and given his fiction to the public; and when examining his fiction, one notices not only a departure from the horror genre in which his father resides (or has been trapped), but also exceptional flashes of writing that is engaging, humorous and insightful.

Before examining Owen's biggest project to date, a look at his short and lesser-known fictions helps establish the range and scope of his writing. Within the first fiction that Owen published, "I Swear I'll Jump" (2000), the reader is given one of Owen's stronger and most engaging works. "I Swear I'll Jump" is a tale involving siblings, their typically combative childhood, their largely familiar adult lives of both excitement and disappointment, and a fortunate if not harrowing opportunity to rekindle a relationship that had been mostly non–existent their entire lives. The "slice-of-life" approach that Owen takes here, and which, to one degree or another, marks most of his oeuvre, works well in that the themes of connection and loss are common but not overly cliché. The result is a genuine involvement with the characters and their lives, which is, on a technical level, aided by a first-person narration that envelopes the early parts of the story with a sense of welcoming and familiarity, resulting in an immersion in the story that may often be met with resistance when a distanced, third-person narrator abruptly injects details into the tale. The main character, Francine Gibbon, or "Frankie" to her brother, eases the reader into the story with rather scathing commentary regarding her brother, Roger, which is universal enough to draw in most any reader. And as Francine relates several short memories to forward her tainted view of her sibling, a conversation, albeit a one-sided one, develops and surrounds the necessary background details with narrative that hardly seems like mere storytelling.

When it comes to fiction, a certain sense of strangeness or distance is typically utilized in order to engage the reader; while familiarity with characters or content is also a tried and tested approach to bringing a reader into a tale, a purposeful disconnect from the story in the form of unknown or mysterious content is just as effective. For "I Swear I'll Jump," Owen King attempts to engage his reader through an exploration of jumping—off cliffs or from airplanes—which serves as more than just a secondary element of the tale used to bring a certain sense of the unknown or exotic into the story. Within "I Swear I'll Jump," which immediately invokes images of suicide (with the notably cliché threat reflected in the title of the story), the act of jumping functions as a risky yet thrilling confrontation with death, but also can be tied to images of "leaps of faith." But as Owen writes of the first jump in this story, it hardly carries any real sense of gravity, as Frankie's brother, Roger, is brought into the story by jumping, or rather parachuting, into Shea Stadium during a Mets game with the following message clearly visible from the inside of his parachute: "**St. Louis is shit. The Mets are a hit**" (O. King, "I Swear" 11). With this first reference to jumping, in which Frankie does not confirm the identity of the jumper as she is watching the game on television until, "My brother removed his goggles. [And then] My stomach gave a queasy dip," Owen establishes the foundation for the use of humor in his fiction with both the crude sentiment displayed on Roger's parachute and Frankie's reaction of nauseating surprise when she learns her brother is behind the parachuting prank (O. King, "I Swear" 11). There is no pretense or hidden meaning behind the free-spirited Roger parachuting into Shea Stadium with a humorous if somewhat vulgar message displayed for thousands of people in the stands and watching the game on television to see, and such humor marks Owen's fiction with a distinction of challenging the norms and modes of fictional expectation.

Although it is somewhat dated to reference Dr. Samuel Johnson and his criticisms of writing and fiction, in the case of Owen King, Johnson's assertion that "it is always a writer's duty to make the world better" is critical to consider when not only examining Owen's fiction but that composed by the rest of his family (474). While an exceptional, or excessive, focus on humor (crude or otherwise) may not always be received as an attempt "to make the world better," Owen seems to seek liberation from the constraints of fictional expectations, or at least those imposed upon writers who are asked to seek serious concerns rather than popular acceptance. And while Owen's fiction at times displays a departure from the spirited and jocose foundation established in "I Swear I'll Jump," Owen is careful to avoid occupying the opposite realm of the writing spectrum of didacticism in his fiction. For example, in returning to the underlying theme of jumping and all that this simple action entails, Roger's description of high-risk jumping is notable for its candor and its casual approach to the topic of death when he addresses the possibility that his hobby will kill him: "Death is a certainty, but the jump is all good, you know?" (O. King, "I Swear" 14). Here Owen, through his character Roger, approaches images of death through the innovative lens of contemporary hobbies, utilizing activities which are finding their way into more and more fiction as they become popular, but also including such an element into his story that goes beyond simply acknowledging its existence. Contemporizing fiction by way of including timely references to particular products, fads or fictions is not uncommon among fiction writers, but actually using a particular idea that is located within a specific time — like Stephen King's use of AC/DC's song "Who Made Who" in his 1990 updated version of *The Stand* — for more than just situating a work within a specific time frame is quite the feat for Owen King. By harnessing the symbolism and breadth of jumping, especially the purported exhilaration of Roger's high risk jumping — "Those last few seconds: imagine how long they last" — Owen takes the readers of "I Swear I'll Jump" beyond the time of the fiction or even the psyche of Roger (O. King, "I Swear" 17). Rather, Owen King adeptly manages what appears to be a side-note to his story and ultimately utilizes it for managing the middle-ground between simple reader appeal and preaching about serious issues such as death. And the gray area of fiction which actively seeks negotiation and experimentation has a willing and exceptional resident in Owen King.

"I Swear I'll Jump" exhibits a wide range of topics and approaches with which Owen King concerns himself and his reader, and some of the more technical elements show that Owen is a writer who takes his craft rather seriously. As "I Swear I'll Jump" ultimately takes Francine and her brother Roger to a scene in which Francine must, too, become a jumper — she finds herself in a secluded wilderness area, surrounded by bees and their stings (to which she is allergic), and her only escape is to jump from a cliff into the water below to escape this threat — Owen gracefully describes not just Frankie's anxiety but also her plunge into the water by writing just six words: "The water elevated to my feet" (O. King, "I Swear" 21). With this short sentence, Owen King accomplishes several feats as an author, especially concerning issues of perception. Not only does this description of Francine's plummet into the waters waiting below capture an inverted feeling of falling by having the water appear to meet the descending narrator, it also provides an instance of unexpected perception that is altered and reversed to parallel Francine's imminent change of perception regarding her brother.

Continuing with Francine's jump, as she recounts her relationship with Roger, including his parachuting prank, she constantly reminds the reader that she dismisses Roger as a reckless and selfish individual. But as Francine jumps into the water and experiences a glimmer of Roger's life, the reader witnesses her reversal of perception and temperament, which is subtly woven into the six words that Owen uses to describe Francine's jump. Although Roger eventually dies when jumping — "Straight down. That's what happened, they told me. There was a fog bank and a concealed rock shaft. He never even pulled his ripcord, never saw a thing. Into the mist, and gone" — Francine's own experience with jumping leads her to accept her brother's death rather than dismissing it as an instance of stupidity (O. King, "I Swear" 22). And while Francine's growth as an individual in just a few shorts pages may be somewhat convenient, depending upon one's reading, Owen does attempt to limit the sentiment and didacticism one might expect in a tale of personal growth and death.

While the ending line that Frankie narrates is a bit heavy-handed in its emotion — "I like to imagine that somewhere he's still drifting down. And the people are cheering for him. And this time I'm cheering, too" — the ultimate presence of forgiveness Frankie suggests, perhaps in response to lost time reflected upon in moments contemplating mortality, allows this particular short story to escape a mawkish reaction and approval based solely on emotions (O. King, "I Swear" 23). True, the inclusion of death and regret as underlying themes in "I Swear I'll Jump" connects the reader with tried and tested methods of prompting appreciation for a work that seeks to reach beyond the page and into the mind and heart of the reader. But Owen's craft, much like his father's, is that which may look to literary predecessors for inspiration but also forges its own path by reaching similar destinations through new pathways. Of course, the terms "original" and "innovative" are implicit with this look at "I Swear I'll Jump," but to use such tired old adjectives hardly does Owen King's writing justice.

Moving from the beginnings of his publishing career to the more recent years, Owen's short story "Nothing Is in Bad Taste" serves a fascinating, albeit temporary, bookend to his young career. Much like "The Cure" and "I Swear I'll Jump," "Nothing Is in Bad Taste" provides a glimpse into fragile and faltering relationships, supplemented by sporadic and sometimes jarring inclusions of humor. Within this tale Owen focuses on familiar people and the easily identifiable world waiting outside the pages of his writings, which can be considered as a bit of a departure from his brother and father. Of course, capturing the realistic within fiction is not exactly noteworthy or unheard of, but the minutiae of "Nothing Is in Bad Taste" highlight does more than merely Owen King's pattern of weaving fictions that seem to exhibit a sense of Attention Deficit Disorder due to the numerous threads of plot that he weaves. In "Nothing Is in Bad Taste," Owen does approach the subject as to what might be considered tasteless, thereby venturing into questions of values that, perhaps, come with a certain generational reverberation. To be sure, "Nothing Is in Bad Taste" does seek a certain audience with certain references, like the inclusion of a Netflix reference, which dates the writing, but Owen King is undoubtedly a writer who also seems to cherish and celebrate his status and position among Generation X. And while he writes to his peers, those who "remember Reagan or Cabbage Patch Dolls or the first space shuttle explosion," he also taps into memories of the generation preceding his own (O. King, "Bad Taste" 61). Whether or not the "Me" generation will readily seek and read Owen's writing is difficult to speculate; simply because he creates links between he and those born in the 1970s and 1980s does not ensure readership from this group either. But the implicit generational gap that "Nothing Is in Bad Taste" attempts to navigate also serves as an appropriate background to story as a whole.

While the title of this story reflects the humor that Owen constantly weaves into his writing, especially as "Nothing Is in Bad Taste" includes visions of "a stroller filled with baby doll limbs" as part of a war protest as well (as an array of jokes made about death), the focus of the story is not entirely about considerations of taste or even values and their influence on perception regarding, among other things, humor (O. King, "Bad Taste" 54). By and large, this short story focuses on the main character, Cheryl, and her assembly of broken or even taboo relationships. In one instance, an early scene involves the death of a homeless person outside of the hospital in which Cheryl works, when this homeless individual, known as the Loading Dock Guy, is run over and killed near the loading docks where he spent most of his days. This small scene carries with it a dark sense of irony in that the Loading Dock Guy, albeit homeless, attempted to help the employees of the hospital by directing traffic away from the loading docks (hence his nickname). However, as Loading Dock Guy is killed at the loading docks by, of all things, a car driven by an inattentive man, the irony is not lost upon Cheryl. Further, the death of Loading Dock Guy gains more dark humor when it is noted that the individual driving the car that killed Loading Dock Guy explains his role in the accident by merely noting, "I just had to park the car, you see" (O. King, "Bad Taste" 51). As this inattentive and indifferent comment is appropriated by Cheryl, it leads to a broken relationship between Cheryl and her friend Meg, who cannot understand or condone Cheryl's seemingly callous fascination with the death of Loading Dock Guy. This broken relationship with Meg, alongside a failing marriage that becomes ruined by Cheryl's infidelity (which the reader discovers in the later pages), presents a clear focus on the question of human relationships. Still, with each relationship being asked to share such a small space in terms of page count, Owen does display a sense of restraint as well as selectivity when choosing to create and explore the small scenes which, together, comprise a story that, depending on one's reading of the title and its nod towards understanding different perceptions, champions not necessarily condoning particular actions that are purportedly done in bad taste but, rather, *understanding* why people make certain choices.

As issues of perception reoccur in Owen King's fiction, it would stand to reason that one of his primary goals with his writing is to help his readers see into worlds, or see through eyes, that the reader would not normally gaze upon. Just as Frankie from "I Swear I'll Jump" comes to understand the thrill of jumping that her brother finds, despite the risks involved, "Nothing Is in Bad Taste" calls to mind the question of whether some subjects of discussion, or certain actions, are universally considered to be abhorred or in bad taste. One issue is whether or not a sense of humor that is certainly dark is indicative of any real negativity. As Cheryl asks, "Do you believe it makes any difference, any difference whatsoever, to the welfare of all the homeless, starving, deformed, and screwed-over peoples of the world, if you laugh at something in bad taste?" (O. King, "Bad Taste" 57). Cheryl's musings seem innocent enough, just as her sense of humor itself seems to be nothing more than a good example of a sharp and refreshingly stinging approach to comedy, as is seen in a ransom note she sends to her husband: "WE HAVE YOUR WIFE'S VAGINA. GIVE US A LIFE IN THE SUBURBS OR YOUR SEX GETS IT" (O. King, "Bad Taste" 60). However, even with Cheryl's use and understanding of humor to dismiss questions of taste (as well as attempt to negotiate new living arrangements with her husband), the ultimate purpose of Owen's examination of humor is not necessarily aimed at defining or redefining boundaries of the comedic. Rather, Owen attempts to direct questions of taste away from the realm of humor, and points the debate towards perception and how one understands the way in which another individual arrives at his or her point of view. To that end, with the political elements of "Nothing Is in Bad Taste" highlighting the political polarity of the American social-scape and the seeming inability to even consider listening to another individual's point of view, Owen asks his readers (although in quite the roundabout way) to consider how something is constructed or perceived to be tasteless.

To clarify, Owen presents the reader with a barrage of politically-founded ideals, including such witticisms as, "Every time a soldier bleeds out in the sand, a liberal gets his wings" (O. King, "Bad Taste" 55). This harsh yet familiar rhetoric that marks the social and political scene in Owen King's America is undoubtedly disconcerting in that these empty and everyday comments warrant examination for some sort of understanding. In other words, it is safe to assume that if a reader were to be offended by or opposed to such a statement, it would not matter — this declaration, albeit heavily charged, is not in bad taste. Rather, it simply expresses, although poorly, a particular political leaning. And with such rhetoric avoiding both outright attachment or endorsement by Owen himself, one sees that "Nothing Is in Bad Taste" serves as a call to avoid knee-jerk reactions to ideas that could be construed as reflecting "bad taste." Therefore, one might conclude that the underlying premise of "Nothing Is in Bad Taste" questions if one is able to dismiss questions or concerns about taste with respect to any issue and, rather, aim at understanding why particular people say and/or believe certain ideals that might be construed as tasteless. Indeed, searching for understanding rather than attempting immediate rebuttal to a notion that one may disagree with for whatever reason is quite a lofty yet worthwhile endeavor.

Beyond speculations as to taste and understanding the thought process behind beliefs or declarations that are taken to be offensive, ignorant, or venomous, the other side to the human condition that Owen King examines in "Nothing Is in Bad Taste" involves the marriage between Cheryl and her husband, Leonard. Quite simply, the story ends with the revelation that Cheryl had been having an affair with a doctor at her hospital and subsequently became impregnated due to her infidelity. While this is not exactly an original or heart-stopping revelation, it does tie the entire story together quite well. With the focus on the human condition, as well as events and occurrences that have become rather mundane regardless of their taboo or offensive nature, such as heated war protests and unfaithful marriages, Owen's look into the crumbling life of Cheryl nonetheless solidifies the declaration of the story's title — that nothing is in bad taste if properly examined and understood. Again, while it would be safe to assume that Owen is not condoning infidelity, or engaging in harsh political discussions that brew hatred rather than promote unity despite differences in opinion, he does posit that, at the very least, understanding can and should be reached regarding any situation. Further, one of Owen's more telling examinations of Cheryl's and Leonard's marriage does not come with an image of disintegration involving a fighting couple, but rather "the separate showers, the glasses of water, the exaggerated politeness, his apology, her apology for making it seem like an apology was necessary, and then sleep, if she could relax enough" (O. King, "Bad Taste" 52). Instead, Owen looks towards the actual intimacy between Cheryl and Leonard, and its measure in the way that they speak to each other (much like how intimate language is explored in Stephen King's *Lisey's Story*), especially concerning the aforementioned dark humor surrounding the death of Loading Dock Guy. As the joke — "'I just had to park the car, you see'" — initially becomes appropriated by both Cheryl and Leonard within their marriage as a genuine example of joy in that they had a joke that they could share with one another, Owen notes, "Before long, though, the usage became corrupted" (O. King, "Bad Taste" 53). In short, as the shared joke involving the death of Loading Dock Guy becomes an example of the language of the two lovers, the disintegration of shared experience and shared meaning helps the reader ultimately understand Cheryl's dissatisfaction with her marriage. The joke itself does not lose any meaning or enjoyment because of taste; it just wears out, as does the marriage between Cheryl and Leonard. Each wants different things, and small enjoyments like dark humor simply do not serve as a strong enough bond for the couple. And while Cheryl's resolution is to engage in an affair with a doctor who seems to promise Cheryl a life that she wants, this does not mean that

Cheryl's actions are in bad taste. They are simply the end result of a chain of events that, when analyzed, points in only one direction — towards a conclusion that could be considered a reflection of bad taste but which can also occupy a different status with another perspective based in understanding rather than judgment.

The First Major Impression: We're All in This Together

Between Owen King's first publication and the last few years of the millennium he published his first book, a collection of short stories preceded by a novella, all of which bear his mark of humor and attempts to navigate the contemporary human condition through what could be considered typical Owen King fashion — by way of a wide variety of lenses and plot strings. With the title story, "We're All in This Together," Owen navigates numerous tales and themes within a relatively short story that covers just over one-hundred pages, and which primarily concerns itself with, as Owen notes, political undertones: "I was morbidly depressed after Bush won the election in 2000. I had this crazy idea he'd stand down because he didn't get the popular vote. It drove me crazy. And I thought about what kind of person would actually do something about it" (Shoard 21). With this sentiment, "We're All in This Together" was born, and while the story has its moments, initial reviews were not always kind: "With time and discipline King may leave behind the op-ed pieces that masquerade as summer fiction" (Zobenica F19). Still, when examining Owen King's fiction, especially in an age in which stagnate and inert fiction finds little readership, a little leniency can be afforded Owen when considering that his writing attempts to embrace the multitudes of everyday life on which his fiction is based and is focused.

Among the varied threads woven in and out of the status quo each day, the political spectrum facing the American populace in the first decade of the millennium has been rather ubiquitous. And as fiction tends to reach into the mainstream not just for material but also to remind itself as to what is important to a potential audience, the American political scene has been one of the most prevalent issues facing Owen King and his readers. However, with the 1990s, criticism of fiction and its focus on the political was not always well received. Alvin Kernan, in his book with the bemoaning title *The Death of Literature*, seems to cringe when he observes the growth of a political presence in fiction in the 1990s, noting, "Texts have become primarily political documents" (86). Although the presence of the political is not necessarily the source of Kernan's distaste, a noted agenda or even bias is, rather, highlighted as an element of fiction that, as Kernan implies, degrades fiction to a point that positions Owen King's largely political story "We're All in This Together" as a mark of stunted growth for fiction and its writers. However, when the social picture surrounding the environment of fiction creation is dominated by a few select events or foci, one cannot hold it against an author to work with the materials that are readily available, such as political strife, discord and division, especially among the reading population.

Regarding the intent of the title story of *We're All in This Together*, Owen states, "What I want the book to say is that all of the people we live with — the different ethnicities, genders, in different parts of the country — we are all in it together. I really believe that people who think the things that I think, and the people who have deep-seated evangelical Christian beliefs, are the people who need to be talking to each other" (Sachs n.p.). And while this nod towards the political divide that was exposed during the 2000 and 2004 elections seems to be a plain undercurrent for Owen's story, he takes care to work with the political clay (an awkward but functional metaphor) rather than let it dry and crumble. To clarify, Owen's examination of the American political and ideological scene of the millennium is connected to the Industrial Workers of the World and the face of this organization, Joe Hillstrom (after which Owen's brother, Joseph Hillstrom King, is named). Owen opening his title story with a quote from Joseph Hillstrom — "DON'T MOURN" — and revisiting the imagery of death throughout the tale (which is also followed by Hillstrom's additional demand to "ORGANIZE") carries the fiction beyond that of mere political criticism and thinly-veiled didacticism (O. King, "We're All in This Together" 1). Still, the connection between the divisive politics of the twenty-first century, and the plight of the worker from the early twentieth-century, wears a bit thin in that the discussions of ideal human cooperation and understanding falls upon deaf ears, or rather purposefully blind eyes. For example, Owen's characterization of Henry McGlaughlin, the grandfather of the main character George Claiborne, is compelling in that Henry is a hard-nosed individual with a union background who is, in some ways, enslaved by his ideals and finds himself constantly berating the American people for following a lost path of sorts:

> In a union, you stood up for the next guy and you never broke ranks and you faced down the bosses and the finks and the goon squads with a solid front. "We're all in this together"; it was the essential promise that an organizer made to the workingmen who risked the livelihood of their families in an action. If another guy's family was hungry, you gave them half of what you had. If another guy came up short on his rent, you turned out your pockets. If another guy needed a hand, you reached out [O. King, "We're All in This Together" 10].

With this reflection upon the union mentality, both Owen and his character Henry begin a series of political musings that, when paired with the depiction of militant pro-lifers who ultimately are responsible for the death of George Claiborne's mother (who worked at Planned Parenthood), the socio-political ideologies and idealisms do become such that a reader engaging the text for story becomes rather burdened with both the overt and hidden engagements with some of the pressing issues of the twenty-first century. This is not to say that "We're All in This Together" is nothing more than a thinly-veiled allegory or Owen King's fictionalized editorial on the political state of America. Rather, as is the case with most fiction, the careful reader of Owen King's fiction must take into account that negotiation is necessary when considering the fiction and the reality behind Owen's writing.

As far as the general plot is concerned, "We're All in This Together" begins with the death of George Claiborne's grandmother, alongside the anger his grandfather, Henry McGlaughlin, has towards George W. Bush becoming president of the United States. One of Henry's most public displays of his anger is a sign that he posts in his front yard with a picture of Al Gore and a declaration that Gore is the *real* president; the plot of "We're All in This Together" mainly begins with Henry's sign being vandalized. "GET OVER IT SHITHEEL! YOU LOST!" reads the graffiti on Henry's sign, and much of the story then focuses on Henry, with the help of his grandson and the neighbor Gil Desjardins, attempting to discover the identity of the vandal, and to, of course, exact some form of revenge on the mystery individual who has only been identified as donning a Richard Nixon mask while vandalizing Henry's sign in the early morning hours (O. King, "We're All in This Together" 20). Moreover, adding to Henry's frustrations, and fueling his suspicions that the vandal is the paperboy Steven Sugar, Henry finds his newspapers on several mornings to be missing certain sections. And as Owen manages this plotline along with the other major thread, which examines George's home life with his mother and her boyfriend (who George irreverently refers to as Dr. Vic, and who, incidentally, "donated money to George W. Bush's campaign"), one notices that there is simply too much happening in this story (O. King, "We're All in this Together" 98). With two major plotlines, along with a heavy political agenda and its use of Joe Hill's union activism, this novella suffers from too many elements that warrant a novel-length treatment for full context and exploration, or an elimination of certain plot elements, because, again, there is simply too much happening.

While the back story provided seems essential to fully understanding the context of the characters, including the tales of his mother's former lovers and his own conception, one must wonder as to how necessary some of the contents really are. Had the story been stretched to the length of a novel, the glimpses into the histories of the characters might function as more than mere story or interesting connections that serve as little more than narrative tangents. For example, as the tension between George and prospective stepfather Vic grows, Owen takes the time to show his readers George's growing distaste for Vic by having George resort to "teaching my prospective stepfather's dogs to fetch their own feces" (O. King, "We're All in This Together" 28). As is the case with most of Owen King's side-stories, a recurring scene in which an angst-riddled teen teaches dogs to retrieve their bowel movements is both startlingly original and rather comical. And while such a scene does clearly show the reader how much George dislikes Vic, it would seem that observing the total lack of communication between these characters would suffice in establishing a particular disconnect between the teen and the doctor.

Although the story has a focus on the humorous beyond the scatological (by way of having George seeing his grandfather smoking marijuana with the elderly neighbor Gil Desjardins), the humor does not deter the supposition that one might become hard-pressed to separate the political discussions and ravings of Henry McGlaughlin from the political leanings of Owen himself. However, Gil seems to serve as the voice of reason in "We're All in This Together," as he looks back on the 2000 election with a noted distaste for each of the major candidates: "*One's a fool from Tennessee who wants to tell us how to live, and the other's a damn fool from Texas who wants to tell us how to live. Either way, we were going to end up with a fool. No difference*" (O. King, "We're All in This Together" 7). But, as one might expect, the story of "We're All in This Together" is not as simple as having an angry character tempered by a reasonable foil. Gil Desjardins, as it turns out, is just as staunch in his support for third-party candidate Ralph Nader as Henry is for Gore. An early indicator of Gil's rather one-sided political thinking has him advocating Nader as the only 2000 presidential candidate "who didn't belong to the system" (O. King, "We're All in This Together" 40). And with this allegiance to Nader, Owen does play Gil against Henry wonderfully as Henry finds it to be his call of duty to jab Gil and Nader at every opportunity, and with such scathing bluntness that his character is further and further developed as a rather myopic individual: "Al Gore did more for working people last night, while he slept in his bed, than Ralph Nader has done in his whole life" (O. King, "We're All in This Together" 36). With this focus on the political, and the treatment of how individuals become so entrenched in their ideals that they draw absolute and definitive lines around them and their beliefs to the point that pettiness and ignorance result, Owen King ensures that "We're All in This Together" does more than utilize current events for story material — he uses story to unveil the darker side to politics that many recognize but do not always confront.

As "We're All in This Together" progresses, George ends up befriending Steven Sugar, at least to a degree, and it is at this point in the story that Owen lets the reader in on an interesting and vital piece of information that pertains to the political differences fueling the early pages of the story. Steven Sugar says to George, "Tell your grandfather I hope he catches that Nixon guy," revealing that he is not the individual behind the vandalism and pranks that have angered George's grandfather and for which Steven had been wrongfully targeted (O. King, "We're All in This Together" 124). The added element of mystery among the tense political, ideological and familiar stages that are erected in the story benefits from this plot twist that Owen hides quite well in the pages preceding Steven Sugar's revealing statement, and even plays with the familiar sense of unfair and unwarranted judgment that Henry passes on Steven in the name of political righteousness. In short, "We're All in This Together" comes down to the unraveling of a mystery surrounding Henry's newspapers, which had been sifted through by Gil (who had published various articles under a pseudonym and just could not wait to purchase his own copies of his work), and the ultimate revelation that Gil is more than just a thief: Gil is uncovered as being the individual behind the vandalism of Henry's Al Gore sign. As noted, Gil's allegiance to Ralph Nader is noted in the early parts of "We're All in This Together," but the literal passion behind Gil's political leanings is not provided, and appropriately so, until the end of the story:

> I was not wise to the history of Gil's relationship with Ralph Nader, to the depth of his wild devotion for the man.... Gil had believed with absolute certainty that he had once stroked Ralph Nader's naked thighs at a masquerade orgy ... [and] it was Gil's testimony that the masked man had returned his thigh-stroking in kind, and with all the compassion and attention that one might have expected from a person who had selflessly dedicated his life to the public good [O. King, "We're All in This Together" 128–9].

Gill justifies his actions by saying of Henry, "He wouldn't shut up about the politics. He couldn't take a little teasing" (O. King, "We're All in This Together" 129). George, however, can hardly contain his surprise at Gil's rationale, believing that the friendship forged between Gil and Henry would preclude actions that might be hazardous to one's health, as evidence by the stress and anxiety which physically and mentally cripples Henry. But this dissention in the name of political ideology imbues "We're All in This Together" with its underlying and darkly universal message: All things, whether they be friendships or even marriages, are negotiable for the sake of one's personal views. And it is with this scathing yet telling review of humanity's capacity for selfishness that "We're All in This Together" finds its core — a blunt and even disturbing examination of fiction's tried and treasured theme, the human condition. As it stands with Owen King, it would seem that there is much work to do among the general population.

Aside from the somewhat difficult navigations regarding politics, personal shortcomings and numerous plotlines that are required when reading "We're All in This Together," Owen King ensures that his fiction goes well beyond mere social critique and by establishing his writing style as one that is enjoyably funny and reflects a particular craft which seeks to create an actual story to surround the climax of the story. With references to 9/11, a mother-son relationship in which communication is limited to passing notes back and forth, taking the time to observe critical moments in George's life (including the loss his virginity just after his mother dies at the hands of "God's Favorite Assholes"), and concluding the story with one final image of a minor character, Steven Sugar, giving an imaginary pep-talk to imaginary troops, readers are given a tale that seems to purposefully blunt the shine of the plot's gems and focal points (O. King, "We're All in This Together" 37). And while this sense of planned obscurity may suggest Owen tries too hard to create a mainstream *literary* story in which ambiguity is favored over clarity, an argument can be made that Owen is simply exercising a sense of responsibility as a writer and an author.

As "We're All in This Together" examines two of the more difficult elements of everyday life—politics and religion—the discerning reader is able to avoid fixating on Owen's prodding prose that tends to be rather harsh in its treatment of Republicans and Christians. For instance, Henry McGlaughlin makes known his views on George W. Bush and the religious fanatics who ultimately kill his daughter by saying, "They [Christians] want everything for themselves, and piss on the rest of the world. We're not even humans to them. Well, they're not even humans to me" (O. King, "We're All in This Together" 55). Henry's statement can easily be interpreted as a veiled critique of organized religion and some of the extreme perceptions and views surrounding those of the Christian faith; but in considering Henry's proclivities for stubbornness and a one-sided understanding of the world—or that the world is, in essence, against him—Owen King creates both a caricature and a portrait of the American Everyman or Everywoman, one that often wants the world to be shaped and fashioned according to his or her desires and without consideration for dissent or plurality. Although such an interpretation of "We're All in This Together" might seem a bit far-fetched or overly misanthropic, Henry McGlaughlin's dominating presence and rhetoric, despite his role as a secondary character and victim of Gil's own political prejudices, acts as an effective summation for the story. To be sure, with Henry's beliefs and opinions, including his rather militant views on Christians (that "the only way to talk to these monsters is to speak in a language they understand," which suggests force and violence is the only effective or universal language), Owen King paints a bleak picture of how the general population communicates (O. King, "We're All in This Together" 22). Additionally, if one were to extend the brute inability to communicate openly (as seen with Henry) and take Owen's treatment of battling ideologies as a metaphor which examines the author-reader relationship, the idea that speaking darkly and directly about humankind's flaws and foibles, and suggesting the audience is a monster of sorts that needs to be forcibly confronted with its ignorance, is not entirely out of the realm of possibility. Although it may be inaccurate to envision Owen King's audience as being comprised of literal or figurative monsters, the notion that communication is often silenced because of an unwillingness or inability to hear other voices is a valid one. And one must commend Owen for his direct writing, which, as the cliché goes, pulls no punches when facing some of the more taboo or even dangerous discussions and ideologies of his general reading public.

We're All in This Together most definitely shows Owen King's range as a writer, and most of this scope can be attributed to the time-frames of his second and third tales in the collection, "Frozen Animals" and "Wonders." Each tale falls in line with Owen's writing as that which is grounded in the realm of the seemingly everyday instead of the supernatural. And despite Owen's noted ability to create engaging characters examined through critically humorous lenses, "Frozen Animals" and "Wonders" do not necessarily represent Owen's best work in terms of overall story. Beginning with "Frozen Animals," the story involves a dentist, Pinet, being taken to a mountain cabin to treat a pregnant wife of a trapper called Kosskoff. Although the treacherous journey to an isolated home constantly threatened by severe weather is interesting (as well as amusing, with Owen taking a brief moment to describe the difficulties of urinating in freezing temperatures), the tale does not entirely sustain the suspense, tension or interest that might be gained within the first few pages. And beyond the criticism that the oddly exotic scene that begins "Frozen Animals" is hardly a capable vehicle for driving the rest of the story, it must also be noted that simply making sense of the story is rather difficult. Simply put, the tale's vague nature could be considered poor craftsmanship. On the other hand, to completely help the reader along with every necessary detail and provide clarification for every implicit element or allusion could quickly grow tiresome; there is something to be said for fiction that manages to walk the line between outright ambiguity and boring detail.

With Harold Bloom serving as one of the staunchest critics against the fiction of Stephen King, it seems somewhat fitting that Bloom indirectly inject his voice into the conversation surrounding Stephen's family. Although Bloom will only briefly enter into the discussion, his views on the short story provide a necessary backdrop to the medium of choice that Owen King favors. As it has been noted that Owen, at times, does not always make information readily available for the reader, Bloom suggests that this decision is one to be cherished, as he states, "Short stories favor the tacit; they compel the reader to be active and to discern explanations that the author avoids" (66). All things considered, the time, location, and purpose of "Frozen Animals" all remain relatively unclear. While "Frozen Animals" primarily creates a purposely vague story that attempts to mirror Pinet's addiction to nitrous oxide, asking the reader to experience a similar disconnect with reality by way of obscure narration does not necessarily work well. Yet, critic Jon Zobenica believes "Frozen Animals" to be "by far the best in the collection [as] this vivid tale is all the more enticing for what it leaves to the imagination" (F19). While imagination is certainly a laudable element in most fiction, especially fiction which leaves excessive detailing of characters to the imagination of the reader, the imaginative elements of "Frozen Animals" do not always combine well with the hazy narrative that attempts to mimic Pinet's disrupted mental processes.

Among the elements that comprise "Frozen Animals," time, location, and dialogue all seem to be rather muddled in this story, especially concerning the use of common contemporary cussing: "Fucking turn around—I can't go [urinate] with you watching me" (O. King, "Frozen Animals" 140). The description of the dentist attempting to urinate in below-freezing conditions is interesting, if not wholly unnecessary to the plot of the story; but with the dialogue exchange including cursing and establishing an inability to urinate not because of the weather but because of an audience, such a contemporary scene of loose language and "stage fright" seems to place the characters in any location but what appears to be the Canadian wild. Yet, Amy Williams, who is Owen's agent, suggests that the multiple obscured threats work well: "In 'Frozen Animals,' [Owen] King achieves a surreal blend of gory, vivid description of unanesthetized dental surgery layered with the drug-addicted dentist's intermittent memories of a happier past" (42). While the gore of the disgusting tooth-removal procedure, including description of the pus and the flow of blood from the mouth of Kosskoff's wife, is rather necessary, especially considering that "the spectacle of tooth-brushing quieted the group," the establishment of time by way of poor personal hygiene does not mesh well with what appears to be the overall aim of the story, which is the theme of memory and nostalgia (O. King, "Frozen Animals" 151). But Pinet's recollections, including the final moment of an odd sexual memory involving the motley crew of characters, are reduced to a single moment of supposed climax in which "Pinet decided that he had imagined the previous evening entirely," which effectively negates any other build up towards Pinet's past (O. King, "Frozen Animals" 155). And while Pinet's back story might make for an interesting read, the lack of development of his memories which precede the barbaric dentistry takes the back-seat in a story with little development beyond what appears to be a rough outline based on a few hazy suppositions involving the trials and tribulations of early oral surgery. And while it is not unheard of for a story to begin within an author's mind based on a single question—"what would happen if..."—some thoughts just do not form into fiction that sustains a focus or interest beyond a single idea or scene. Balance, of course, is always difficult to manage in fiction, especially regarding details and other developments, but when a certain sense of balance is perceived to be tipping towards dearth of detail and story, latitude becomes less and less of an option for a writer.

While merits and deficits follow all fiction, especially as issues of taste and interest are so varied among readers, any absolute or definitive assessment of any fiction is impossible. And as "Frozen Animals" captures the reader with a scene of disturbingly disgusting dentistry that, like a car accident, has the onlooker at pains to look away or become otherwise disengaged, the third inclusion in *We're All in This Together* serves up a similar portion of fiction that engages in light of, and in spite of, its actual story. "Wonders," at first glance, appears to be a story of sports nostalgia, taking place at Coney Island in, roughly, the 1930s. With racism and the fascination with cinema emerging as noted presences in the story, the temporal location of "Wonders," like in "Frozen Animals," is a matter of educated guesswork — which is actually one of the more acceptable omissions made, as the timelessness of a story can be literally woven into the plot.

In looking at "Wonders," and the wonderment one finds in navigating through the elements of sport, film, race, gender and the taboo, Owen King seems to create a maze out of this story, especially with a main character, Eckstein, who is given no first name. Within "Wonders" it is difficult to determine where one's focus should be placed, although the story does ultimately end with the Coney Island Wonders all physically beating down a heckler that had constantly berated the one black member of the Wonders. With Cleatus "Woodpecker" Burnham, the lone black character in this story (as Owen notes that "there weren't any other Negroes in the Hudson League; it was against the rules, but Coney Island had an entertainment exemption for special attractions"), the author draws attention to the race tensions and ignorant exoticism surrounding Burnham which effectively establishes the story as one placed within the early twentieth century ("Wonders" 158). But beyond Burnham's trials and tribulations within the ballpark and the dugout (as his fellow baseball players also haunt and taunt him because of his black skin), the issue of race is only one of the ugly faces which stare back at the reader in this story.

Among the most startling images to be found in "Wonders" is that of the "freaks" which serve as entertainment during the baseball games that mark the daily passage of time in the tale. The initial introduction of the freaks, from the seemingly innocuous Backwards Man to the slightly more disturbing Purple Girl, is awkwardly placed into the backdrop of the baseball theme. The freaks do not immediately add to the story in that their presence is veiled and obscured by their position as entertainment, as backdrop characters. With these numerous minor elements, like Burnham's ethnicity and the brief glimpses into the fictional world of the cinema and the film about vampires, *Black Mansion*, that occasionally frightens Eckstein ("Eckstein wanted proof that it was all make-believe, that *Black Mansion* wasn't true"), Owen asks his readers to constantly shift their gaze, but not necessarily because of lazy plotting or poorly managed content (O. King, "Wonders" 170). Although the several horrific elements of "Wonders" parallels the numerous plot threads that one sees in Owen's other fictions, the film, the racism, the freaks, and Eckstein's eventual impregnation of his girlfriend Lillian reminds readers of the complexities of real life, that there is hardly ever a time in an individual's existence that one and only one issue is asking to be resolved. Of course, with an extensive analysis of each of the horrors that Owen weaves into "Wonders," much commentary can be derived. For instance, the elements of fictional fright from the vampire movie *Black Mansion* becomes, at the very least, a point of brief conversation between Eckstein and Burnham, as each player discusses his fright at the possibility of vampires existing despite their awareness that vampires are fictional creatures. Although a discussion of the cinema and the wonderment of fiction and fantasy serves as a touching common ground between these two characters, along with Eckstein's sympathy for the treatment that Burnham receives from their teammates and their fans, the cinematic discussion fails to do much else besides serve as a fleeting link between two individuals that highlights issues of fright.

Despite the feeling that the sub-plots of "Wonders" are meant to harmoniously co-exist and come together for a larger narrative, suggesting that equal time and treatment will be given to these plot threads, "Wonders" ultimately places its focus on Lillian's unwanted pregnancy. And while the ugliness associated with unwanted children, born or unborn, shares a position in the dark and cold recesses of the public consciousness, such a desolate, destructive and divisive plot element is just another in a series of fictional fractures that Owen uses to make "Wonders" resemble a broken mirror of sorts — that which casts a distorted and troubling reflection back to the reader, but which is still an accurate reflection, especially when considering the possibility that the reader casts a purposefully broken gaze onto the disturbing elements of his or her society. With little left in the literary world in terms of originality, it seems as if all writers have left to explore is the taboo and unspoken, which follows from a Gothic influence but which also implies that if readers are to stay current with fiction and the society which it reflects, some of the only stories which remain are those that have been pushed all the way back to the outskirts, such as abortion. But writing fiction solely based on the socially unacceptable or the grotesquely horrific is hardly the core of Owen King's fiction. Still, in "Wonders" Owen takes his readers down Wretch Lane, the dark alleys of Coney Island where Eckstein learns that the freaks he sees at his baseball games are his only option for aborting his and Lillian's child. Alongside the tensions of a nighttime abortion in a dwelling reserved for society's outcasts, Owen does not hesitate to add to the grotesqueness of his story by describing the moments preceding the abortion to be performed by a two-headed woman:

> Eckstein noticed something move inside the jar. He wiped a hand across the film of dust. A knot of thick white worms, like ropes of taffy, squirmed at the bottom of the glass.
> "What are those for?" he asked.
> "They eat it," said Jenny Two Heads. "That's they job."
> He took a place by the table and held Lillian's hand. The freak flipped up Lillian's dress, and with a savage swipe, tore away the girl's underwear. "You won't want em after this, honey," she said [O. King, "Wonders" 174].

As Owen takes the reader further and further into the uncomfortable territory of abortion, he continues to unflinchingly tell of the pain and anguish inevitably involved. Depicting the abortionist as being blunt to the point of callousness as she tears Lillian's underwear from her body, even as Lillian's fear and immense sorrow has been established — "Someday I'm going to have beautiful babies.... You'll just be a used-up ballplayer in some jerkwater town" — Owen continues with the scene (O. King, "Wonders" 172). Ultimately, the scene takes the reader to a conclusion in which the abortionist reveals that Eckstein and Lillian had nothing to fear in terms of their pregnancy: "Your works ain't no good. Your works don't work. Rotten fruit. They ain't no babies ever comin from there. Fuck all you want and there won't never be any" (O. King, "Wonders" 175). While the words that the abortionist speaks are hardly comforting, despite the strange feeling that the abortionist finds it relieving (if not darkly amusing) that Lillian did not need to have an abortion in the first place, the harsh reality of Lillian being barren resonates not only with an odd sort of irony, but also a real sense of tragedy. The characters and the readers of "Wonders" face more than Lillian's broken dream: they all face a sense of indifference and apathy towards the simplistic yet endearing hope for a young woman to have a family and realize the American Dream that, as seems to be more common than not, is looked at as nothing more than an empty, fanciful desire.

The brutal nature and scope of "Wonders," from an abortion clinic run by circus freaks to the racially charged environment of the era in which the story is set, certainly garners attention. But for what reasons or even at what cost? *New York Times* critic Jon Zobenica claims that Owen's grotesque imagery within "Wonders" functions as little more than a transparent soap-box. However, aside from the grotesque elements of "Wonders," and the simplistic reduction of the "freaks" as nothing more than a gimmick that Owen utilizes, one sees an engaging sense of irony and critical commentary emerge. The freaks, which are mainly used for entertainment, are also used to engage in acts generally deemed socially unacceptable, like pre–or extra-marital sex and abortion. Perhaps Owen's most gruesome yet convincing insight in this tale is creating a functional, if not disheartening, link between social outcasts and social taboos. By placing the "freaks" into roles of entertainers, prostitutes and surgeons for hire, he actually empowers these outcasts. By having them occupy positions that may be considered rather low or even repulsive, the "freaks" are positioned as individuals which are, to an extent, desired, even needed, by a community that outwardly shuns these people while also aiming to oppress such individuals.

But the critical irony is that even with the distance and degradation involved, the "freaks" become a foundational immersion in the community despite any professed outrages. And it is with these "freaks" and their necessitated position in the community, as both entertainment at the baseball games and as problem solvers living in the dark recesses of the community, that perhaps the ultimate focus of "Wonders" becomes clear — as the game of baseball can no longer function as a form of escape or even livelihood. While baseball, and its often redemptive powers, appears to provide some sort of solace for Eckstein and his teammates, this sport becomes more and more of a distraction, an intrusion, on the story. Although "Wonders" is broken down in terms of narrative structure by way of a game-by-game accounting of the plot events, the constant look into the other elements of Eckstein's life suggests that there is often more pressing issues in the shadows of one's life than where an individual foolishly places the spotlight, like on a mere sport.

There is a joke I once heard from my father, Lee McAleer, in which a man at an interview is asked about his worst quality, and he responds with a single word: "Brevity." Correspondingly, in analyzing the fiction of Owen King, brevity often comes across as one of his less than desirable traits. For example, while twenty pages hardly seems to be brief in many writing respects, twenty pages is all that Owen King gives to his short story "Snake"; and those twenty pages hardly allow for any story to develop. Within this story, Owen once again looks into the lives of everyday people, presenting a story of a divorced man, Ken Ackerly, and his son Frank. The set-up for the story tells readers that "Frank was sixteen years old, a junior in high school, but his long, stringy black hair made him look older. He wore a water-stained trench coat and old canvas sneakers with ripped soles. His parents were divorced and it was one of his father's weekends" (O. King, "Snake" 179). Owen provides further detail, as might be expected, by noting that Ken Ackerly is a borderline alcoholic, and that he has a particular charm and charisma — "His father could still make him smile, could make anyone smile, even Frank's mother" (O. King, "Snake" 181). However, a charismatic alcoholic cannot sustain a story, no matter how entertaining he or she is, and creating a story about a troubled teen within a broken home cannot be sustained merely because of its anticipated familiarity to the average reader.

On the subject of potential detriments, "Snake" also contains political commentary that seems common to Owen's fiction. Yet beyond the brief commentary on commercialism and politics that "Snake" provides, via Frank's time spent at the mall and his father's views on the primary setting of the story — "Ken called it the Reagan Mall, and if he was hammered enough, he could be counted on to give a lecture on the subject, about how ever since Ronnie the country was like a dumb kid who had eaten a bunch of lead paint chips" — one of the more redeeming qualities of this story is its own examination of fiction (O. King, "Snake" 182). As "Snake" shifts focus from questions of the family (as well as politics and economics), much of the story becomes concerned with the issue of fiction, as evidenced by somewhat lengthy descriptions of Frank's reading tastes, which include the mystery genre. As "Snake" follows Frank Ackerly through a run-down mall and into a bookstore where he satiates his hunger for mystery fiction, the mystery which ultimately interests Frank the most is the story surrounding an aging hippie, Jimmy "Leatherneck" Federicci, who is at the mall with his pet snake, Julius Squeezer, and his attempt to make money by selling pictures of shoppers posing with the snake. Regarding the first interaction between Frank and "Leatherneck," Owen marks the scene with Frank encountering Jimmy and Julius with his typical touch of humor, taking care to note a sign Jimmy has made regarding his pet: "Warning: Julius Squeezer WILL eat ASSHOLES!!!" (O. King, "Snake" 185). But in dismissing the humor, along with other minor details that often seem to have little direction or purpose other than a perfunctory attempt to paint a mental picture, "Snake" moves into the realm of the metafictional, with Jimmy Federicci telling a curious Frank about how he acquired the boa constrictor:

> She [an angry lover] slips the old Squeezer in bed with me after I'm asleep one night, expecting him to bite my ass or something. I wake up, feeling a little tickle around my feet, and think I've kicked off the sheets. That's when I see Julius here, curling all over my legs. For a second, I think I'm fucked, but then I realize he's only a boa, and I sit right up and start cuddling with the big son-of-a-bitch [O. King, "Snake" 188].

While the story behind the "Leatherneck's" original acquaintance with Julius Squeezer is interesting to Frank for its seeming uniqueness as well as exoticness, "Leatherneck" goes on to suggest that there is more to his story than befriending a snake. Sure enough, "Leatherneck" suggests that his former lover met an untimely end at his hand for her strange and ineffective attempt at murder. But just as Frank finds it difficult to believe that "Leatherneck" was able to successfully smuggle a boa constrictor into the United States, he also boldly proclaims to "Leatherneck," "You didn't kill anyone. No way, I don't believe you" (O. King, "Snake" 193). And while Frank's noted distaste for lying is told to be the root of his confrontation with "Leatherneck," Frank later reflects, "He had busted an old hippie for lying. It had been a nasty thing to do" (O. King, "Snake" 194). With this introspective move, it would seem reasonable to conclude that "Snake" might then turn towards a key revelation or resolution regarding Frank's detachment from the world and its people, regardless of their varying levels of honesty. However, when it comes to either expectation or convention, Owen King is more than willing to break from such restraints.

With "Snake" mirroring "Frozen Animals" in terms of the limited scope as well as the seeming lack of profound truth to be found in the end of the story, one sees a willing pattern in Owen's fiction to, above all else, simply tell a story. And while stories, at least those with a certain dramatic flair, tend to play up the mundane, "Snake" follows in the mold of the Owen King canon by recognizing that an excessive amount of drama is, despite what the formulas of fiction call for, not always realistic. With "Snake," the main character, Frank, simply visits a mall, encounters a shady, lying hippie, and then falls upon the mercy of said hippie for a ride home when his father fails to pick him up. And while the lack of parental responsibility could have been examined or inflated, as could have been the case with "Leatherneck" agreeing to give Frank a ride home because Frank possessed marijuana that he agreed to share with the very same man he embarrassed earlier, "Snake" purposely omits any exaggerated or embellished analysis of these relationships and interactions. The story, like many other fictions, still provides a few loose lines for the reader to bite at, including the praise that "Leatherneck" ultimately bestows upon Frank — "You're a good kid, Frank. Only sale I made all day. You didn't even want a Polaroid. I could see that. You were just being cool, that's all. Your dad is missing out"— and this simplicity is hardly an indication of poor writing (O. King, "Snake" 197). Although Harold Bloom suggests that displeasure is likely to result from a story like "Snake," as "short stories are not parables or wise sayings, and so cannot be fragments; we ask them for the pleasure of closure," he suggests that no enjoyment can be derived from a story in which there is only the slightest hint that Frank and his father will forge a strong relationship (31). And when Frank notes at the end of the story that his father is "okay.... He's got some good stories," such a sentiment is a far cry from genuine closure (O. King, "Snake" 197). But ending a story just before some sort of climax, no matter how anti–climactic the establishment of a functional father-son bond may be, is just the sort of bold maneuvering within contemporary fiction for which Owen King should be lauded rather than chided.

Among the stories that make up *We're All in This Together*, "My Second Wife" concludes the cornucopia of fiction, and does so with perhaps the most polished and engaging opening within the collection: "When my wife left me for another man I called my brother Wayne" (O. King, "My Second Wife" 199). The simple opening, with the immediate reference to a character that the reader can only identify as the narrator's sibling, along with the early establishment of conflict, brings the reader into the story quickly yet smoothly. Of course, the story does not maintain any semblance of the simple or the ordinary when the narrator describes a road-trip he takes with his brother, who is looking to acquire a car in Starke, Florida:

> Wayne explained that the town of Starke was the seat of the Florida electric chair, and the car belonged to Virgil Pendergast — the so-called Sportscar Splatterer — a psychopath of no small renown. Four summers earlier the Sportscar Splatterer had run down three squeegee men in Tampa before a neighbor spied Virgil Pendergast out in his driveway, digging clotted meat from the grille of his Jaguar [O. King, "My Second Wife" 201].

More than anything, the dark humor attached to Owen's description of a serial killer cleaning his latest kill from his vehicle is an attempt not to shock the reader but rather to create a foundation for the character of Wayne. The narrator, Stan, may be the ultimate focus of this tale, which recounts a long journey to Florida and a series of strangely amusing events (including a confrontation with an emu) but the oddity dubbed Wayne, who, incidentally, had been "expelled for trying to crossbreed marijuana with seaweed," is, again, another example of Owen's fiction taking on the form of a somewhat thin mosaic of events and people aimed at covering numerous plot threads rather than focusing on a single element (O. King, "My Second Wife" 213). And once again this variety does have its problematic aspects. For example, as Stan and his brother Wayne make their way to Florida, Stan recounts a scene in which he and Wayne smoke marijuana with an elderly couple, and while a brief recollection of smoking weed with an unassuming couple is entertaining because of its seeming lack of reality, the most important element of this scene is how the elderly man discusses and celebrates his sister's memory loss. While Stan offers sympathy and condolence for the sister's dwindling mental capacities, the elderly man replies, "Why [are you sorry]? ... She's happy. She's daddy's little girl again. Think about it. She's got her whole life in front of her" (O. King, "My Second Wife" 204). The alternative perspective offered on losing one's memories is refreshing and insightful, which is something to be celebrated despite the mildly forced insertion into "My Second Wife." But, again, such a rejection of convention or seamless narrative is an exceptionally notable and engaging element of Owen King's fiction.

In addition to the noted repetition of numerous stories-within-stories that mark Owen's fiction, the presence of humor in "My Second Wife" reiterates Owen's predilections as a writer. But with the constant use of humor in his varied fictions, it is rather difficult to gauge what Owen's ultimate goal might be. Whether one is discussing the layers and complexities of, say, satire, or examining the crudity and offensiveness of juvenile humor, the question of comedy is never easy to address when it comes to fiction. William Boerman-Cornell suggests, "Most successful writers use humor as a way to get their audience's attention" (66). So one might guess that Owen is simply utilizing his skills as a humorist to merely gain favor with any potential reader. As Owen describes Stan's first impressions of his ex-wife's home with comical religious caricatures, including "book covers [that] showed elaborately painted action scenes: Jesus smashing the moneychangers' table with a kung fu kick, and David taking a chainsaw to Goliath's spewing jugular," it is difficult to stifle laughter at such a scene of ridiculousness and perhaps religious ridicule (O. King, "My Second Wife" 207). As Jon Zobenica notes, "Even if the story called 'My Second Wife'—with its combustible toe jam, its dead emu in the motel bathtub and its transgender incest—is several yucks over the recommended allowance, [Owen] King's unapologetic urge to entertain is still a trait to be encouraged" (F19). One can only hope that readers who encounter Owen King feel the same way, as humor is an essential structural element of Owen's fiction.

Moving past the comedic elements of Owen King's writing is possible, especially when one notes hardly a touch of the jocose in "Wonders," for example. Just as it is essential to shed the burdens of generic expectation or avoid an extensive analysis of any writer through only one lens, "My Second Wife" is almost impossible to negotiate without noticing, at the very least, the absurd at just about every turn. For instance, when Stan agrees to marry a stranger just to have sex with her — "Jesse said we needed to get married before we consummated our love. Her Uncle Bob was a minister and he could do it" — the sham wedding and empty process of matrimony simply reeks of the fantastically bizarre (O. King, "My Second Wife" 216). And considering that Stan and his second wife, Jesse, consummate their marriage in a trailer park, invoking images of *The Jerry Springer Show* (on which Jesse, unsurprisingly, appears at the end of this tale), in addition to Stan discovering that Jesse wears a necklace bearing dozens of plastic rings similar to the trumpery that Stan wears after he weds her, the silliness of the story gleams so brightly that just about any nod towards seriousness is all but impossible to see. However, even among the mockeries of partnerships and loving unions, which include Wayne running off with Virgil Pendergast's wife, Yolanda (who enlists the assistance of a voodoo man to raise her dead husband), "My Second Wife" does find time to return to the provocative opening of the story, which has Stan reflecting upon his recent divorce.

In the end, Stan's first wife, Paula, reunites with him after her lover files for bankruptcy, which not only suggests that Paula is a fickle and perhaps materialistic individual (or a seemingly accurate caricature of the stereotypical modern American woman), but that Stan is merely one lonely individual. Stan's willing blindness to his first wife's indiscretions and selfishness places him in the role, not uncommon in fiction, of the weak male who succumbs to a dominant female presence. Yet one would do well to split hairs and view Stan as a man who is more than just weak and lonely: he is an encapsulation of the stubbornly delusional man whose unsure assessment of his marriage after separation — "We are happy, I think" — leaves readers with no smiles whatsoever (O. King, "My Second Wife" 221). That is, unless the reader finds joy in one man's inability to shed his restraints of passivity and thinly constructed need for fulfillment by just about any individual that will give it to him. Of course, happiness can be found in reflecting upon the fact that one is not in Stan's position of weak-willed entrapment, or that Stan's position is also one of his own making (because he experiences his depression and a renewed yet strained marriage as a sort of karmic retribution for his own unfaithfulness while married to Paula). There may be little that is amusing about a couple whose marital bedrock is anything but solid. But even a little irony, accompanied by a headline for *The Jerry Springer Show* which reads, "THE WOMAN WHO BECAME A MAN AFTER MARRYING OVER A HUNDRED MEN AND HER BROTHER-LOVER" (a headline which connects Stan to the spectacle of strangeness of Americans seeking entertainment no matter what the cost), carries just the right amount of humor for most discerning readers (O.

King, "My Second Wife" 222). And for all the purported imbalances found in Owen King's fiction, the masterful blend of dark irony and slapstick in "My Second Wife" beckons readers to a writer whose young and hopeful career should be nurtured so that it continues to grow.

Conclusion — Another Taste of the Com(ed)ic: Who Can Save Us Now? *(with "The Meerkat")*

From beginning to end, the fiction of Owen King displays a range of fictional focus as well as ability. But given the variety that Owen King offers, at least in terms of stories which contain plots that are often overshadowed by the secondary threads of story, what, then, is one supposed to take from the fiction of Owen King? One could do worse than encounter a few well-worded insights and some crude laughs to temper any semblance of political or personal grandstanding that might be gleaned from reading his fiction. But even with the preceding examination of Owen King and his fiction, the multiplicity that marks his writing still leaves a lingering question for his audience: How is one supposed to approach the fiction of Owen King? What purpose does it serve? For that matter, what can be reasonably concluded by noting and examining his approaches to the craft, including his constant draw to humor and subtle if not sporadic attempts to craft his writing in a way that reflects exceptionally careful and planned prose? By one account, Amy Williams suggests, "Freaks and weirdos — external symptoms of his protagonists' inner struggles — people [Owen] King's shorter stories, which strive to balance the lurid with a reach for emotional truth" (40). Amy Williams' overview of Owen King's writing, and his taste for the strange as a gimmick of sorts that is tempered by an inherent gravity of seriousness that can be lost amidst the carnival of odd images and occurrences that populate his fictions, reminds readers that Owen is a writer who never loses sight of the power of the literary form. Such a form, that which considers and embraces the reality from which all fiction stems, perseveres even in Owen's most recent fiction, "The Meerkat."

As a tale in the comic vein, "The Meerkat" is admittedly just another superhero story with no great aspirations or profound insights into the human condition. Still, "The Meerkat," like most any story, comes with several layers of plot and meaning. With the hero of the tale, Wade Hanes, transforming into a humanoid meerkat and using his newfound agility and keen animalistic senses in a manner befitting a superhero, the back story in "The Meerkat," along with the back and forth action among Washington, D.C., Cleveland, and the Kalahari Desert, merely blends into a rather typical story. There is action, including a giant Soviet robot named Peaceful Ivan wreaking havoc on the city of Cleveland, as well as questions of love and loss, especially when Wade becomes transformed into a meerkat and his girlfriend leaves him. More to the discussion of love, Owen tells how Wade's recruiter, Doris Krimsky, eventually fell out of favor with her husband by having her explain, "He said he couldn't live with a person who used their mind to wipe their ass" (O. King, "The Meerkat" 126). Once again, Owen provides his story with juvenile humor, but with the light-hearted nature of "The Meerkat," as well as the undercurrent of superpowers running through the text, the image of cleaning oneself after a bowel movement with telekinesis is hardly out of place. Further, aside from an amusing look at personal hygiene, "The Meerkat" is consciously constructed as a story that, much like the rest of Owen King's fiction, is under no delusion of grandeur or literary excellence (which is not an unfavorable element, or dismissing criticism, of "The Meerkat" or its author).

As Owen himself has suggested that stories do not always have to be ground-breaking or awe-inspiring, "The Meerkat" wraps itself in a shroud of *story* that savors the unpretentious treatments of the mundane, including issues of love and death. Further, "The Meerkat" carries itself along a rather familiar plotline of heroic uncertainty that is erased with the need to rectify conflict, and it concludes with an expected ending of good triumphing over evil, as is typical within a superhero story even if the hero is hardly an image of grandiosity. Owen delicately and bluntly closes the tale with Wade reunited with his girlfriend: "The rest of what passed between them isn't necessary to the story, which is primarily a yarn about how a fearless superhero saved his city" (O. King, "The Meerkat" 157). Of course, there is much more to "The Meerkat" than a simple story following a rather familiar plotline, but as Owen reminds his readers that he really does not aim for much more than just a *story*, he makes no apologies for not adding any ostensible elements of sophistication or illumination. *Story* simply needs engaging events, and "The Meerkat" possesses a particular uniqueness via a man as a superhero under an unconventional moniker and visage. Still, even though "The Meerkat" can be reduced to a series of words and images that simply add up to a mildly undistinguished tale, Owen King nonetheless supplies a few insightful comments through his fictional creations to provide a mild level of metafictional depth to the story. For instance, he precedes the perfectly typical conclusion with a few nods towards death and heartbreak when his hero Wade notes, "No one dies or gets their hearts broken in the comics. It's different in real life" (O. King, "The Meerkat" 143). And it is with this sentiment — that there will always be a noted difference between real life and fiction, between expectations and realizations— that Owen King truly makes his mark as a writer of fiction. He reminds readers of all walks that sometimes fiction is simply a story wanting to be read.

With an analysis of Owen King's fiction producing, above all else, ambivalence, especially concerning questions of Owen's ability alongside his heritage, all criticism must reach the conclusion that he is, at the very least, very knowledgeable and focuses quite well on his craft. Further, Owen King's fiction asks little of his readers other than an open and willing eye. This is not to say that he is simply a writer seeking an audience for the purpose of achieving the status of "writer." To the contrary, Owen's fiction serves as a foothold for the new generation of writers who not only seek and desire publication, but wish to compose writing that loses pretension and gains the reader's lenient and patient ensnarement in a story that is, above all else, a story. In Owen's own words, he confirms that his goals are rather simple: "I just want to write well, and tell stories well" (Sachs n.p.). Despite concerns surrounding Owen's ability to manage the numerous elements of his stories, and that his constant jocosity does not always serve the purpose of promoting genuine joy, his success is to be found in his purposefully unapologetic approach to fiction and the real-world inanity that undergirds his writing. The willingness, and ability, to probe the numerous idiocies and fanaticisms of his surroundings and peers, and to do so with the hope that subtly confronting such lesser traits and qualities can be done with a smile on the faces of both the author and reader, is a literary treasure trove that, no matter how polished or rough the contents may be, shines with an austerity that, fortuitously, seems to run in the bloodlines of the family King.

4

More Than a Matriarch: Tabitha King's Canon

The fiction of Tabitha King has a public starting point of 1981 with the publication of her first novel, *Small World*, but this single novel is anything but the beginning of the Tabitha King story. While Tabitha has been credited with jumpstarting her husband's career by literally rescuing the manuscript of Stephen's first published novel, *Carrie*, from the trash, and as biographers of Stephen have taken some time to detail Tabitha's own history (including her education at the University of Maine-Orono and as a member of the Spruce family, whom Stephen notes in the dedications of several of his novels), Tabitha's life and fiction are almost always overshadowed by the literary elephant in her own living room. And while, for instance, Tabitha's poetry might have never reached the eyes of the reading public without her husband, who provides a complete version of Tabitha's poem "A Gradual Canticle for Augustine" in his 2000 non–fiction book *On Writing*, her writing must be considered as an entity separate from her husband's oeuvre. This does not eliminate the usefulness of Stephen's fiction as a point of comparison, or contrast; but while it should go without saying that Tabitha's fiction is fully able to stand on its own without the imminent influence of or connection to her husband's writing, the early critical returns suggest otherwise.

With respect to Tabitha's poetry and her published fictions, there is something to be said for her husband's popularity and notoriety, especially as Stephen King collectors, through various channels and the Internet, seek Stephen's early work. One such early publication is the 1970 issue of *Moth*, which not only contains the first publications of Stephen's poems "The Dark Man," "Donovan's Brain" and "Silence" (which have been republished in *The Devil's Wine*), but also contains the first appearance of Tabitha's poetry, including the aforementioned "A Gradual Canticle for Augustine" and the poems "Elegy for Ike," "Note I from Herodotus," and "Nonsong." And aside from this footnote of sorts, which is just one in a wide selection of instances in which Tabitha's writing is inextricably bound to her husband's, it must be noted that situations such as this recalls the ostensible and often regrettable pull by critics and scholars to bring Tabitha into the growing academic conversation on Stephen King, especially regarding his treatment of female characters, rather than attempting to at least create some distance between the two artists.

Concerning the female presence, however, it is said of Stephen that "although [Stephen] King must be praised for this accurate and potent rendition of Everyman in the late twentieth century, his representations of Everywoman often provoke hostility as well as admiration" (Lant and Thompson 4). Consequently, the focus on the female character that marks Tabitha's fiction seems to be an opportune and appropriate locale for examining and juxtaposing Stephen's fiction. This focus on the female, however convenient it may be in terms of contrast between the King family patriarch and matriarch, is, again, just one in a series of examples of the literary net that has entrapped Tabitha King. And while this is not to belabor the point that Tabitha is a writer in her own right, or that juxtapositions between her writing and her husbands are necessarily tainted, it is nonetheless critical for readers and critics to read Tabitha King through a lens which acknowledges and works around the narrow prescriptions that her marriage and career have been subjected to.

When approaching Tabitha's fiction, which is largely concerned with the everyday occurrences within the small town, and even within the domestic home fronts which populate the small town, a focus on her setting is essential to understanding her intentions not as a writer, but as a *female* writer: "Unless we acknowledge and study the pervasive powers of the home plot, we cannot fully know what it has meant to be a woman and an artist in America" (Romines 18). The domestic settings of Tabitha's fiction, along with the overt sexual tensions and instances that do not always populate the writing of the rest of the King family, most certainly place her work within a sphere of literature that can be classified as largely feminine. But, like any other female writer, Tabitha's particular take on and representation of the female is not universal or wholly revealing of certain truths either denied or missed by male authors. Her writing and her treatment of the female, in many cases, is merely an example of how classification can constrict the scope of an author's work, which subsequently limits the ways in which one reads and analyzes Tabitha King's fiction. While there is no denying the more dominant presence of the female in her writing when compared to the fictions of her husband and two sons, there is much more to Tabitha King and her writing than her sex and gender.

In examining the fictions of Tabitha King, and also attempting to isolate her and her work so as to examine them without the bias imposed by her husband's fiction, a purposeful resistance to definition is paramount. For example, with her first novel, *Small World*, being classified as a science fiction work, disappointment is likely to follow a reading of this text, as *Small World* only relies upon elements of science fiction in a passing manner. To focus on the science fiction elements of a novel aimed at more than technological speculation is, of course, quite the discredit to Tabitha and her first book, which, among other things, examines not just the consequences of a blind faith in technology, but also, and more importantly, the dynamics of the family and the lengths to which a mother will go to protect her children. Further, her last novel, *Candles Burning* (which is a collaboration of sorts with the deceased Michael McDowell, who is likely best known for authoring the movie *Beetlejuice*), being classified as a contemporary Southern Gothic text is just as misleading.

Candles Burning may take place predominantly in the South, but the sporadic supernatural inclusions and the sustained focus on the literal growth and development of the main character, Calley Dakin, douses the fires of the few Gothic elements. However, there are critics who look at the latest movements in the Gothic genre as those which do not necessarily hold to the more traditional elements of the Gothic novel, which is concerned with a celebration of death and ruination: "Contemporary Gothic is not preoccupied with the end of the world but with the end of innocence" (Spooner 23). In this statement, it is rather convenient to aim and expand the boundaries of the Gothic by considering "the end of innocence" as a new Gothic direction, especially as a loss of innocence, and even sustaining a fascinated focus on the steps leading to a character's loss of a relatively untarnished world view, is hardly a new transformation of the Gothic.

In other words, expanding the realm of the Gothic to that which is attached with a common element of simply growing up and becoming more and more immersed in a world overwhelmed not by purity but by deceit and destruction is a weak attempt to create a literary umbrella of sorts for most any fiction which has a character grow from childhood into his or her teen years and beyond. And while Calley Dakin is faced with the trauma of her father's gruesome death and the literal specters of her family's history, positioning her tale firmly in the realm of the Gothic misses the rest of the novel as originally conceived by McDowell and then completed by Ms. King. Further, as Jeffrey Andrew Weinstock defines the Female Gothic as "a category of literature in which female authors utilize Gothic themes in order to address specifically female concerns," his assessment of the genre and its gendered lens reading is that which can be widened to the point of usefulness, or rather forced applicability (1). However, as indicated, no matter how gendered Calley's personal developments are, including her first menstrual cycle, her larger issues are hardly Gothic or even Female Gothic.

While this general rejection of generic classification for Tabitha King's fiction may seem to be a random or reckless introduction and approach to her fiction, such a foundation must be established because placing Tabitha King into a corner, as has befallen her husband, is an act that diminishes her writing. To be blunt, and to reiterate the sentiments which open this chapter, Tabitha King is not always known as a novelist. She is, of course, known as Stephen

King's wife, and that particular title is not always helpful when attempting to examine her fiction. As Tabitha says of her and her marriage to Stephen, "He's one of the most interesting writers in America, but people put him in a box, and I get boxed, too, because I'm married to him" (W. Davis B1). By taking Tabitha outside of the literary box in which her husband resides, readers and critics note quite the difference between Tabitha and Stephen. For instance, William Davis notes that, on a very basic level, "Although also deeply rooted in Maine, her [Tabitha's] novels are free of the horror and gore found in most of Stephen King's work" (B1). Without the expected elements of the horrific that are either constructed or forcibly inserted into Stephen's fiction, Tabitha's stories are reasonably considered as more concerned with reality and effectively exploring the everyday occurrences, as well as the everyday nuances, of the American Everyman and Everywoman. Even with a general focus away from the horrific, as is the case with the aforementioned *Small World* and its reported science-fiction plot, Tabitha does craft her fiction in a rather dramatic way: "Although no one has ever faulted her grasp of the nuances and social dynamics of small-town life, some critics have found King's prose purple and her plots soap-operalike" (W. Davis B1). And for any faults that one can find within the soap opera, those which likely stem from an elitist aesthetic which condemns anything not ostensibly created to be wholly artistic or which falls under any number of other artificially created categories of artistic merit, it can be said, and celebrated, of Tabitha King that her fiction effectively captures her reader.

Even when Tabitha King is not writing fiction, she laces her words with a notable flair and wit that almost transforms her writing into a conversation that she has with her audience. Among the works that make up her canon, a small selection of non–fiction writings provides a certain depth when investigating her concerns and her style. To wit, with her 1979 article titled "Living with the Boogeyman," she honestly and insightfully portrays the growing fame of her husband and establishes it as anything but the macabre backdrop that curious readers might expect: "There is a children's story about a boy who has monsters in his closet. Eventually, he takes them all in bed with him, after he discovers they're just as frightened of the dark as he is. I love that story; it is *my* autobiography" (177). Additionally, when Tabitha was commissioned to serve as a photographer and a contributor to *Mid-Life Confidential: The Rock Bottom Remainders Tour America with Three Chords and an Attitude* (1994), she reflects upon her time touring with her husband's band (which also included other popular writers like Dave Barry and Amy Tan) with a comical edge that suggests her contributions as a writer and photographer were not adequately compensated, titling her contribution to the collection "I Didn't Get Paid Enough." But beyond these two minor non–fiction inclusions in Tabitha King's collection of writings is her chronicling of the Maine Girls High School Basketball Championship of 1993–1994. This self-published work stemmed originally from a growing national interest in Cindy Blodgett and the Lawrence Bulldogs in Maine. Tabitha contextualizes her account of the story, titled *Playing Like a Girl*: "In the summer of 1993 I was assigned by *Sports Illustrated* to write a piece about the final high school season of Cindy Blodgett ... [but] *Sports Illustrated* then killed the piece" (i). However, when reviewing Cindy Blodgett's story as recounted by Tabitha, who notes, "'The Best of Maine's Best,' the *Bangor Daily News* called Cindy Blodgett," it is little wonder that Tabitha, with the help of her brother, Christopher Spruce, ensured that Ms. Blodgett's story be told (9). Setting aside, however, that Cindy Blodgett's tale culminates with her ending her high school career as Maine's all-time leading scorer in *both* men's and women's basketball, Tabitha King writes of Blodgett's senior season with both a touch of the dramatic and with a selective restraint that gives justice to the sportsmanship inevitably connected to high school sports. For example, when Tabitha notes that "no matter what kind of night she's had, Cindy comes off the floor aware she's made mistakes, that she could have been better," she captures the essence of a basketball player who serves as an example of humble humanity that easily extends to most any walk of life, including an author (9). Indeed, through all the discussion of the camaraderie and agony that shows the duality of high school life and high school athletics, Tabitha ensures that the *story* behind the statistics and factual events shines through.

To Tabitha's credit, she finds a way to give voice to an important element of her community, much in the same way a local Friday-night sportscast will highlight its own community news as it relates to high school sports. And when Tabitha captures Blodgett on paper, she, in many ways, characterizes Blodgett as a hero, almost as if she were a character in one of Tabitha's novels. As Tabitha portrays Blodgett, perhaps the most compelling line from *Playing Like a Girl* summarizes Blodgett, and maybe even Tabitha's own writing, with a single question: "What's the point of doing it unless you do it all the way?" (42). And while effort is not always an accurate or meaningful measure of athleticism or, say, writing ability, Tabitha King can certainly be classified as a writer who genuinely gives all of herself to her craft. And while she has not gained the audience that other writers have, she is nonetheless due a level of appreciation.

More Than Science Fiction: Small World

One of the most pressing concerns that the fiction writer faces is that of originality. With literary criticism, "which is bullshit, by the way," at least as far as Owen King implies in his short story "We're All in This Together," much has been written in the way of examining the form of fiction and attempting to create particular guidelines for creation (110). In the 1945 study by James

N. Young, *101 Plots: Used and Abused*, he asserts that reality-based fictions are less than inspired and essentially unworthy of any reader as he declares, "Stories out of real life ... are almost invariably worthless" (7). To justify this claim, which suggests that perhaps speculative fiction is by its very nature of more use and value to the ordinary reader than a text primarily founded upon real or common events, Young also states "Life, which scribbles in accordance with no plan, is a poor technician" (7). With this, Young seeks to establish that *plotting* is tantamount to success for the fiction writer. And with the call for originality by way of a certain strangeness or unfamiliarity that is necessarily accompanied by carefully constructed plots, it stands to reason that texts which follow this formula seek to be accepted as not only literary but also "worthwhile." However, when literature is reduced to the capturing of the human condition, reality often pervades and overshadows the largely invented or unfamiliar elements of, for example, science fiction or fantasy.

When it comes to the human condition and any recognizable elements or noted oddities that encroach on the highly varied lives of Tabitha King's potential audience, the careful reader can see past the transparent channels that writers use to convey particular truisms about their fellow humans. With that, Tabitha says of *Small World*, "It was a book about power," suggesting that any generic boundaries can be broken down by a simple look at the roots of the novel's plot as that which treats a common element of the human condition (Shattuck 62). But even with the explorations of common social concerns, both in the form of power struggles and the technological boons and burdens that have developed over the last several decades, which bookend Tabitha's writing career, *Small World* is, strangely, reduced to a novel about sex. With blurb-like ramblings which call this novel a "torrid affair" and "a real whopper," along with a provocative picture of a statuesque brunette in revealing workout attire (at least for the Signet paperback edition), one sees that Tabitha King's writing is immediately showered with misleading categorizations and irresponsible reductive sentiments that brand her as a writer who, besides being married to Stephen King, is focused on a highly sexual plot perhaps because of her gender (Yamamoto 814). Sex does play its part in *Small World*, and it is telling to trace the treatment of sex and sexuality within Tabitha King's fictions as a stark contrast to the veiled sexual elements of Stephen King's fictions— think of the somewhat trite and clichéd sex scene which opens *Gerald's Game*, as handcuffs are used in the Burlingames' sex-capades (never minding their ultimate use as a plot tool to keep Jesse Burlingame trapped in her bedroom). But solely because Tabitha appears to have a clearer understanding of sex and its complications than her husband, at least as their treatments of sex within fiction are concerned, to consider Tabitha King and her first novel as nothing more than sex with science fiction as a background element is to grossly misread *Small World*.

The label of science fiction is likely the best *initial* summation of *Small*

World in that Tabitha invokes one of the most well-known science fiction writers of the twentieth century, Arthur C. Clarke, to open the door to her novel and its speculative foundations. She ultimately suggests that the lack of explanation that her story provides for the technological innovations at play should be forgiven, as Clarke's "third law" indicates that science should be viewed as an acceptable mystery related to, if not sharing the very same properties of magic. More specifically, Tabitha pays further homage to Clarke when she describes the structured and scientific approaches of her nerdish character, Roger Tinker, as being "akin [to] the naming all the names of God," which is a reference to Clarke's short story "The Nine Billion Names of God" (T. King, *Small World* 11). Of course, Tinker's surname is a thin moniker that adds to the experimental nature of the novel and its scientific links, but *Small World* is primarily concerned not with the awe and wonder of science but rather with the significant lives of intricately connected characters, one of which is the daughter of fictional President Michael Hardesty. Still, the science fiction elements cannot go unnoticed, but when considering the rest of Tabitha's fictional canon, any sustained focus on speculative fiction, or generic distinction, distracts the reader from Tabitha's constant examination of human relationships in all their varieties and in all their multiple settings with their plethora of anomalous quirks. James Gunn even suggests that science fiction tends not to focus on the real or everyday world: "The fictional world represented [in science fiction] is not the world of the here and now or even there and then but the fantastic world of unfamiliar events and developments" (6). And with *Small World*, readers are introduced to more than just Tabitha King's first story—they are introduced to the first in a line of many misleading perceptions surrounding her writing, whether such views concern genre or familiarity to the public by way of her marriage.

The opening pages of *Small World* not only introduce readers to Tabitha King's first novel, they also introduce readers to a prominent cast of characters and create a particular tension within the story (as a notable theft occurs within the first few pages). The plot of *Small World* is rather simple and, to put it plainly, small, in most every sense of the word—it is a story that concerns itself with a woman seeking a rather ill-conceived revenge. While such a summary is undoubtedly limited and reductionist, it nonetheless asks that attention be directed to a selection of other elements which comprise the story and lead readers down the path of reading, understanding, enjoying, and critiquing Tabitha King's fiction. As *Small World* brings readers into a rather minute world mainly concerned with, say, a half-dozen characters of importance, many of the peripheral elements of the tale warrant a brief look in terms of piecing together the literary puzzle of Tabitha King as a writer. With the first page of *Small World*, Tabitha King gives her readers not only a rather poetic glimpse into a world she attempts to clearly create before the reader's eyes, but she also displays both a linguistic power and a seeming reliance on descriptive verbiage that can be construed as excessive. For example, the opening lines of *Small World* read as follows:

> Bells chimed a soft release. Roger Tinker was alone in a three-sided cell, one element in a honeycomb maze of partitions that displayed the museum's collection. The light falling from the skylights had the honeyed richness of late afternoon. Dust motes swam through the diffuse golden streams and vanished into the angled shadows of the walls. The whisperings of departing visitors and the "good-days" of the staff intruded on the ecclesiastical silence like muffled prayers [T. King, *Small World* 3].

Admittedly, such a look at the choice of words is a narrow look at a novel which does play with themes of the minute. But language is almost always one of the most important elements of a text, in that it serves as either a transparent and open door for readers, or as a brick wall that needs to be scaled. With Tabitha, aside from a few instances in which her language borders on the overbearingly poetic, her first novel sets the scene for a canon which is marked by story that, no matter how real, trivial or fantastical, is engrossing.

The stage of *Small World* is set with a look at a lonely and miserable child whose father happens to be the president of the United States. Dorothy Hardesty Douglass, known as Dolly as a child, is given a miniature replica of the White House when she is young, and her fascination with the house serves as an escape for the lonely child. It also births an adult obsession with the literal small world involved in miniature models. Dolly's obsessions do not always overwhelm her life the way some obsessions or additions may for other individuals, but Dolly's rather isolated and self-imposed reclusiveness does detach her from her son and her grandchildren, whose mother, Lucy Douglass, is despised by Dolly regardless of Lucy's tremendous craft with miniature models. Aside from this foundation for the story which ultimately focuses on Dolly's obsessions and developed lack of sanity, *Small World* introduces quite a wide cast of characters—from Nick Weiler, who is a former lover of Dolly's and current beau for Lucy, to Leighton Sartoris, a painter who lives in Maine (of all places) and is known for his painting of a childhood Dolly. Besides these characters, and the previously mentioned Roger Tinker (from whom the science in this science fiction stems), there is Leyna Shaw, a reporter who has wronged Dolly by calling her Dolly on national television. Now, aside from the seeds of vengeance and, perhaps, sociopathic elements which grow in Dolly Hardesty, Tabitha weaves, perhaps, too many threads into this story by naming dozens of characters and discussing their relationships by way of marriage or other connections within the first twenty pages. Of course, one can appreciate Tabitha crafting a story in which the reader is not burdened with needless build-up or the introduction of germane characters much later in the story. But the imbalance within the early pages is a bit of a tough obstacle. Nevertheless, with a touch of patience, the reader is rewarded.

Promising (according to the useless blurb found on the cover of the paperback version of *Small World*) "sex and evil that packs a punch," Tabitha's first novel is an intriguing look into the elements of power involved in science fiction. Although sex is not absent in this novel, it is a far cry from the sex one might expect from a romance or a passing scene discussing the natural sexual elements of a mainstream marriage. In short, *Small World* moves into its plot of revenge with Dolly Hardesty ultimately enlisting the help of Roger Tinker and his minimizer, of which he says, "There's probably only two or three people in the whole world capable of understanding how it works, assuming they had the proper theoretical information. And me, of course, and I'm not too sure myself sometimes that I've got it right." This can be read as either a cop-out from the standpoint of fictional accuracy, or as a metafictional reflection of Tabitha's nod towards the inexplicable "magic" behind science fiction that she alludes to in the tale's epigraphs (T. King, *Small World* 64). But the science of the story and the partnership between Dolly and Roger is anything but magical or happenstance in terms of the plot, which sees Leyna Shaw "minimized" and forced to exist in Dolly's miniature White House. The undercurrents of *Small World* and the details which explain how Leyna came to be "minimized" are critical to the story and its treatment of power, primarily by way of explaining not the science of the minimizer, but the rationale behind Roger's allegiance to Dolly.

In terms of the sex that the cover blurb magnifies, Dolly is a character who, essentially, preys on weak individuals, using an uncanny ability to identify people's weaknesses, whether it be Lucy Douglass' love for her children or Roger Tinker's inexperience with sex. As *Small World* progresses to the point where Roger agrees to minimize things, including people, for Dolly's obsessions and revenges, she uses the one things she has that Roger wants as a bargaining chip: sex. Although, as Tabitha notes that the initial sex between Dolly and Roger was a bit lackluster, or perhaps disappointing ("Sex was not as he imagined it"), Dolly realizes that Roger's inexperience with sex can be used against him in that his expectations for sex can only be measured through the sex that Dolly allows him to have with her (T. King, *Small World* 72). Dolly does allow Roger to act out a few sexual fantasies, including pretending to be Captain Kirk from *Star Trek* while having sex with Dolly, but such a scene in which it would appear that Dolly is being demeaned is, nonetheless, an exercise of her power over Roger in that his sexual fantasies are limited to pure imagination rather than elaborate, titillating costumes and bedroom activities which warrant the need for safety words. And while Dolly exercises power over Roger through sex, she exercises power of size and domination over Leyna Shaw when Leyna is minimized and placed into Dolly's miniature White House. As far as the story goes, this power functions as more than just a means of propelling the plot — Leyna Shaw commits suicide to escape Dolly's mechanisms, which can be considered as just another power display in that Leyna usurps Dolly's dominance by taking her own life.

With Leyna Shaw's suicide, Dolly's obsession with power pushes her to declare to herself, "She must have new tenants for her White House" (T. King, *Small World* 222). Ultimately, the individuals targeted to become denizens for the miniature White House are Dolly's grandchildren. However, Lucy learns from Roger that Dolly plans on shrinking the children and taking them, and Lucy eventually kills Dolly by pushing her out a window — but only after the children are minimized by Dolly. Eventually, Lucy and Nick are shrunk to join the kids as Roger works to find a way to reverse the minimizing (even though Roger Tinker notes earlier that "the process isn't reversible. You can't unminimize something") (T. King, *Small World* 105). With all this leading to the end of the tale, Tabitha ends by noting that Lucy and her children survived, which is not only reflective of the novel's earlier sentiment that "what can't be changed must be endured," but also suggests that there is more to a story than pure resolution (T. King, *Small World* 143). In this case, the reader may not know if Lucy and her children are able to resume a normal life, but that is hardly the point of the story.

It is interesting but not entirely telling to note that Tabitha provides a metafictional reference to her husband's work in *Small World*, as a miniature Leyna Shaw navigates the miniature White House, full of anxiety and paranoia but also believing that "she was being silly, giving into the jim-jams, on the strength of fiction. It wasn't as if the elevator in the Overlook Hotel had really existed, really been haunted" (T. King, *Small World* 166). Still, with a somewhat open-ended conclusion, the point of *Small World*, just like any fiction, opens for debate, despite the claims of the author (and the actual content of the book) that the tale was primarily about power. But if one were to approach *Small World* and examine the fruitless endeavors for power that the book examines, such a reading would give the book, and Tabitha's contribution to the examination of human folly within this tale, due credit.

Tabitha King's Maine: Introducing the Nodd's Ridge Stories

First impressions of Tabitha King's fiction, at least based on the titles of her writing in conjunction with the blurbs that grace the covers, tend to parallel the career of magician David Copperfield in that they are noted measures of misdirection. *Caretakers*, for example, is reported to be "a haunting novel about love against all odds," which suggests that the text finds its tension not just in images of the horrific but also the class differences between the blue-collar character Joe Nevars and the character of high society named Torrie Christopher. While the story does explore the lives that each of these characters lead and subtly plays upon the hands-on work that Nevars is cornered into (juxtaposed against the rather elitist leanings of the Christopher household in terms of careers in medicine and archaeology), the separation that these characters faced, based on economical factors, hardly received any extended treatment in the story itself. Although the eager Marxist critic would undoubtedly magnify the varied socio-economic conditions that shaped the main characters, *Caretakers* primarily functions as the doorway into Tabitha King's invented small town of Nodd's Ridge, a town that is no more haunting than any small town of the American social-scape. Of course, most discerning readers tend to ignore the deluded and diluted encapsulations of fiction that accompany most books, but when it has already been noted that Tabitha King faces the burden of being married to Stephen King, it is both interesting and discouraging to see that her fiction is hardly endeared to her potential readers through misleading synopses.

While this initial foray into the Nodd's Ridge writings of Tabitha King seems to merely belabor the minor point that her fiction, like that of many others, is positioned in a literary mine-field of sorts that readers must carefully and maddeningly navigate, it actually serves as an appropriate lead-in to her actual writing. With the multiple angles of interest, expectation, and revelation that surround Tabitha King's fiction, any venture into her writing necessitates, at minimum, a selective eye that can purposefully dismiss elements of her biography and other expectations which might fundamentally alter one's reading experience. The Signet paperback printing of Tabitha's novel *One on One*, for example, suggests that "falling in love is a contact sport," and despite the rough allusion to sex, as well as the pun which connects the love story to the athletic backdrop of high school basketball found in the pages of this text, there is hardly anything revealing about the actual story itself from this rather inane attempt to ensnare readers through a somewhat empty summary of the story. While there are scenes of brutality in *One on One* in which one of its main characters, Deanie Gauthier (otherwise dubbed "the Mutant" as a reflection of her reported failure to conform to an appropriate feminine identity), has to have emergency surgery to remove a chain from her face which was ground into her skin by a rather physical confrontation with her mother's boyfriend, the actual love story that undergirds *One on One* can hardly be effectively captured by the attempted witticism found on the cover of this book. Although the criticism surrounding marketing and other means of presenting Tabitha King's fiction to the reading public is largely out of Tabitha's control, such is an important plot element to the entire context of Tabitha King's fiction.

Defining and isolating themes or categories of literature is not always easy or, for that matter, fruitful. Further, any attempts to accurately capture and present fiction to the public for consumption is anything but an exact science. Consider, for instance, Mary Shelley's *Frankenstein*, with its positioning within the Gothic as well as the genre of science fiction, not to mention the feminist elements to be found in this text (as the main storyline takes place over a rather telling time frame of nine months). With the battle for classification that *Frankenstein* faces, it serves as a parallel to Tabitha's fiction both in terms of categorization and gender concerns. Seeking categories of literature and seeking to sift through the critical impositions of limited categorization (and restrictive expectations that are also attributed to a writer's gender) contributes to the muddled scene surrounding the Nodd's Ridge tales, as well as the rest of Tabitha's collection of writings. Dale Spender suggests in her analysis of women's writing titled *The Writer or the Sex?* that "one of the reasons that women have been discouraged from writing — and that their writing has been dismissed — is that the *woman* writer has presented an alternative world" (194). Although this statement does not function as a catch-all for women's literature, or necessarily point towards the alternative world allusion provided by the science fiction elements of Tabitha's first novel *Small World*, the play with "reality" in terms of innovation and imagination, or even elements such as character and setting, is an appropriate insight to Tabitha King's body of work.

In short, with Tabitha King facing impositions of genre, biography and biology, she attempts to draw a distinct line between her *person* and her *profession*. With expectations ranging from seeking horror and death in her fiction to slanted impositions placed upon her work because of her gender, Tabitha refreshingly declares, "You see, I'm not a lady. I'm a writer" ("Dump on Vulgarity" 13). Assuredly, Tabitha suggests that much of the foundation on which gendered critical analyses of her writing rests is in need of revision. For example, while the Nodd's Ridge stories can be seen, at times, as tales concerned with the small town and the additional microcosms of the domestic spaces that comprise the Maine small town, Dale Spender suggests that this element of Tabitha's fiction is simply a matter of course: "For women writers, art and domesticity have been inextricably linked" (121). And when the expectation of a domestic setting is met with the suggestion that this location is inevitably Gothic, as Gail Turley Houston observes a movement of the Gothic "from exotic to trivialized domestic spaces," it would seem that any attempt to move Tabitha and her fiction from these spheres is an exercise in futility (3). However, the domineering pull and sway of gender and genre is rarely left alone when it comes to literature, and the domesticity that is explored in Tabitha's fictions faces an inappropriate and inaccurate repackaging when one solely focuses on literary boundaries rather than initially approaching a text on a holistic level. Then again, any call to examine a text only in its entirety is all but impossible, as extended examinations often must analyze the parts of a given text; but to have one's analysis informed and narrowed by overly restrictive lenses asks for different approaches.

Although a purely generic or gendered analysis of Tabitha King is as limiting as viewing her writing as a mere offshoot of Stephen King's fiction, this is not to say that particular glimpses into Tabitha's writing by way of the Gothic or the feminine is without merit. For example, when Fred Botting describes the Gothic as a genre concerned with the "embodiments and evocations of cultural anxieties," he suggests that the Gothic, as both a genre and a means of artistic expression, tends to be intimately linked with the social scene on which a work of art is founded (2). Therefore, invocations of the Gothic need not always be concerned with death and decay, but rather the pressing social concerns of a given time period or even from within a specific location. And as Tabitha King's writing stems from similar social and cultural sources as that of her husband's, Tabitha's "Gothic" engagement with her world is hardly an attempt to feed off the success of Stephen's work within the stereotypical Gothic frame. To that end, when Tabitha King creates Nodd's Ridge and places both the freedoms and pressures of small-town life into her fictions, she may be utilizing a Gothic approach to confronting angst and worry, especially that with which she is largely familiar. But she is also simply weaving and crafting a story based on recognizable settings and figures which she feels warrants a fictionalized treatment. And with the notion of the small town serving as the backdrop for Tabitha's Nodd's Ridge novels, one immediately sees that the perceived quaintness and simplicity of the small town is anything but what these common impressions convey.

A (Hi)Story Begins: Caretakers

The first novel in the Nodd's Ridge series, *Caretakers*, finds itself in quite the predicament in terms of establishing a starting point for both an imminent series of books as well as the internal elements of the fictions which includes the crafted history and back-story of the town itself and its denizens. With the obstacle of clearly establishing a foundation for an entire town, and also managing to tell a specific piece of this town's history as it concerns the two main characters, Joe Nevars and Torrie Christopher, *Caretakers*, in many ways, is quite the ambitious novel. In one instance, with the setting of the small town seemingly dominating the text as both a background element and the constant thread which ties together the characters and their histories, Tabitha creates a novel that appears to engage in the revelatory discourses of obscured American life that her husband treats in his own fictions. In other words, when renowned Stephen King scholar Tony Magistrale says, "King's portraits of American suburban life are often alarmingly accurate: under the surface, in the modest split-level home with central heating, occupied by college-educated parents and children with potential for future success, lurk some disquieting realities," his analysis of the function of the small town in fiction suggests that Nodd's Ridge, too, provides a telling examination of a relatively misunderstood American microcosm (52). But beyond expectations of class divergences, as alluded to by the ubiquitous Cadillac of the alcoholic archaeologist Torrie Christopher, *Caretakers* takes on much more than just the inner workings of the community.

As is the case with most works of fiction, the reader is often introduced to a particular work by various means of advertising, and one of the most intimate advertisements attached to any book, as already discussed, is blurbs and summaries that are inscribed on the book itself. But such notations, like the reviews which often arise, tend to be either misleading or outright fabricated. For example, Barbara Parker's review of *Caretakers* suggests that the novel is "a dark but moving tale, sensitively written"; while one can only speculate as to the care and sensitivity on behalf of a given writer (in this case, Tabitha King), the empty words that Parker uses pose a few problems for the novel (1503). The invocation of the work "dark" may seem to be an appropriate connection to the "haunting" nature of the book that the publishers have attributed to the story, but most any reading, whether overly theorized or grounded in simple pleasure, finds great difficulty in deeming *Caretakers* a novel that is overly dark. Perhaps the darkest element of the text is the strained relationships that its characters face, and the revelation that its main characters had an affair which resulted in a child; but the passing or mundane nature of secrecy in a small town does not seem to be anything as darkly noteworthy.

By some accounts, the most shocking scenes of the Nodd's Ridge series are those which occur or are detailed outside this novel, including a brutal rape in *The Trap* and the clear revelation that the death of the child Joe Nevars fathered with Torrie is actually murder by the hand of Joe's wife. When these events are taken into account, along with the strong dramatics of the entire Nodd's Ridge series, it would stand to reason that the "darkness" which early reviewers impose upon Tabitha's fiction does indeed take hold — but not in the same way as it does in Stephen's novels. All things considered, Tabitha is her own writer and, like her sons, garners both praise and criticism on her own merits. *Caretakers* and the rest of the Nodd's Ridge tales may possess a very real sense of darkness that is essential to both the plot and the plotting of the stories, but one must be careful in sweepingly dubbing Tabitha's writing as dark, as such a summative critique is undoubtedly empty.

Moving to the actual novel, *Caretakers* carries within its pages a notable two-fold goal: relaying a particular story from the town of Nodd's Ridge while also looking beyond the primary plot's magnifications and casting a gaze towards the larger social and historical story. The course of the novel introduces readers to what appears to be both unnerving and common occurrences for Anytown, U.S.A.— including a house fire, numerous deaths, and the public fallout of various relationships among the citizenry — which easily establishes a traumatic and dramatic undercurrent for the story at hand. But the minor events which receive extended treatment in this novel reminds readers that, in many ways, *Caretakers* functions as little more than a recursive timeline that acts as a loose historical foundation for the four Nodd's Ridge novels that follow, three of which mainly focus on one of Torrie Christopher's lovers, Reuben Styles. But all stories must start somewhere, and Tabitha must be credited for having a plan in place for her creation in that the extensive historical coverage that she provides includes a level of detail that is often absent in stories of the large, or epic, scale.

Caretakers takes the reader through a wide selection of appreciated historical snapshots, and the chapter titles remind the audience of the movement within the text: "Holy Saturday 1982," "Summer 1912," "Fall 1956," "Fall 1956," "Spring 1951," "Fall 1953," "Spring 1967," "Spring 1957," "Fall 1966," "Winter 1917," "Summer/Fall 1962," "Summer 1961," "Summer 1962," "Fall 1949," "Winter 1949/Summer 1952," "Summer 1941," "Spring 1959," "Fall 1956," "Fall 1956," "Spring 1968," "Summer 1958," "Summer 1977." However, this constant movement did not find favor with early reviewers, who found Tabitha's approach to the issue of time as rather problematic: "One flaw that detracts from the effectiveness of *Caretakers* is the random sequence of the flashbacks. Mrs. King follows a haphazard scheme ... without any obvious plan" (Bass BR27). Each chapter, although announced as a particular period of time, moves between the indicated time period of the chapter's title and the story's present day (1982), with temporally jarring results. Keeping track of dates and history is difficult enough outside of a novel, and while it is possible, and necessary, for the careful reader to follow the histories of the characters in a piece of fiction, it is mildly disconcerting to think of pleasure reading as that which necessitates taking notes. Such is the case with reading a notably difficult text, like Thomas Pynchon's *The Crying of Lot 49*, or *One Hundred Years of Solitude* by Gabriel García Márquez (in which contemporary paperback editions tend to provide a detailed family tree to guide the reader through this novel which contains several related characters with the same name). But to return to the question of time, the historical flashbacks could be said to parallel, for example, Stephen King's *It*, in which readers are asked to move between 1957–8 and 1984–5, and also negotiate the wider historical scope of the novel, which takes readers into the eighteenth century and even farther back in time. And while *It* often balances a careful examination of the past and present alongside the characters that exist in these times, *Caretakers* tips this scale in favor of time. But, as noted, the foundational purpose of this novel purposely takes precedence, and yet it still manages to present a cast of characters and an excellent display of literary craft that bodes well for the rest of Tabitha's series.

Like any adept writer, Tabitha King shows a strong predilection for creating memorable characters. And while the reasons behind particular characters' noteworthiness vary, as is the case with Joe Nevars (who is the first character to be introduced in her Nodd's Ridge tales, and who is wonderfully crafted as a realistically dual-minded character that displays both care and rage), the characters largely propel both the novel and the reader in *Caretakers* and the subsequent Nodd's Ridge novels. And while *character* is only one of many components to any fiction, *Caretakers* is careful to establish a noted complexity beyond just the people that populate Tabitha's fictions, such as the intricate timeline established in the novel that is present in Tabitha's other novels. When one reads Tabitha's fiction and sees that her attention to detail, plot, character, setting, and just about any other major or minor element of the fictional creation, is anything but limited or small in scope or treatment, one then sees that Tabitha genuinely attempts to create fictions that are more than thinly-drawn caricatures of the world at large. And while such layering can be criticized as being overly elaborate or even confusing for the reader, Tabitha reflects upon her writing that "I think it's too bad there's such an emphasis on stripped-down stories, because people's lives aren't.... A novel should be, to me, something where there's a whole lot going on, the way it is in reality. In other words, I'm not a minimalist" (Shattuck 62). Tabitha's noted endeavors to create fiction that is real to the point that it effectively mimics the layered and convoluted everyday occurrences of everyday life is not just a pattern to observe in her writing; it is a point of critique that she cannot avoid, despite her justification for the labyrinthine constructions of her fictions.

Returning to the characters that function as a basis for *Caretakers* and as a point of reference for the rest of the Nodd's Ridge population, it is easy to see that Tabitha creates multi-dimensional characters that compliment the twisting and somewhat opaque timeline of her core series. In the case of *Caretakers*, readers may come to understand Torrie Christopher and her alcoholism (not to mention her other flaws), in that she loses two children and finds herself in both a loveless marriage and various predicaments of threat (which include a near-rape scene near the novel's conclusion). Further, Joe Nevars is drawn in such a way that he becomes believably and sympathetically real. Aside from Joe Nevars' position as a friend and confidant for Torrie Christopher, he is developed as a man who is trapped in a loveless marriage. He literally strikes out against his wife, Cora: "'I can't take this no more,' he said, and punched her in the face. And into his other fist, hitting her so hard it jarred him" (T. King, *Caretakers* 138). This physicality, this abuse, may be somewhat tempered in that Cora is despised by just about everyone in Nodd's Ridge, from Torrie—"When I get to hell, want me to say hello to Cora?"—to Cora's own daughter (Joe's step-daughter), who implies that any beating that Cora receives from Joe is not necessarily condonable but understandable because of Cora's stubborn and malicious persona (T. King, *Caretakers* 74). Further, Tabitha is careful to provide an accounting for Cora, who recalls being molested by her father in addition to his indifference to the suicide of her first husband, who was reported to have killed himself as an escape from his marriage to Cora. And while such character developments can be seen as typical in terms of the tensions and dramatic effects they bring to the tale, one must also consider that such developments carry more than just fictional formulas or gimmicks.

In this instance they transform the story of *Caretakers* from a historical foundation for a series of novels sharing the same setting to a notable novel with the depth of development one expects from a skilled writer, one who knows how to add depth to a character for the purpose of forwarding a story rather than merely fulfilling some sort of forged requirement for fiction. But the extensive characterization that Tabitha's creations receive is not without its pit falls.

Although it would be grossly reductionist to consider Tabitha King's writing as that which is sustained through a handful of compelling scenes and/or characters in each of her novels, such a pattern can be noted. In *Pearl*, for example, the title character, Pearl Dickenson, is a divorced African American woman who finds herself living in a small and largely Caucasian town, and while the story takes readers to and through the turbulence of Pearl's love life as it develops in Nodd's Ridge, perhaps the most intricate and interesting element of the story is Pearl's ethnicity. As Tabitha plays up Pearl's skin tone, as well as her gender, in the early pages of the novel, and positions Pearl as a strong presence in the town (both in spite of and because of her biology), it seems as if the tale finds a precipitous drop off when the plot has Pearl negotiate the judgments not of race and sex but rather of morality as she shuffles between two sexual partners and must wade through each individual's personal history (which is, of course, intricately tied to the history of Nodd's Ridge). But this focus on Pearl's involvement in the history of the town, by navigating through its past and becoming inextricably tied to its present and future, is a remarkable element of Pearl's creation and characterization, especially when compared to how the rest of Nodd's Ridge population, by one degree or another, is deftly woven into the story of the town itself by way of notably dramatic and/or traumatic events which constantly ripple throughout Tabitha's imagination and stories.

By looking at Tabitha's characters, as well as *Caretakers*, as threads which are woven in and out of the larger Nodd's Ridge tale, the selective and sporadic historical highlights can be seen as careful plotting rather than whimsical writing. With *Caretakers*, despite its own primary story which unceremoniously reaches back into the personal histories of Torrie Christopher and Joe Nevers (so much so that some of their life experiences do become lost, if not negligible, as the series concludes), there are several instances within the overarching tale that serve as placeholders of the plot that are developed further in the series. In one instance, as readers become acquainted with Torrie's children, Joe comments that Torrie's daughter seems to resemble Joe's sister: "Your India's the spit of Gussie at that age" (T. King, *Caretakers* 187). While this strange comment is unveiled as *Caretakers* progresses and reveals a single sexual encounter between Torrie and Joe, one of the most genuinely mysterious scenes of this book, which is not wholly unwrapped until the conclusion of the entire Nodd's Ridge series, involves not India Christopher's birth, but her death. As Tabitha sets the scene, she has the old caretaker, Joe Nevars, along with his heir-apparent, Rueben Styles (with whom readers become much more acquainted in the third novel of this series), working on the roof of the Christopher home. From this vantage point they see out onto the lake near which the Christopher home sits. There they see Torrie on the lake with her surviving children, David and India (as Tommy Christopher had passed away after being hit in the head by a wild pitch during a communal baseball game). However, as the scene progresses, readers are told, "There was a crack, the doe jumped and fell, as a second crack broke like a thunderclap over the water," suggesting that hunters near the lake took poor aim at their prey and killed the child (T. King, *Caretakers* 109). This second gunshot does in fact kill India. "But the Sabbatos County coroner called India's death a 'misadventure.'... As it was, there was no body and no bullet," so readers are left with a scene of sorrow and misery that does not become completely untied in the novel (T. King, *Caretakers* 111). Such tension is noteworthy for its effectiveness in creating interest in the people and events of Nodd's Ridge, especially as Tabitha provides enough information to suggest that despite what the authorities on the Ridge concluded, India's death is but one of many events that cannot be fully understood in pure isolation.

It is ultimately suggested that India's death is no accident, and that it is Joe's largely estranged wife Cora who waits, watches, and murders India, with the convenient pretense of a hunting accident to cover her deeds. But the murder of Joe's illegitimate child is not entirely explained. Even though Joe suggests, as he lays dying underneath Torrie's Cadillac, that Cora's jealously and rage at Joe's relationship with Torrie prompted Cora to kill India ("India was mine. Cora couldn't stand me having anything 'twas my own. She took her away from me"), there is, again, a real sense of disbelief that enters the tale (T. King, *Caretakers* 324). While this reflection by Joe suggests that Cora murdered India, the convoluted scenes involving the sex act between Joe and Torrie which led to India's birth, along with Torrie's inability to clearly remember that she and Joe had sex (in that she was drunk during their encounter), does not fully or clearly reveal what is learned in later books — which is that Cora does in fact kill India. Part of the disbelief stems from the idea that India's death is purportedly orchestrated to a point of perfection that is all but impossible, and part of the disbelief comes from the inability of the reader to gain a strong hold on the plot and its occurrences.

Again, within *Caretakers*, readers are left with an overarching sense of mystery, aided by numerous references to the flaw in India's eye as a noted link to Joe's genealogy, and his recognition of the same distinct mark in his sister's eye. In later novels, the imperfection in the Nevars line is played up so much that all familial connections are clearly established, but *Caretakers* remains mysterious to the point that it all but demands a reading of the later novels so that a given reader can begin to complete the historical and contemporary picture begun in *Caretakers*. Although Tabitha reminds her audience of the clandestine nature of Nodd's Ridge as the novel concludes ("The Ridge. It's like a great big secret. The only way you could know it all would be to be born here"), she sets her readers up to continue with the series (T. King, *Caretakers* 333). As her readers are literal and figurative outsiders, Tabitha creates a need to satiate any curiosity that has developed by reading *Caretakers*, the secrets alluded to in this novel are enough to warrant not just additional books, but also continued readership. However, *Caretakers* is, above all else, a foundational novel that does have some difficulty in holding up under the weight of potential story brought into the actual story of Torrie and Joe facing their mortality, which is a story that is apparently not enough of a story in and of itself to garner most of the novel's focus and treatment throughout its pages.

Caretakers is a book best described as "almost"—or as a text that almost realizes its potential. It is a story that tends to take on too many subplots and historical accounts to satisfyingly capture the love and respect that Joe Nevars and Torrie Christopher appear to have for one another. As it were, the story ends not with a sense of "hope and courage," as reported by Judy Bass ("Although overridingly tragic, *Caretakers* yields glimpses of hope and courage"), but with an excerpt of Torrie's last article published before her death in 1982 (BR27). Such an ending serves as a glimpse into Torrie's constantly interrupted and fragmented life, one which sees her lose two of her children, her best friend, and her career before any of these elements of her life are afforded any real semblance of animation, which hardly offers any hope when reflecting that most lifelines of those who live in Nodd's Ridge seem to be severed before any real growth is afforded.

Breaching the Home: The Trap *(aka* Wolves at the Door*)*

One of the main criticisms of *Caretakers* has been that it is a thread of a larger story, and because of the future potential for this tale and the semblance of grandiosity that a series of stories implies, it is difficult to fully grasp the story which *will* be told, despite relatively easy access to the story *being* told. In many ways, as it is difficult, as well as disrespectful, to judge an author's writing on the parts of his or her fictions, the nature of the serial novel does create an obstacle in terms of examining a fiction as a whole, which is preferable to isolated and perhaps slanted criticisms based on minor elements of a story. Nonetheless, Tabitha King's second installment in her Nodd's Ridge series, *The Trap*, is hard to navigate in terms of its placement in the entire series, even from a retrospective point of view which looks back to the story after reading the last three novels (which primarily focus on the history of Rueben Styles, a seemingly minor character from *Caretakers* whose witnessing of India Christopher's death is only a minor part of his own well-documented history in the later parts of this series). But even with *The Trap* serving as what seems to be a minor piece of the Nodd's Ridge puzzle, especially as the main character, Olivia Russell, only makes a few minor appearances in the rest of the series (and Walter Mackenzie, not Joe Nevars, is the current caretaker for the Ridge), this does not mean that this novel is lacking in terms of its own plot and characters. In many ways, *The Trap* functions as a stand-alone novel that only shares a familiar setting with the rest of the Nodd's Ridge tales, although it does find itself firmly situated in the larger history of the entire story behind the series. But like any familial relationship, connection and kinship by way of blood, literal or literary, can only account for so much.

One of the earliest instances in *The Trap* which separates this tale from the rest in Tabitha's series is that the main characters, the Russell family—Olivia (Liv), Pat, Sarah and Travis—are outsiders to the overarching story and to Nodd's Ridge, as Tabitha notes that the first scene of this novel examines the Russell family's "first summer in Nodd's Ridge" (T. King, *The Trap* 2). As Tabitha also positions this family as outsiders, people whose story will only briefly be touched upon in later books in this series, she seems to break down her own series from the inside, even though the theme of community is carried out in the story, which suggests that Nodd's Ridge does not solely belong to its original denizens. However, while *The Trap* does not fully incorporate the Russell family into the Ridge, it does provide a few glimpses into the darker corners of the town, with particular attention given to the Nighswander family, a collection of drunks and misfits who essentially terrorize the entire Nodd's Ridge area. Even within the first few pages, this gaggle of delinquents—Rand and Ricky Nighswander, along with their step-brother Gordy Tweed—makes a critical effect on the story in that they encounter Olivia Rusell and hassle her to a degree that is criminal. Rand Nighwander concludes his first meeting with Olivia by waving his penis at her in a mocking manner that, incidentally, also serves as a foreshadowing for the later scenes of the novel.

But this treatment of Olivia as a woman, an outsider, is not wholly solidified in the early chapters, as one local, Helen Alden, takes a shine to Olivia. Their brief and cordial relationship includes a tour of Helen's home—complete with a secret passage that is critical to the plot of the story—and a discussion of a string of robberies that have taken place on the Ridge (with the aforementioned Nighswander boys as the primary suspects). At this, Helen suggests that a Machiavellian mindset is warranted: "A prince being thus obliged to know how to act the beast must imitate the fox and the lion, for the lion cannot protect himself from traps, and the fox cannot defend himself from wolves. Therefore be a fox to recognize traps, and a lion to frighten the wolves" (T. King, *The Trap* 45). As is the case with Rand Nighswander's penis and the secret passage in Helen Alden's home, this literary reference is just one of many preliminary cases of foreshadowed plot development that Tabitha brings to this tale, and although Helen Alden takes a liking to Olivia, she and her family still seems to encroach upon the story as outsiders. This suggests, as far as the construction of *The Trap* goes, that (despite the previous claim that examining fiction based on its parts is detrimental to the reading experience and more than discourteous to the author) this particular novel seems to deconstruct itself in terms of its focus, as the numerous peripheral yet critical elements of the story all but eliminate a genuine center.

Among the obstacles created in *The Trap* which makes a genuine center of the novel difficult to find is Pat Russell's screenplay, *Firefight*, serving as a background for the story by way of its examination of Vietnam veterans fighting for their lives while readjusting to civilian life. On the one hand, Tabitha's crafting of this story within the story is rather effective, and one might even want to see this tale in its entirety played out or written, which brings a particular distraction for the underlying story. On the other hand, Pat Russell's project serves as a constant point of tension for the Russell family, in that his career often takes precedence over any family development as Pat is constantly traveling to California. This leaves his boy, Travis, to not only develop a distaste for their home in Nodd's Ridge, but to also observe the toll that this crumbling family structure has on his mother, Olivia: "Daddy's never home, and you cry all the time" (T. King, *The Trap* 79). Further, this wonderfully intelligent insight by Travis is preceded by his initial awareness of the harm his father's career has on the family when he states, "I hate you ... [and] I hate your stupid movie!" (T. King, *The Trap* 16). This early establishment of the somewhat dysfunctional family is certainly important as far as the story is concerned, especially as the family ultimately splits, with Pat taking his stock, angst-filled teenage daughter to California so he can finish his screenplay, while Olivia and Travis spend time in Nodd's Ridge. Further developing a rift in the family is the odd if not Oedipal relationship between Olivia and Travis, aided by Travis' familiar use of his mother's first name when he addresses her. Even with these instances illustrating an unstable family unit, perhaps the most interesting aspect of the crumbling Russell family is not Pat's career, or that he buys a house in California without first consulting his wife, but his cocaine use.

Pat's cocaine habit is somewhat telling, as Stephen's chronicled struggles with the same drug align temporally with the 1985 publication of *The Trap*. Catherine A. Lundie notes, "Authors do not produce texts solely out of private experience," and reminds readers that the source material for fiction is hardly ever fully fictional (Lundie 2). And while Lundie's reminder as to the nature of fiction is originally connected to the construction of American ghost stories penned by women in a literary period dominated by men, the suggestion that fiction is hardly ever created in pure isolation makes Pat's cocaine use quite compelling when connected to Tabitha's life beyond her typewriter. Then again, this particular drug, although seemingly a minor element of the story (despite Olivia's powerful reprimand, "Wanted to find out how it was to fuck your wife on a rush of coke?"), makes quite a strong reappearance in the latter half of the novel (T. King, *The Trap* 74). Of course, there is much missed or dismissed in fast-forwarding from the initial and familial discord to the aftereffects of the noted geographical separation that appears to function as a precursor to an imminent split between Olivia and Pat. But when looking at *The Trap* from a standpoint which seeks its most profound and memorable qualities, some parts of the story do, unfortunately, become negligible.

Briefly setting the inclusion of cocaine aside and directing focus to the Nighswanders, as their role in the story becomes much more important than a drug, it is noted that these individuals are responsible for the rash of crime spreading across the ridge. The story naturally positions these males to entrap Olivia in her home where Rand Nighswander ultimately rapes her. Aside from the rape, which is one of the most disturbing yet important scenes in the novel, the elements of sex and power, which play vital roles in Tabitha's first book *Small World*, are developed well in advance of Rand's violation of Olivia. On the one hand, Rand is a product of an environment which treats women and sex in a demeaning and domineering way, as evidenced by one scene in which Rand beds a woman at home, to which his father replies, "Used to be me breakin' 'em in" (T. King, *The Trap* 190). This unnerving dialogue serves up quite the commentary on the state of the American family in which denigrating women is considered to be a family pastime, and that sex is often seen as an activity in which males are said to create their identities as *men*, even though Tabitha suggests in a wonderfully blunt and accurate statement that "It takes two to make a whore" (T. King, *The Trap* 92). But there is much more to sex and rape in *The Trap* (specifically the brutal rape of Olivia, which begins when she is hit so hard in her face that she actually loses a few teeth) than a few glimpses into the truly dysfunctional family life of the Nighswander clan.

The sexual acts in *The Trap* are established as displays of power rather than intimate encounters, especially as it is revealed that Gordy Tweed, who is already in a role of subservience as the step-brother to the Nighswanders, had to fellate his step-brother Ricky, and had even been sodomized by Ricky. And with all this context regarding the function of sex, it is clear that Rand's eventual *rapes* of Olivia are in line with the standard disturbing source of rape as a means of power rather than thrill or titillation. And this is where Tabitha King creatively and provocatively brings her treatment of rape to a level that not even her husband could muster. Tyson Blue says of the previously examined "Man with a Belly" that Stephen King's treatment of rape "is nowhere near as brutally effective and repulsive as the excruciatingly-graphic rape sequence crafted by Tabitha King in her 1984 novel *The Trap*" (51). This is not to say that Tabitha is disturbed or more connected to the genuinely repulsive than Stephen, but it does suggest an understanding of sex and rape, as well as a willingness to confront it, beyond Stephen's. Although Stephen does come close to capturing the reality of rape's brutality in his recent novel *Under the Dome* when several characters gang-rape Sammy (Samantha) Bushey, one notices a hesitancy to describe the horrific act itself in that the only real examination of the rape itself is almost absent, as the narrator only ventures to note that the worst of the rapists "had gone at her hard" (King, *Under the Dome* 355). Stephen King's fans have seen limited treatments of rape like this before in *The Stand* when the only real description of Nadine Cross' rape by Randall Flagg is that her hair turns completely white; and this reluctance to examine the truly horrific, or this inability to fully examine the world of sex and its terrible derivatives, carries many implications. But beyond this separation regarding examinations of sex and rape between Stephen and Tabitha King is the long and devastating violation at the heart of *The Trap*, which carries with it perhaps the darkly shining moment in Tabitha King's oeuvre.

To the heart of *The Trap* and perhaps Tabitha King's canon is the rape of Olivia Russell by Rand Nighswander. As Olivia is hurting from having her teeth literally knocked out to also being "coked up" (as Pat Russell's drug of choice finds its way back into the story), Tabitha provides an initially basic description of rape that is as compassionate as one might expect: "For an instant, Liv could do nothing. He was hurting her, he was inside her, fucking her, tearing her. He was raping her. Nothing she had ever read or heard or imagined had prepared her in any way for the reality of rape" (T. King, *The Trap* 223). But Tabitha proceeds to ensure that this scene becomes memorable beyond the standpoint of brutal violence, especially as imprinting images of rape upon her readers should have more of a point than just memories of a disturbing scene. In short, Tabitha has Olivia, to put it simply if crudely, fuck her rapist: "You asked for it, she thought. You bastard. And then she tightened her vaginal muscles" (T. King, *The Trap* 224). As Olivia attempts to gain some semblance of control over her attacker, she realizes that even though she is being raped, she can fight back, at least to a degree by speeding up the rape — by forcing Rand to climax prematurely, she does what she can to end her rape and alleviate some of the dread involved: "Her own terror receded. She didn't need to fuck him to death. It was enough to humiliate him" (T. King, *The Trap* 224). To be sure, Tabitha's treatment of rape is not only very blunt, but is also innovative from the standpoint of the victim-victimizer relationship described, as Olivia, in one respect, essentially rapes her rapist. Of course, this is not exactly empowerment on Olivia's part because she is, no matter what, a rape victim, but the initial turn of events in which Olivia weakens her attacker by fucking back is a very powerful scene.

Although Olivia has, in some ways, wrested power and control from her rapist by essentially raping him, Tabitha creates genuine horror when she has Rand rape Olivia for a second time. This time, as "He [Rand] placed one hand firmly on her pubis, and began to insert small quantities of the powder into her vagina," Tabitha not only creates the ultimate horror in an additional rape that, despite Olivia's previous efforts, will be completed to the attacker's satisfaction by removing power from Olivia by numbing her vagina, Tabitha takes care to detail the scene (T. King, *The Trap* 226). Again, while the details may seem inconsequential or downright despicable, one must give credit where credit is due and note that Tabitha King is anything but shy when it comes to the dark and horrific occurrences of the world. As Tabitha herself notes, "Every character I have ever imagined was rooted in some aspect of myself, including the nasty ones. I'm not saying I'm a rapist or an alcoholic, but it's my job to imagine what it would be like to be such a person" (Rogak 128). Such an imagination may be seen as sickly, but Tabitha's job of imagining is not necessarily concerned with the unimaginable — one only need watch the nightly newscast to see numerous instances of imagination run amok. Still, it is within this imagination, or at least a keen awareness of the happenings within her own society, that Tabitha does provide a fictional temperament for the darkness of *The Trap*, as she sees to it that the Nighswander boys all die by the time the book concludes, which could be viewed as an exceptionally karmic ending. However, in the realm of fiction, readers often suspend disbelief, as it serves to be more of an obstacle than a form of saving grace regarding the reading process; and with the reader setting aside slanted perceptions of reality and believability, *The Trap* is able to effectively and hauntingly move into its conclusion.

To be brief, as Olivia ultimately endures Rand Nighswander's rapes and escapes her home with Travis, she and her son find themselves only able to flee as far as the nearby home of Helen Alden, which is, unbeknownst to the Nighswanders, rigged with trip-wires connected to shotguns. As Olivia and Travis are, fortuitously, able to avoid tripping one of these traps when they flee into the Alden house, her pursuers are not as lucky: "Ricky hooted and kicked the door a third time. It fell slowly, heavily inward. He hooted again and jumped through the door frame. He felt the slight constriction of the wire as his chest hit it but there was no time to even wonder what it was before the shotgun went off" (T. King, *The Trap* 260). With Ricky Nighswander, as well as Gordy Tweed, out of the picture, the only "wolf" left for Olivia (and, by proxy, Helen Alden) to trap is the monster Rand, who is ultimately lured into the chimney from the roof. As he frees himself from this temporary prison, he flees the hearth (where Olivia has set a fire) and trips a wire like his brother and is killed by shotgun fire. Of course, this brief encapsulation of the concluding pages do not do the story justice, which ultimately concerns itself with literal justice, as Helen Alden is accused of murdering the Nighswander boys by way of her rigged home, although Olivia's "testimony ... moved the jury to find Miss Alden guilty not of murder but of manslaughter, and to recommend a lenient sentence" (T. King, *The Trap* 307). Outside of the courthouse, readers see the Russell family mostly reunited and looking towards a future where they, primarily Olivia, can then heal, which is sealed by the tale's concluding image of the safety and comforts of home including a cheesy nod towards *The Wizard of Oz* that could have easily been omitted.

While this final note leaves a rather sour impression on the reader, this minor element does not reduce the book to a second-tier fiction. Indeed, as reviewer JoAnn Vicarel says, "despite some unpolished writing and a few incongruities, King has produced a gripping story with an electrifying climax and first-rate heroine," and the sustained perseverance as well as adaptability on behalf of Olivia helps to overshadow the perceived foibles within the text (rev. of *The Trap* 158). Among these potential flaws is another instance in the Tabitha King canon which connects her work to her husband's, as she references specific towns and locales, specifically Togus and Shawshank Prison, along with another metafictional reference to the Stephen King canon in which she notes the reading tastes of the new caretaker, Walter McKenzie, whose favorite fictions "were by J.C. Devereaux, who was really a woman named Bobbie Anderson who lived only a hundred miles northeast in Haven, a wide place in the road on the way to Derry and Bangor" (T. King, *The Trap* 138). Still, no matter how much Tabitha King's fictions bleed into those of her husband, and no matter how issues of taste may decry some of her authorial decisions and creations, she really begins to establish herself as a writer who can and will hold a mirror up for her reader to see reflections of the darkest corners of the troubled society which influences her imagination and craft. And while some of these corners are more troubling than others, especially in terms of ostensible, physical brutality in the form of rape, for example, Tabitha and her Nodd's Ridge tales do not stop with a handful of tragedies and complex personal histories. Nodd's Ridge may be a small town, but even a small town carries with it an infinitude of stories, both endearing and troubling.

Race and the Small Town: Pearl

The third novel in the Nodd's Ridge series continues Tabitha King's pattern of looking into her fictional creation primarily through a single character; and within this novel the title character, Pearl Dickenson, is given the honor of the spotlight. Pearl's connection to Nodd's Ridge is found through her bloodlines, as she is the grand-niece of the recently deceased Joe Nevars. But while Pearl is connected to the town because of her genes, one particular element of her genetic makeup stands out above all else, and it is not her gender. Pearl Dickenson is black, and she is the only black character with any noted role in Tabitha King's fiction, which pushes one's focus, and potential criticisms, right to this aspect of *Pearl*. Although some critics might view this character as a feeble attempt to engage issues of race that have become more and more prevalent during Tabitha's lifetime, Pearl cannot be reduced to a stock black character, or even treated as such, as has been the case in Stephen King's fiction.

Some have given Stephen King credit for creating strong African American characters. Samantha Figliola says, "[Stephen] King's black characters from Hallorann to Hanlon are heroic because they have not allowed their exposure to evil to destroy their capacity to love. They are healers for people who need their strength and greater knowledge" (56). But the catalytic yet isolated role that these characters take on, alongside Tabitha's character Pearl, are not always seen as heroic or even accurate. Quite noticeably, the role that the black character plays in Stephen King's canon, and to some extent in *Pearl*, has piqued the curiosity of critics who have all but demonized King for the role that black characters take on in his fiction, including John Coffey from *The Green Mile*, whose divine touch heals Paul Edgecombe and Melinda Moore but cannot save him from the electric chair and the ire of his predominantly white peers. This "magical negro" analysis carries with it some weight and validity with which the discerning reader can re-enter Stephen's more racially charged works, even though Stephen King is hesitant to accept such readings of his fiction. He says, for example, that "the idea of Coffey being a superman is just plain wrong" (S. King, "Steve's Take" 14). With *Pearl*, the title character is not a superwoman, although she is admittedly a very strong character who willingly enters the small town of Nodd's Ridge, even though "the range of ethnic groups was overwhelmingly Northern European" (T. King, *Pearl* 21). As she faces the stereotypical short-sightedness and ignorance that is believed to indelibly mark small-town U.S.A.—"Goddammit, Reuben. I ain't ignorant. I seen *The Cosby Show*. I know a Negro when I see one"—Pearl's experience in Nodd's Ridge as an African American woman becomes less and less of an issue as the novel maneuvers through a plot primarily concerned with love and the ghosts of the past (T. King, *Pearl* 22). As the issue of race becomes a background element that is rarely highlighted, perhaps this element of the text can be interpreted as a sign of hope concerning the role of race in the larger American social-scape of the late 1980s; yet the flashbacks to Pearl's childhood and her single mother bring up issues of race in terms of temporality, and the connection to discussions of race involved in Stephen King's *The Shining*, as Tabitha King reveals that Pearl grew up in the company of a familiar African American face—Dick Hallorann. And while this connection to Stephen King's own imagined fictional world(s) is just one of several that are to be found in Tabitha King's fictions, and which add to the overarching story and accompanying concerns that populate Stephen's fictions, this decision by Tabitha is not an attempt to jump on the coattails of her husband.

Tabitha's conscious weaving of her stories into the larger backdrop of her husband's work creates a conversation of credence and validity in that their treatments of the human condition—that of death and despair, as well as issues of sexuality, childhood innocence and the issues of race which run through American history—finds a certain believability and consistency through repetition. As Tabitha notes in *Pearl* that the title character has drawn certain conclusions about the small town in which she establishes her residence, including the notion that "I thought nobody locked their doors up here, everyone was so honest," this reverberant image of Maine and the surrounding areas is more than just common ground between Tabitha and Stephen (T. King, *Pearl* 16). It is a wide window through which each asks their respective readers to look in order to see a world that is ambivalently innocent and ignorant, much like the rest of the American landscape. Just as the narrator for *Pearl* notes that "learning the other ways into Nodd's Ridge, the back roads, takes a lifetime of living there," Tabitha King's extensive knowledge of the social norms and actions of her Maine are to be trusted, as is her treatment of Pearl and her initial obstacles of becoming integrated and accepted in Nodd's Ridge (T. King, *Pearl* 11). Further, as Tabitha continues with the geographical backdrop of Maine to position her tales, and when her first major minority character enters into her oeuvre, it is rather fitting to have such a character's trials and tribulations become enhanced by the geography. It is an excellent layering of time and place, along with an awareness of the criticisms that have faced her husband and his treatment of African American characters in a largely Caucasian cast, that *Pearl* becomes both an honest and believable treatment of race relations in the waning years of the twentieth century.

In looking beyond Pearl Dickenson's race and the small-town atmosphere that Tabitha adeptly creates through the book, especially concerning the networking that takes place involving the accurately assumed brevity of a secret in such a location, readers are treated to the typical components of a Tabitha King novel. There are instances of sincere and accurate humor, as when Sam Styles (the main character of the following Nodd's Ridge novel, *One on One*) sarcastically comments to his troubled sister, Karen, "Got your period? ... That should be a relief" (T. King, *Pearl* 59). Supplementing the humorous insights into the Styles family, which pales in comparison to the Nighswander family from *The Trap*, are a wide selection of seemingly happenstance or convenient notes that help further establish the history of Nodd's Ridge and its citizens. Beyond the notations that Reuben Styles' son, Frank, is in the Navy and fighting in the first Gulf War, along with a brief mention of Sam Styles' nighttime problems—wetting the bed—that receive extended treatment in *The Book of Reuben*, *Pearl* ultimately focuses on a love triangle between the title character, Reuben Styles, and a minor character from *Caretakers*: David Christopher.

In *Pearl*, David Christopher, Torrie Christopher's only surviving child, enters the story with some acerbic wit when he asks Rueben Styles' daughter, Karen, "You still here breaking hearts and zippers?" (T. King, *Pearl* 77). Of course, Tabitha takes the time to repeatedly note that Karen's breasts are similar to the breasts of Kissy Mellors (large) from Tabitha's second stand-alone novel,

Survivor, and this sexually charged depiction of Karen does more than just continue a trend in content for Tabitha's writing. In many ways it sets the entire scene of the novel, which not only takes time to repeatedly remind readers that "Reuben Styles is a well-endowed farmboy," but also that David Christopher is bi-sexual, adding a new dimension of sex and sexuality to a series that has already confronted, among other sexual actions, affairs and rapes (T. King, *Pearl* 124). Then again, as Tabitha notes, "Sex doesn't stop in bed" (T. King, *Pearl* 186). While such a focus might detract from the actual plot of the tale, which, at its core, is dependent upon the byproducts of sex (Pearl's lineage is highlighted when she is labeled "the bastard child of Elizabeth Madden,") it is nonetheless refreshing to see Tabitha continue to be able to write of sex, as well as its derivatives and repercussions, in that this particular element of her writing seems to be a market that she has cornered, so to speak, within the King family (T. King, *Pearl* 139). As always, reducing a writer to a single component of his or her writing is limiting, but one must wonder why Tabitha is so comfortable with sex as a topic in her fiction.

With respect to the story of *Pearl* in its entirety, it seems to follow the pattern established with *Caretakers* in that it moves readers along a specific moment of history in the town of Nodd's Ridge, and almost with no purpose beyond sharing a snapshot of the town's people and their daily lives at a particularly dramatic and eventful moment. In many ways the construction of the tale is both burdened and blessed with a variety of stories within the main story. JoAnn Vicarel's review of *Pearl* suggests that the multiplicity within the story is the bedrock of the narrative, in that this book is "a contemporary tale of real people struggling with teen rebellion, the aftermath of divorce, aging, loneliness, and abuse. An unforgettable reading experience" (rev. of *Pearl* 85). Of course, it is hard to deny that *Pearl* comes with its share of sub-plots that add to both this specific story and the story of Nodd's Ridge, and the breadth of such stories is important to consider when reflecting back upon *Pearl*. However, even given such varied sub-plots as abuse in its many forms (especially spousal), death (including murder and abortion), and a dog that refuses to stay leashed (allowing Tabitha to make yet another connection between her fiction and her husband's, as this stray dog leads to a *Cujo* reference), perhaps it is best to primarily examine *Pearl* for its strengths in terms of sex and race, as well as gender and the larger tale that Tabitha must manage.

In keeping with an examination of *Pearl* which considers its keen dissection of sex and the complex relationships that can form around this act, one of the most telling lines of the story, along the lines of Tabitha's insightful analyses of human relationships and the complications that the joy of sex can bring, is when Reuben discovers that Pearl has also been sleeping with David Christopher. At this revelation, Reuben says, "Don't you see, Pearl, it's like you've been sleeping with Sam [Reuben's son]. I've known David since he was a baby" (T. King, *Pearl* 337). On the one hand, this line establishes Reuben's dominating masculine identity in that he finds a way to demean Pearl for sleeping with another man while Reuben was sleeping with her. On the other hand, this establishes more story for the series in that Reuben's familiarity with David has yet to be fully explored, and that one must read Reuben as a character who can extend beyond the narrow categorizations of the sexually territorial and adept man because his relationship with David seems to be more than just a passing acquaintance. And this suggests that in addition to the strengths of Tabitha's story in terms of its thematically accurate depictions of race and sex, there is a larger story that she is still attempting to weave. And she ensures that among the sexual and racial tensions of *Pearl*, readers do not forget the specific location in which this book is situated. As the love triangle between Pearl, David and Reuben pushes David over the edge of his noted mental instabilities (which David thrives on and considers eccentricities more than anything), David attempts to commit suicide. In this instance, suicide aside, David's masculinity overshadows his largely gender-neutral and bi-sexual character, as he, like Reuben, finds Pearl's perceived promiscuity to be a threat and a measure of his insufficiencies as a man and a person.

But as is the case with Pearl's race becoming a background issue in the text, David's insecurities become hidden, as does his suicide attempt when, as his efforts to drown himself in Lake Keywadin results in one of the most unbelievable yet thrilling events in the Nodd's Ridge series. David's suicide attempt, which sees him sink to the bottom of the lake and become entangled with whatever lies there, actually jars loose the corpse of his dead sister, India. Such coincidence, of course, is not uncommon in fiction, and in this particular case it serves as a means of further connecting *Pearl* to the rest of the Nodd's Ridge tales, as well as providing David Christopher a means of reconciling his own inner demons by finally confronting the death of his sister. Also noteworthy is that Reuben confirms his own knowledge of India's markedly secret parentage when he informs Pearl that she is actually related to India Christopher: "That little wedge of tarnish that's copper in your eye was gold in hers. Same place, eleven o'clock on the iris. Gussie [Pearl's mother and Joe Nevar's sister] had it, you have it" (T. King, *Pearl* 348). Of course, this knowledge may seem to suggest a level of incest between Pearl and David as the connections of their genealogy become clearer, but perhaps more importantly than reading into issues of sexuality and biological relationships is the overwhelming sense of closure with which *Pearl* ends. As the opening pages of the book look to the local graveyard, which makes some critics forge connections between Tabitha and her husband by way of the death imagery, the final pages, too, concern themselves with death. And as Tabitha plays with her audience a bit by suggesting the funeral in the final scene will be for David Christopher, she reveals that this final scene does not mark the end of one character's life, but rather consists of a cathartic celebration of another character's life:

And David, in white linen, came through the gapped line of the elms, thin and serious, his eyes hidden behind glasses. Taking them off, he met her gaze and smiled and walked toward them. He took her other, ringless, hand and the three of them turned to watch the undertaker remove India's coffin from the hearse [T. King, *Pearl* 363].

This ending is certainly more than just a touching scene in which David Christopher is able to close one of the most difficult chapters of his own life; it is also a scene by which Tabitha has, to a degree, painted herself into a corner concerning her series.

With the most suspenseful moment of the Nodd's Ridge stories literally laid to rest at the end of *Pearl*, one must wonder as to what else might propel Tabitha to continue chronicling the people and the history of this town, or what might motivate any reader to continue with any sense of concern or interest. As far as Tabitha, as a writer, is concerned, there is something to be said for an active imagination and a blank slate that desires to be filled with thoughts, and in many ways this simplified outlook on the Nodd's Ridge tales is accurate—despite the tensions, mysteries, explorations and insights that the novels provide, they are difficult to connect beyond a few shared stories, such as India Christopher's death, and a collection of characters that share a specific location. In other words, it is difficult to sort through these stories as a whole in that the snapshots of specific characters and events is so selective that the gaps in story and imagination are frustrating to the reader who wants a complete history with a balanced examination of as many characters as possible. Of course, this desire by the audience is nothing more than an exercise in greed, but there is something to be said for a collection of novels that leave many questions unanswered and which ultimately focus on one particular family among a large cast of individuals whose own stories would undoubtedly make for enjoyable and insightful reading. But rather than bemoan Tabitha's unceremonious departure from the publishing world when her husband moved from Viking to Scribner (which ultimately resulted in Tabitha being without an editor or a willing publisher), readers would do well to find pleasure and satisfaction in what the publishing world has made available—novels that may be criticized for their consistently domestic settings and overly dramatic plots, but are nonetheless indicative of a writer with quite the range for theme and content.

Courtship on the Court: One on One

As the title of the fourth novel in the Nodd's Ridge novels suggests, the theme of sports dominates this installment of Tabitha King's main corpus. Although the focus of the story resembles the sexually charged fictions in the same small town as the previous three installments in this series, the foregrounded element of athletics, and high-school athletics at that, looks to be a strange maneuvering into young adult fiction, as teenage characters have primarily served Tabitha as background characters at this point in her career. In terms of the sporting side to *One on One*, however, the constant references to the Red Sox in Tabitha's fiction, as well as Stephen King's fiction, suggests a particular value placed on sports and athletic competition within the King family. At the very least, Stephen's 2004 non–fiction collaboration with Stewart O'Nan, *Faithful*, serves as a reminder of the influence that sports have on the New England region, and the fascination with the Red Sox and the years of distress that follow the team — especially the 1986 World Series and Bill Buckner's error, which is revisited numerous times in Tabitha's fiction — suggests that *One on One*'s athletic foundation is merely a reflection of the real-world interest and obsession with sports that permeates Tabitha's life and community.

One on One examines the aspects of small town life beyond the stereotypical expectations of secrecy and drama, and encompasses the function of sports that is, in many ways, an American universal: "While sports seem frequently to be little more than a feel-good distraction for a disposable culture, it is just as often something in which we invest the deepest part of ourselves" (Cocchiarale and Emmert xvii). While it is perhaps erroneous to think of the reader as being exceptionally invested in *One on One* for its use of athletics as a primary thread for the story, the characters in this story, especially Sam Styles and Deanie Gauthier, show not just a passion for sport but almost a dependence on basketball to provide order and even meaning for their lives. These two outsiders find themselves as integral, important members of their respective team communities, suggesting that sport is more than just a means of competition or enjoyable spectacle within the novel.

Although high school basketball is, in many ways, the heart of *One on One*, a core which confirms the assessment that sport has a value beyond mere entertainment (especially for the athletes), it nonetheless becomes a background element for the book and the reader, which is refreshing in the sense that Tabitha is able to create a fiction concerned with the development of characters rather than the excitement of sport to gain readership. While the male and female squads of the Greenspark Indians may ultimately each win their respective state basketball titles, there is much more to *One on One* than simple sport. Still, the ultimate success of *One on One* led to Tabitha's own non-fiction piece on the ubiquitous presence of sports in Maine, titled *Playing Like a Girl*, which chronicles the 1993–1994 senior season of Maine's high school basketball sensation Cindy Blodgett (and which initially caught the attention of the nation by way of *Sports Illustrated*). While the use and examination of athletics is not exactly an oddity in Tabitha's fiction when considering the larger social engagement with sports surrounding Tabitha in her home state of Maine, the story of Sam Styles and Deanie Gauthier, the fictional basketball stars of Greenspark Academy in *One on One*, does have its strange aspects. But, more than anything, the story of Sam and Deanie is another instance of a compelling romance which does extend beyond mere hormones and near-cliché sexual exploits.

One on One, from the standpoint which focuses on the ages of the primary characters, is a tale of high school which captures the politics and romances, as well as the rivalries and partnerships, among awkward, developing teens, not to mention all the booze, drugs and sex that seem to be stereotypical of any examination of the lives of those under the age of twenty. To wit, *One on One*, according to Jan Blodgett (no known relation to the aforementioned Cindy Blodgett), "successfully evokes the excitement of small-town high school sports and the underlying tension her plot requires," suggesting that Tabitha is careful to extend the focus of her novel beyond the athletic backdrop, which she does (192). For instance, while the concerns of the adolescent at times seem to be rather distanced or trivial from both the larger world and many readers, Tabitha King is able to effectively capture the worries and desires of the teenage characters in *One on One*, providing an accurate and believable snapshot of high school life and high school characters beyond the beating pulse of the athletic presence that most high schools witness, complete with the mundane and dramatic elements that construct real life and the fictional foundation of the text itself. As far as rules and regulations are concerned for the athletes that populate the story, each is largely concerned with athletic eligibility, which can be affected by alcohol, tobacco, drugs, and sexual relations, as such general guidelines for behavior are common to the various codes of conduct to which high school athletes are asked to adhere.

But even more than the general and common concerns which direct and often dictate the behaviors of Tabitha's characters, especially the main male character Sam Styles, son of Reuben Styles and new step-son of Pearl Dickenson (who has given birth to Reuben's fourth child, a daughter provocatively named India), Tabitha creates the perfect contrast for Sam in Deanie Gauthier, the star of the female basketball squad at Greenspark who "got her skinny ass kicked out of the game against Breckenfield for diving into the bleachers to punch out an abusive fan" (T. King, *One on One* 12). Deanie's proclivities towards violence, or at least that which opposes the status quo (as evidenced by her shaved head and network of piercings and chains which connect her piercings), appears to set her up as one of the most despicable characters in the novel. Yet she does earn quite the level of sympathy, as she is dubbed the Mutant by her peers who only see a troubled teen rather than a troubled individual in need of help. And just as *The Trap* and *Pearl* focus on the main female characters with a sense of curiosity and sympathy, Deanie Gauthier and her particular troubles and eventual victories become the glue for *One on One* in terms of plot and reader interest.

Athletic competition may be the center-point of *One on One*, especially in terms of the somewhat repetitive and trying construction of the plot, in that the reader is constantly aware that regardless of the character's personal developments beyond the basketball court, the plot will repeat itself and return to the game at the tale's center. To be sure, there is an almost excessive amount of prose aimed at capturing the action of the numerous games played by both the boys' and girls' squads throughout the course of the novel. And while the details do not always bleed into the realm of boredom, it is an awkward balance that Tabitha tries to strike between fictional sports reporter and fiction writer. But aside from such a critique on the athletic events and their presentation in *One on One*, the importance that basketball eventually takes for Deanie Gauthier cannot be dismissed. Her growth as a basketball player in many ways is almost inevitable considering the larger scope of the story; but it is indeed Deanie's growth within the game of basketball that allow readers to fully grasp the complexities of this character and fully understand the atrocities that have befallen this troubled young woman.

With respect to the early descriptions of Deanie as a violent spectacle whose presence on the basketball court inspires fear (not because of her ability but because of her appearance and demeanor), it seems almost strange for such a strong yet violent women to be taken seriously as a cornerstone for the novel. However, when it comes to such first impressions of Deanie, it must be considered that this character is hardly an anomaly or a gimmick aimed at garnering morbidly curious readers who wish to follow the next outrageous exhibition of a female character who is likened to a circus sideshow. Rather, as Josephine G. Hendin suggests, "Violent women are embodiments of modernity defined as alarming and exciting change. Their depiction in fiction and media holds an enlarging mirror up to transformations in intimacy, family life, and citizenship" (55). Following this line of reasoning, one can then see that Deanie Gauthier is a character whose consistent status as the other, the outsider, or an image to behold but not necessarily engage or even take seriously, suggests a reflection of the American culture in which women have begun to finally redefine the conceptions and misconceptions of the female gender. But this is not to say that the transformed female, whether in terms of minor alterations or seemingly large-scale transformations as displayed through Deanie, is readily or easily accepted. As Deanie finds exceptional resistance among her attempts to carve a niche for herself in a culture and town that is hesitant to embrace change or individuals outside the mainstream, her struggles are chronicled as a reflection of the difficulties most any female must endure to find some semblance of comfort, relief, solace or acceptance in a male-dominated landscape.

Navigating the complexity of Deanie Gauthier as a female who struggles to find a place in her surrounding community is primarily concerned with where she lives, how she presents herself to the outside world, and how she is both used and viewed as a sexual object. As far as Deanie's home life is concerned, she finds the freedom to smoke marijuana in a household that almost necessitates the escape that pot affords her, especially concerning her mother's live-in boyfriend, Tony, who molests Deanie at most every chance he gets: "He comes back and turns off the radio again and lets her have the last couple hits while he fools around with her. She does what he wants so he will go away and let her do her homework" (T. King, *One on One* 29). While such a scene is, without doubt, disturbing and disgusting, it functions as a vital piece to the story, the crux of Deanie's psychological make-up that flows from her bedroom, where she cannot find any safety, to the outside world that promises just as little succor.

To clarify, the only place in Nodd's Ridge where Deanie finds any refuge is an abandoned mill, and it should go without saying that an abandoned structure hardly suffices as a locale of security. However, it is in this abandoned mill, originally erected by the Styles clan in 1849, that Deanie ultimately finds a glimmer of hope when it becomes a place where she and Sam Styles first have sex. "Making love" is too far removed from the initial sexual encounters between Deanie and Sam, but this leap to sex in an abandoned building not only provides a foundation for the rest of the novel in which Sam is able to see past her defenses, but also leaves many gaps in the story and its treatment of Deanie as a struggling female. Returning to Deanie being constantly molested by Tony, and even utilized as a mere object of sex by her drug-dealing boyfriend J. C. Chapin, Tabitha clearly establishes Deanie as a figure who attempts to both confront and negate her victimhood by way of how she presents herself to the outside world and even through how she views herself. In the matter of how Deanie attempts to mitigate or even erase the abuses that she endures, she decorates her bedroom with mirrors, which brings the reader uncomfortably and unflinchingly close to the psyche of Deanie amidst the molestations, noting that she can (and does) actually watch herself being molested. Deanie's almost casual observations of being violated by Tony cannot, however, be reduced to indifference or acceptance — rather, she attempts to communicate her predicament through her appearance and her seemingly delinquent actions, which results in mixed messages, to say the least.

As *One on One* slowly brings Sam and Deanie together as friends and lovers, Sam becomes one of the few individuals in the novel to understand how and why Deanie constructs her identity as one almost devoid of any feminine traces. At one point when Sam gains access to Deanie's room, he is overcome with a sense of discomfort by the mirrors and the tattered decorations, but he ultimately comes to understand that her shaved head, aggressively frightening demeanor and otherwise dirty appearance is, primarily, a reflection of who she actually is: "The room of hers is nearly as horrible as the cubby in the Mill — worse, with those frigging creepy mirrors. Her belongings are as pathetic as a refugee's. It occurs to him now that she made a style of holes and rags because that was what she had—turned them into a kind of sarcastic joke by flaunting them" (T. King, *One on One* 341). With this scene, Tabitha King not only creates a keen sense of understanding for Sam, but also the reader, especially when she notes why Deanie voluntarily constructs her identity as that of the fractured, broken outsider. Deanie, aside from being an individual fraught with numerous demons who has little else to work with or reference when creating an image for the world to see, attempts to portray herself as a broken individual to keep people at a distance. In some ways this is an exercise of power for her, especially as she positions herself to seduce Sam not necessarily because she wants to, but because she can: "She knows things about him. How scared he is. Of her. It's a trip having power over him. Knowing he's cherry. He's going to be a pushover" (T. King, *One on One* 173). As Deanie learns that Sam is a virgin, a male who is unfamiliar with sex and would likely become enraptured even at the sight of bare breasts, she seemingly coerces Sam into having sex with her—because she can.

Although this is an exercise of power on Deanie's part, this is not necessarily a scene reminiscent of rape. But it is an instance in which Deanie exercises a particular power in that sex with her can never really be about sex in and of itself. Sex with Deanie Gauthier, because of her personal trials and dark history (as blatantly advertised through her self-created demeanor and image), is a breakdown of traditionally male-conceived expectations of sex in which "the object, not the experience, is considered to be sexy" (Gallop 138). Accordingly, Deanie Gauthier attempts to remove enjoyment of the sex-object—the woman as enjoyed by the man—by voluntarily pushing herself into the role of the Mutant, as an undesirable object that promises no enjoyable sexual experience. This is not only a role that she accepts (as her own life circumstances are seen by her peers as reason to place her in this outsider's role), but this is also a role she perpetuates because it seems to give her some sort of satisfaction, a sense of control in a world that has not allowed her any semblance of sovereignty before.

To focus on Deanie Gauthier and her plight seems to be rather depressing, as *One on One* takes its audience through more than 500 pages of her troubled life, which finds even more trouble when she is physically abused by her mother's boyfriend, Tony, who ultimately murders Judy Gauthier, but only after he has beaten Deanie to the point that his punches to her face actually embed her chains into her flesh. This occurrence happens at a point in the novel when it seems that Deanie is on the verge of a normal life, as her relationship with Sam Styles has extended beyond games of power and manipulation, which is quite the accomplishment considering that Tabitha bluntly notes early in the text how such a relationship is almost impossible: "Guys don't know how to be friends to girls without screwing them" (T. King, *One on One* 161). But the pressures and constant obstacles that Deanie Gauthier faces simply reflect the difficulties of the world in which Tabitha writes, especially concerning the female. For instance, Tabitha notes in her article "Dump on Vulgarity" that "there are dozens of ugly words for women, nearly all reducing them to their sexual organs ... but there are *none* for white males of equal weight and ugliness" (T. King, "Dump on Vulgarity" 9–10). With this she provides a bluntly accurate reminder of the societal and linguistic oppressions that females must face on a daily basis. Perhaps this is why Tabitha, when discussing Deanie's private parts, constantly utilizes the term "sex," especially as Tabitha has shown no compunction with crude sexual vernacular in the rest of her body of stories. "Cock," "cunt," and "pussy," for example, can all be found in the pages of Tabitha King's fiction, ranging from the comedic discussions of, say, "delivering take-out pussy" to the mere use of such words perhaps as a means of shocking the audience with audacity if not transparency, reflecting her desire to speak freely without judgment as to why she uses terms that seem to be off-putting or un-ladylike (T. King, *One on One* 86). But with *One on One*, Tabitha takes a noted turn of sorts and uses a more formal term when referring to Deanie Gauthier's genitals, perhaps a move meant not to further isolate Deanie but to provide her with some humanity that her classmates and family have denied her.

Such a conclusion concerning Tabitha's careful use of language points towards the potential happy ending for Deanie, suggesting that even a few flashes of decency that she is afforded can prove to be rather promising for this troubled young woman. And while Deanie Gauthier, no longer as the Mutant but just Deanie in the novel's final pages, can look towards the future with Sam Styles by her side, Tabitha King remains true to the tough world that provides the foundation for *One on One* and ensures that a happy ending for this novel is only a *possibility* rather than a certainty. *One on One* concludes with one of the better, and smoother, endings in Tabitha's canon, confirming the assertion that this book creates "a complex bond [between Sam and Deanie], composed of both pain and hope, that King makes believable and captivating" (Blodgett 192). In short, Deanie moves in with Sam, and the novel then concludes one year after what becomes an inconsequential state championship for both the men's and women's basketball teams. The actual last lines come after Sam attends parent-teacher conferences on Deanie's behalf, as she still has one year of high school left to complete. As the teachers recount the story behind Sam and Deanie, the novel finishes with an appropriate uncertainty:

"What happens to them?" the young woman asks.
The older teacher shrugs. "Sometimes they grow up together quite successfully," she says. "You can never tell" [T. King, *One on One* 525].

With ambiguity awaiting Sam, Deanie and their audience, *One on One* essentially closes the entire Nodd's Ridge series, despite a fifth novel, *The Book of Reuben*, being published a year later. Of course, concluding a series with the hazy future of two infatuated teenagers may not end the series on an expected note, or one that firmly ties up all loose ends that remain unresolved at the end of *The Book of Reuben*, but is it necessarily detrimental to the entire Nodd's Ridge series to be asked to imagine what will take place once the author is finished with the story? Certainly not. But there is a bit of a chore awaiting readers who are reminded that *One on One* is part of a larger story, as Tabitha King notes, "Castle Rock and Derry, of course, were first mapped fictionally by another novelist who was kind enough to allow me to add to their histories. For those of you who are familiar with Castle Rock, the basketball season related in this particular yarn occurs in the spring before Mr. Leland Gaunt opened his curio shop in the Rock" (*One on One* 526). Linking *One on One* the destruction of Castle Rock in *Needful Things* hardly brings any new insights to Tabitha's tale, or any more hint at closure. But there is something to be said for a story that, despite the indication that no more tales will be told about Nodd's Ridge, does not have to end. Yet one is left to wonder if the modern reader will take the reins that Tabitha King has left for the imaginative reader, the rare individual that holds to the belief that while closure, or climax, may be pleasurable, it does not compare to the entire journey.

One Man's Tale: The Book of Reuben

The nature of the serial novel tends to indicate a sense of closure or completeness, yet Tabitha King challenges this notion, or expectation, with the final novel in the Nodd's Ridge series, *The Book of Reuben*. In terms of closure, this last book avoids any sense of finality, as the text chronicles the life of Reuben Styles, who is one of the only characters in Nodd's Ridge to be present in all five of these books, and concludes with his courtship of Pearl Dickenson, circling readers to the beginning of the third book in this series. As this ending clearly ties *The Book of Reuben* to the preceding stories in the series, the conclusion of this novel is only one instance in which this novel relies heavily upon earlier texts for full meaning. The serial novel is that which constantly moves back and forth between current texts and prior tales to complete the story at hand, but a careful balance must be struck if one part of the series is to stand on its own and tell a story that uses the previous tales as guidelines rather than excessive buttressing supports. And while the conclusion to *The Book of Reuben* is not exactly clever or profound in terms of concluding this particular tale, as it redirects the reader to *Pearl* and a life that readers also see further develop in *One on One* ("It was time, Reuben thought, time to get on with his life"), there are instances of plotting firmly grounded in the story itself that create a book solely focused on a single character who, it seems, merely happens to be written into the Nodd's Ridge community (T. King, *The Book* of *Reuben* 432). Although *The Book of Reuben* is bookended with a story that is perhaps overly reliant on the rest of the Nodd's Ridge tales for context and effect, it nonetheless continues an exceptional pattern of Tabitha King's canon of fiction that thoroughly explores the histories and psyches of its characters. But it should be said that for a series devoted to an entire town, it is disappointing that the concluding story of this town focuses mainly on just a single character, bringing to the fore a microcosm of the town that, regardless of the intricate web of back story and communal connections, is not necessarily representative of the town as a whole.

Although *The Book of Reuben* does provide a sweeping examination of Nodd's Ridge which includes insights either previously ignored or not yet imagined by Tabitha King, it is, as the title suggests, largely the story of a single character: Reuben Styles. This narrowness may be reflective of the character concerns from the previous novels, perhaps resulting in a sense of dissatisfaction that could be extended to the rest of the stories because of their approach to an entire town through a few select characters and ultimately a single family of no real import or sway beyond serving as numbers for the population total (even though the Styles, as is noted in *One on One*, have reportedly been in Nodd's Ridge since its founding). The importance of the Styles family seems negligible in that their *presence* seems to be the only lasting imprint on the town. This is not to say that the Styles' existence is overwhelmingly positive or negative, or even that they have any ostensible or measurable influence on the town. Rather, like most families in Nodd's Ridge, they exist, and their stories become known to the rest of the town and the curious reader. Specifically concerning Reuben, however, his story is that of an alcoholic who loses his father to suicide (or, rather, a self-administered "treatment" for a cancer diagnosis), and who is introduced to the world of sex by Torrie Christopher. The affair with Torrie primarily sets the stage for his strained marriage to Laura Haggerty, who may not have been married to Reuben when he had sex with Torrie but was nonetheless involved with him. But in terms of the entire story behind this series, Reuben's encounters with Torrie clarifies for readers exactly why he is so connected to David Christopher, which is not entirely important for this last book in Tabitha King's series but which does offer a needed reexamination of the third book in the Nodd's Ridge tales.

In *Pearl*, Reuben tells his future wife that when she slept with David, it was as if she had slept with Reuben's son, Sam, indicating that Reuben and David had some sort of connected history resulting in a friendship constructed as if they were father and son. But this history between Reuben and David is so completely hidden and muddled in *Pearl* that the story, from the perspective of Reuben's sense of disgust for Pearl's multiple sexual partners (beyond his own masculine insecurities), seems to unravel because of the lack of clarity. But *The Book of Reuben* highlights Reuben's affair with Torrie Christopher and his first glimpse of the troubled young boy who, reportedly, becomes a son-like figure to Reuben: "A boy, Reuben assumed — the woman addressed him by a male name. But he needed a haircut so badly he certainly would be accused in the local schoolyard of being a sissy if not an outright queer" (T. King, *The Book of Reuben* 40). Aside from David's ambiguous sexuality in terms of appearance and preference, which is explored to a degree in *The Book of Reuben* and which comes to a rather amusing crossroads in *Pearl* (beyond David's involvement with the title character), as he teases Reuben that *both* of the Styles children promise great sex, his presence in Reuben's story is largely sporadic. But in the few scenes that David and Reuben share, there are quite a few profound moments.

In sorting through the few threads that readers are given regarding Reuben's relationship to David, sex is ultimately the catalyst which brings these two individuals together. Or, more specifically, it is the sex between Torrie and Reuben that pushes the two male characters together and, at times, apart. From Torrie's initially blunt come-on to Reuben — "You want to screw me, don't you?" — to David smelling his mother's perfume and her alcohol at Reuben's Texaco station, one might conclude that the relationship between David and Reuben, which is essential to the plot of *Pearl* and which is not entirely clarified or developed in that book, is also overshadowed and treated sporadically in *The Book of Reuben* (T. King, *The Book of Reuben* 69). Perhaps this sentiment is simply a reaction to what can be construed as an excessive examination, or at least focus, on the sexually charged nature of this text. Although the story does shift its focus to Reuben's sexually frustrated life with his frigid wife, Laura, the relationship that Reuben has with David is almost a lost story in and of itself, much in the way that the aftermath surrounding Rueben's father's suicide goes unexplored. One of the key lost occurrences in *The Book of Reuben* is what happens to Reuben's father after he commits suicide in that a pack of dogs on the Styleses' land begin to eat the corpse: "It wasn't their fault. The dogs had just done what came natural to them, but that didn't change the fact they'd tasted a man's blood and eaten of his body" (T. King, *The Book of Reuben* 56). This particular element surrounding the death of Reuben's father has great potential for serving as a recurring theme or vision throughout the rest of the novel, as Rueben seemingly leads anything but a charmed life; however, the agony of burning animals is, sadly, not explored further. But, as this scene can be drawn as a parallel to the undeveloped story concerning Reuben and his surrogate fatherhood of David Christopher, Tabitha King does provide much in the way of powerful narration with only a few select scenes.

Despite the focus on sex within the first and last sections of *The Book of Reuben*, which hardly seems to be out of the realm of Tabitha King's fiction, readers are finally given some insight into Reuben's strange friendship with David Christopher, as well being given the back story to his failed marriage with Laura Haggerty. Concerning David and Reuben, it was stated that their relationship is founded upon sex, which not only becomes more complicated when revisiting their continued bond through sex and an unknowingly shared sexual partner in *Pearl*, but which is founded on an innocent yet pragmatic discovery in that David ultimately learns of Reuben's affair with Torrie Christopher by accidentally walking in on them. The dialogue which follows this scene is quite telling of the mindset of both Reuben and David, and as to how their relationship will develop throughout the rest of the series:

> "I'm sorry," Reuben said [to David].
> "For what? Fucking my mother?"
> "For not locking the door."
> David smiled. "Very nice distinction. You needn't bother. You're not anything new under the sun. She likes young stupid guys with dirty hands" [T. King, *The Book of Reuben* 98].

With this simple and honest exchange, Reuben and David begin a relationship of mutual respect, one that is tested more and more as *The Book of Reuben* unfolds, and especially in *Pearl*. But perhaps the most important bond that is formed between these two characters is through the death of India Christopher. As Tabitha notes in *Caretakers*, Reuben is at the Christopher household the day that India is shot and killed. And as Tabitha reiterates the common views concerning India's death that are originally established in *Caretakers* by noting, "The state police investigators admitted the odds of an accidental between-the-eyes shot was astronomical, but they had two witnesses to it," she then immediately dispels any myths of freak occurrences as far as Reuben and David are concerned (*The Book of Reuben* 109). In a scene that is absent from *Caretakers*, as well as *Pearl*, which places quite the burden on *The Book of Reuben* to answer many of the unresolved issues which haunt Nodd's Ridge, Tabitha has Reuben and David immediately confer regarding India's death:

> "David, you know it wasn't an accident, don't you?"
> David stared at him through a long silence and past him into bitter distance.
> "Yes," he whispered [T. King, *The Book of Reuben* 107].

With this dialogue, Tabitha brings Reuben and David's relationship into clear focus, forever linking them together with the knowledge that India's death is not an accident, which is made more troublesome because their suspicions do not really escape their own discussion on the matter. Neither Reuben nor David seek the full truth behind India's murder, even though Reuben might be able to deduce that Cora Nevars is responsible, since he knows of India's lineage by way of the flaw in her eye which is a noted mark of the Nevars family. Interestingly and sadly, Reuben's knowledge of India's lineage leads not to an arrest, but rather a self-investigation into questions of morals and ethics which, incidentally, become the foundation behind the religious aspects of the later scenes in *The Book of Reuben*. In short, Reuben believes, "They were all lesser people for it. Only the child, the little girl, was innocent. [But] He'd never breathe a word to anyone concerning the child's likely paternity"

(T. King, *The Book of Reuben* 96). Again, there is no clear indication as to why Reuben might keep his silence about India's genealogy, other than to protect David from the possibility of vicious rumor and scandal that seems to thrive in the small town. All readers are left with is speculation, which may be empowering in that the audience is able to craft their own explanations and insist upon plot elements that please them and their tastes; but this does not bode well for the actual story that Tabitha King writes.

Such mismanagement of the plot, although likely common within any fiction if any given reader is critical enough with his or her investigations into a plot and its devices, could be read as being a mere symptom of a story with too many threads. For example, as previously noted, the discussions and insights into sex within this book are numerous, and although these passages provide exceptional insight into the burden that Reuben's penis becomes, including his slanted yet honest look at his impending marriage—"Two thousand dollars to screw a girl he had already promised to marry? If he paid for her fancy wedding, did she mean she would let him fuck her once before the wedding, or twice, or anytime he wanted?"—it is exceptionally difficult for the reader to constantly be drawn into Reuben's bedroom when there is so much else occurring (T. King, *The Book of Reuben* 196). With that said, perhaps some of the most spectacular scenes of *The Book of Reuben* (or, rather, scenes of noted spectacle) involve the legal and religious peripherals surrounding Reuben's failed marriage. As Tabitha writes of Laura's growing distance from Reuben, while either ignoring or dismissing Reuben's alcoholic tendencies and earlier indiscretions involving Torrie Christopher and Sunny Lunt's ex-wife Joyce, she provides a rather scathing view of religion that dominates the rest of the tale. For example, as an economical criticism of religion, Tabitha notes that Reuben "had heard stories about people in her [Laura's] church working three jobs to increase their tithes" (T. King, *The Book of Reuben* 307). More to the point, while the growing divide between Reuben and Laura by way of sex becomes further complicated by their differing views on religion—"My immortal soul, if I have one, is my business. My wife is welcome to attend her own"—the story takes on a noted duality in terms of irony and focus (T. King, *The Book of Reuben* 279). In terms of irony, Laura's growing fascination and involvement with religion culminates in an affair with the Reverend Smart. This affair, which leads to the production of a sex tape that garners a level of infamy among the Nodd's Ridge community (again, sex creeps into the picture), creates a plot twist worth noting in that Laura's "holier-than-thou" act with Reuben is undercut because she commits adultery—and thoroughly enjoys the sex involved, which is in stark contrast to her previous and frigid sex life with Reuben. But beyond this irony, which easily paints Laura as a vindictive and conniving woman (while Reuben gains a level of sympathy by way of character contrast to his now-monstrous wife), is the vehicle of religion as a tool of deceit and division rather than truth and harmony.

The Styles household remains relatively unexposed to religion throughout the course of *The Book of Reuben*, which suggests that its characters have a rather clean and clear perception of religion. In other words, with little involvement in the church or any noted professions of faith, the Styles, especially the children, are positioned as not necessarily susceptible individuals but rather those with clear lenses with which to view religion. That is to say, when the Styles all begin to accompany Laura to her church and become subject, and subjected, to the Reverend Smart's sermons, the reactions that result are reportedly without bias. When Sammy Styles says to Reuben, "Daddy Chu-chu-church is scary. Duh-duh-do I have to guh-guh-go?" the reader is given a clear construction of not necessarily religion, but its potential for discord when placed into particular hands (T. King, *The Book of Reuben* 299). With the Reverend Smart fulfilling the role of a hellfire and brimstone preacher with an agenda, and Reuben telling him bluntly that his preaching is little more than transparent rhetoric that does little to uplift the congregation (specifically telling Smart, "You're scaring the shit out of my kids"), the story utilizes another tried and tested thematic of conflict that actually blends quite well with the sexual strife of the novel (T. King, *The Book of Reuben* 303). But just as religion has become an easy vehicle, or target, within fiction, critics have noted that Tabitha does not always create believable fiction: "The novel's major weakness is that Laura is never presented as a particularly sympathetic character, so it's hard to understand why Reuben is attracted to her or why he keeps trying to accommodate her" (Pearl 130). Ultimately, even the conclusion of this story suggests a certain weakness, especially considering that the end of Reuben's tale is the beginning of Pearl Dickenson's tale, which then leads to *One on One* and leaves the story of Nodd's Ridge concluding with the image of Sam Styles and Deanie Gauthier attempting to create a life together, which hardly seems appropriate as an ending to a series focused on an entire town.

Further, with this exceptionally fast conclusion to be found in Tabitha's text, summing up the aftermath of Reuben's failed marriage, as well as devoting a paragraph to the events of *The Trap* and essentially giving the last chapters over to the events of *Pearl*, Reuben's story culminates in the convenient notion in which Reuben thinks, "If Pearl Dickenson had come to town while he and Laura had still been married, he'd have cheated on Laura with Pearl without a twinge of conscience" (T. King, *The Book of Reuben* 430–1). Of course, without a prior knowledge or reading of *Pearl*, this line would likely only confirm Reuben's sexual leanings and solidify the constant thread of sexuality that runs rampant throughout *The Book of Reuben*. But that is both the danger and the joy of the serial novel — knowing that the foundations and events of the larger story are in a constant state of flux which requires constant attention, but which can be difficult to piece together, whether one is crafting or consuming the tale, especially when the seams of the serial novel clearly show. Examining the Nodd's Ridge tales in isolation from one another is a bit of a disservice to the intertwined nature of these stories. However, just as is the case with Stephen King's *Dark Tower* series, a collection of books that branches out and captures the stories from numerous other fictions in Stephen's canon, a complete capturing of the entire story, as well as each story on its own, is a difficult task. While the nature of this book is to provide an initial criticism and evaluation of the King family fictions, certain drawbacks are noted but hopefully set aside for the sake of exposure and beginning the discussion at hand.

Any in-depth look at the history of Nodd's Ridge would make for an engaging and insightful study, especially considering the link that Nodd's Ridge has to Stephen King's own Castle Rock (and, therefore, to the rest of Stephen's canon), but for now the focus lays on Tabitha and her efforts to not only bring her readers into the small towns of Maine through varied doorways, but also into realms of intimacy and the home-front that escape the fictions of her other family members. Even in celebrating Tabitha King and her fiction, or broaching issues, characters and locations that are not always found within the fiction of her husband and sons, the critical eye must remain open. This is not an invitation to scour the pages of her fiction for deficiencies prompted by constructive concerns or by way of taste, but one must approach her fiction, or any fiction for that matter, with a discerning eye. And in the case of Tabitha King, that discerning eye would do well to look at the inter-textual bridges that she creates between her works and her husband's. As Tabitha connects *One on One* to *Needful Things* by way of geographical and temporal proximity, she is also subtle in some of her other forged connections: "They could all recite gruesome legendary deaths of kids—the one hit in the mouth by a baseball that poisoned his heart with the stuff at its center, the one who tried to fly off the barn roof, the one who got turned into hamburger by the train, the one who got murdered by the crazy old homo" (T. King, *The Book of Reuben* 37). Of these deaths, the death of a young child by way of a baseball game is a death of Tabitha's own making, which she details in *Caretakers*, but the others seemingly belong to the wide range of death found in Stephen King's canon, especially the death of the boy who is hit by a train (think Ray Brower from "The Body"). Such connections may suggest that Tabitha's fiction is inextricably linked to Stephen's (especially as she utilizes familiar surnames in her fiction such as Tozier, Clutterbuck, Priest and Malenfant), and that their fictions, together, comprise a single story that necessitates reading all of their individual writings. Then again, much like how a marriage is made up of two people to form a single union, with the individuals involved each retaining their separate identities, it would be best to look at Tabitha King's fiction as that which is entirely her own, regardless of any connections her writing has to her husband's canon. And perhaps the desire to separate herself from her husband, in terms of fiction (but not necessarily in terms of setting), is why the end of Tabitha's career as a solo writer moves from the series to the stand-alone novel *Survivor*, which may not take readers from Maine, but which does reacquaint audiences with much of the same writing that Tabitha has established as her own.

From Maine to ... Maine: Survivor

With the Nodd's Ridge series complete, or at least finished (in that the lives of its denizens really receive no conclusive endings or clear resolutions by the time the last Nodd's Ridge novel was published), Tabitha King nears what appears to be the end of her career with *Survivor*. Moving right into the content of this first stand-alone tale in Tabitha's canon in fifteen years, *Survivor* is a gripping story that adeptly draws the reader into a world of fiction that resembles a believable soap opera. It is, according to reviewer Marylaine Block, a tale that "is as good as anything King has done previously" (89). Of course, such measures of success are arbitrary and open for debate, and even though it might be agreed that Block is correct in her assessment that *Survivor* is truly a "compelling *psychological* drama," any text that ventures into the realm of the dramatic and sustains a focus on the character's psyches is not good by any intrinsic measure (89, emphasis added). Although there is quite the voyeuristic pull within *Survivor* created by the narrator's constant psychological explorations, it is a story that, perhaps as an accidental metaphor (considering Kissy Mellors' profession as a photographer), appears to be little more than a series of snapshots, or slices of story that tell the reader of the occurrences from one scene to the next.

The numerous scenes of *Survivor* which encompass several years of action and activity do not always come together under the guise of a traditional story with a tightly-woven plot and an inevitable and compelling climax. What the story does, however, is provide an intimate examination of the psyches of its characters, especially the female protagonist, which seems to position Tabitha in a place opposite her husband and his characters. As Chelsea Quinn Yarbro says of Stephen King, "It is disheartening when a writer with so much talent and strength and vision is not able to develop a believable woman character between the ages of seventeen and sixty" (49). Tabitha King may have a noted advantage over her husband when it comes to capturing the essence of femininity and the psyche of the female, but this element of *Survivor* is but one of several plot threads which comprises a tale that is largely inviting because of its somewhat voyeuristic examination of *people*, with the issue of gender only highlighted from time to time. While the novel also explores the world of sports that Tabitha first examines in *One on One*, and also visits familiar scenes of broken families and the rapid communication of rumor and hearsay within the fictional Maine town of Peltry, there seems to be a missing catalyst of sorts for the story which fully ties it together, much in the way that a projector connects the thousands of singular images that comprise a reel of film.

Regardless of the initial critiques which look at the story of *Survivor* from a distanced vantage point, the text does carry several instances of immediate gratification and satisfaction in terms of its content and construction. First and foremost, with a suddenness that could be construed as gimmickry akin to that which Stephen King uses in his 2006 novel *Cell*, *Survivor* opens with death. This initial scene in which numerous lives are intertwined by way of death serves as an underlying thread through the story, as the main character, Kissy Mellors, not only eventually becomes a lover of the man, James Houston, held responsible for the death of one woman, Diane Greenan, but she also befriends the grandmother of the other victim, Ruth Prashker, who is put into a coma because of the accident. On the somewhat tangential note of a woman who slips into a coma, Tabitha takes care to note that the grandmother, Mrs. Cronin, "read to Ruth from a novel about a man who had recovered from a coma and discovered himself to be clairvoyant" (T. King, *Survivor* 75). Of course, this is an obvious reference to *The Dead Zone* and is just one of many inter-textual references and links that Tabitha creates between her fiction and her husband's. But to, again, direct focus towards Tabitha's metafictional treatments distracts from the underlying sexual tensions of *Survivor*, which carry the novel into several sexually charged scenes for which Tabitha can be said to have a particular fascination, if not mastery.

Some of the sexual elements of *Survivor* are rather juvenile, as evidenced by Kissy Mellors' nickname of Kissy *Melons* and the attention that her chest receives from her future husband, Mike Burke: "He had not considered himself a tit man, but hers would get anyone's attention. And then they had that amazing quality all tits, big or small, did: there were two of them. A fact that might indeed be proof that God had a dick" (T. King, *Survivor* 54). But even with such juvenile insights into questions of sex, including that of Kissy's first husband, Junior Clootie, who loses a girlfriend in the first pages of *Survivor* and says, "Diane was a blip in my life. She's dead and I don't feel all that much. A little bit amazed that someone I used to fuck is dead," Tabitha does more than merely depict her male characters as insensitive or obsessed with images and ideas of sex, no matter how morbid (T. King, *Survivor* 37). Tabitha's focus on sex within the first several chapters of *Survivor* continues a trend in her fiction to discuss not only an issue that the other writers in her family tend to shy away from (with exceptions, of course, including the sexually charged plotline of Joe Hill's novel *Horns*), but to remind her readers how much of an overwhelming effect sex has on the human mind. Further, Junior Clootie's commentary that he feels strange knowing that someone he had slept with was dead (and that the only feeling he felt was a certain awkwardness rather than loss) establishes a particular axiom for the story that seems to be rather reflective of the culture surrounding Tabitha's writing career: that sex and love do not always cross paths.

The most believable, if not repetitive, parts of *Survivor* include the multiple routes involved in sex and, to a lesser extent, love. This story primarily focuses on the relationship between Kissy Mellors and Junior Clootie, a college hockey standout who dreams of playing major-league hockey and does so (although, mainly, for a fictional Denver Drovers team, which seems to conflict with the inclusion of the non-fictional Wayne Gretzky in the story). But beyond a simple investigation into the relationship between two individuals essentially brought together by death, *Survivor* examines both the dramatic and believable developments in this relationship—from petty confrontations to divorce-causing circumstances. Long story short, with Kissy and Junior building a relationship as Junior makes the transition to major league hockey, he, as one might expect, ultimately struggles with his career. As his attempt to solidify his footing in a life of athletics becomes Junior's primary focus, the many distractions associated with contemporary professional athletes infringes upon Junior's life and career. As Junior navigates the professional ranks, he becomes deeply involved in drug abuse and infidelity, which is only discovered when he passes gonorrhea to Kissy. Despite any professions of love from Junior to Kissy, the largely absent declarations and displays of genuine affection or devotion provide *Survivor* with both a convenient dramatic element and an honest investigation into the human condition.

When considering fiction, especially Tabitha King's fiction, as an examination of common yet often obscured, or even dramatized, elements of daily life, one must wonder when and where a line is drawn in terms of repetition. With Tabitha King, one of the most constant if not overbearing focal points of her craft involves sex; *Survivor*, despite being over 500 pages in paperback, does not escape this narrow theme. From moments of what appear to be genuine affection to admonishments concerning an excessive focus on sex (such as when Junior Clootie's father tells him, "You only got the one career. Don't let your dick run your life, Junior,"), such critical yet circular concerns are troubling (T. King, *Survivor* 150). On the one hand, Tabitha King may be painted into a corner regarding her fictional accounts of sex and its overwhelmingly ubiquitous presence in her novels. On the other, one might consider that there is, perhaps, a sincere and profound reason Tabitha goes to the well, so to speak, so often, much like how Toni Morrison has consistently focused her fiction on the African American experience. For Morrison, it seems as if her fiction revisits the African American experience not because she has anything new to say regarding the concerns about the atrocities that many African Americans have endured throughout the history of the United States, but because her readers, imagined and actual, have not necessarily acted upon the fiction which seems to ask for personal reform. While it would be unfair to consider Morrison, or Tabitha King for that matter, as preachy or didactic writers, it might be reasoned that these writers simply revisit specific themes and situations because their audience has yet to engage the text in any way beyond a certain distanced interest.

While the African American experience has been noted and has resulted in some positive forward movement, there are times when it seems as if all channels directed towards change within this arena are being aimed at indifferent individuals. And while the large issue of sex may not function as an exceptional or credibly analogous parallel to the African American experience in the novels of Toni Morrison, one only need to look at afternoon television shows like *Jerry Springer* to see that any messages of caution, insight or self-awareness regarding sex that Tabitha King focuses on have seemingly gone unnoticed. Of course, the fiction of Tabitha King has not been mainstreamed, academically or otherwise, to the point that Toni Morrison has, but in considering that her analyses of sex are not all that uncommon, the disturbing scenes of sexual dominance and ignorance that mark Tabitha's fiction might be explained as fixtures in her canon because her readers are unable to read past the drama involved, which is quite the disheartening snapshot of contemporary reading audiences.

Even as much of Tabitha King's readership is presumed to be primarily enraptured and enthralled with the sexual tensions and dramas of her fiction, while perhaps missing the larger implications of such content, Tabitha does not escape the backlash of critics that have commented on the dramatic elements of her writing, which suggests a writer merely pandering to an audience. As *Survivor* takes Kissy Mellors into the arms of James Houston, the man behind the wheel of the deadly crash which opens the text, it is ultimately revealed James actually impregnates Kissy. This entices readers through scandal, as well as purposefully denying important information, in that James is not revealed to be the father of Kissy's child, Dynah, until more than four hundred pages of story have passed. Further, there is no real explanation for her tryst with James Houston, although there is an interesting twist to their sex in that when they begin making love, Kissy has a tampon in her vagina, and they start intercourse without removing the tampon. But even with this strange, and perhaps humorous, sexual encounter, there hardly seems to be anything enlightening that stems from this scene.

Of course, not all fiction is aimed at being profound or is constructed with the intent to be exceptionally serious from start to finish. But there simply seems to be something lacking in the constant drama of *Survivor*, from the obsessive jealousy which consumes Junior Clootie—"While he was out there breaking his ass, she [Kissy] was being somebody else's piece of ass"—to a brief examination of statutory rape in which Junior's Russain teammate, Deker, impregnates Junior's underage sister, Bernie (T. King, *Survivor* 223). But much like the development of Kissy's child, Dynah, the birth of Bernie's child (as well as several other sub-plots) almost becomes lost, just as the tale itself becomes rather lost when, with only one hundred pages left in the novel, Kissy divorces Junior and marries Mike Burke. This particular relationship, like the marriage to Junior, is dominated by strife, as well as critical examinations of the insecure male, in that Mike finds his convenient marriage to Kissy to be constantly on the verge of crumbling, despite his excessively controlling demeanor. Indeed, during one of the few times in which he and Kissy have sex, Tabitha reaches into his mind and tells the reader of Mike's recognition of the fragile marriage as well as his inability to concede that, perhaps, the marriage would just not work: "With all his heart, he cheered on his sperm, the fast strong ones that were racing up her tubes in search of an egg. She wouldn't leave him if she caught, he was certain of it" (T. King, *Survivor* 381). Mike's surety that impregnating Kissy would lead not to a stable marriage, but perhaps to one that would not dissolve certainly reflects the common social practice of pregnancy serving as the ultimate tie that binds. Interestingly enough, if not accidentally, the survival of Mike's marriage to Kissy is, in his mind, dependent upon the survival of his sperm to ultimately produce a child, suggesting, at last, a sense of clarity for the novel concerning the implications that the title holds. But not even the imagery of successfully kindling a viable life form as a catalyst for holding a marriage together can be seen as a clear indication of the purpose of the novel, or its allusions to the whimsical and inexplicable nature of why some things, like marriages, survive or rot away.

As *Survivor* nears its end, with Kissy merely moving through life and her empty marriage to Mike Burke, the novel comes to a close through the doorway of death. But there really is no sense of closure for the book itself. The final scene of *Survivor* witnesses Kissy and her current husband (and third lover in the book) engage in a rather physical confrontation, with Mike Burke ultimately drowning in the river. While Kissy survives the altercation, as she, too, ends up in the river during her fight with and flight from Mike (which seems to be purposeful in its imagery and symbolism akin to the final scene of Kate Chopin's *The Awakening*, which sees its own strong female character floating in the water at the tale's conclusion), the novel simply ends at that point. Kissy seems to display a sense of regret for her failed marriage with Junior, as the last page tells the reader of Kissy's longing: "'Where's Junior?' she asked herself aloud. She needed him; she might be able to get warm again if he would hold her. She leaned back and closed her eyes, and on the wind there rose a distant plaintive siren" (T. King, *Survivor* 463). With this somewhat odd and rather unsatisfying ending, one thing to consider is the overarching domestic thematic of this novel, as it is primarily concerned with the daily lives of Kissy Mellors and her *family*. Further, as it is suggested that, "survival and its costs are a persistent concern of the home plot," perhaps the ending that Tabitha constructs is appropriate to the degree that Kissy yearns for a return to a semblance of security, or at least comfort, in the arms of her first husband (Romines 296). But in order to survive and create a stable family life for her daughter, she had to seek refuge in the home of the police officer who, ironically, turns on her. Then again, the ending readers encounter in *Survivor* is not the original ending that Tabitha planned, and the convoluted conclusion might be better viewed as not a particular generic fashioning but rather an altered ending which highlights the woes of everyday life. At the end of *Survivor* it cannot be clearly deduced if Kissy survives the temperatures or the tide of the river, and it remains to be seen if she returns to a life with her first husband; but perhaps that uncertainty is ultimately woven into the plot to suggest survival truly has no clear endings. Perhaps the best conclusion to draw from this novel is that survival is not a goal with a clear ending but a constant occurrence that cannot ever really be reached.

Conclusion — Words of the Deceased: Candles Burning *(with Michael McDowell)*

While Stephen King toured and promoted his 2006 novel *Lisey's Story*, he not only mentioned Tabitha's catalytic role in producing the novel, he also made it a point to let his audiences know that his wife had recently completed a new novel. This minor plug cannot solely account for the sales of the book titled *Candles Burning*, but this particular point in Tabitha's career as a writer functioned as a crossroads of sorts. As Stephen did his best to increase awareness of Tabitha's latest, and perhaps last, writing project, the book itself was promoted well, as it was easily accessible by way of the fading book chains, and was also appealing because of its curious composition. *Candles Burning*, as is described in the book's forward, is a collaboration of sorts in that Tabitha finished a novel that her friend and fellow novelist Michael McDowell began to write before his rather unexpected death. Such a collaboration is hardly a collaboration at all in that Tabitha really sought to complete the book more than write alongside McDowell; and while some reviewers found the tandem to be more than just functional—"King completes it beautifully as to tone, aura, and flavor"—the book itself is nonetheless an anomaly and a curiosity (Olson 38). The anomalous nature of the book stems from each author's inability to work in tandem (as death, not time or space or ego, separated each author), and the resulting text serves as a curiosity akin to a creative writing exercise in which one student begins a story while another student finishes the story without any input from the original writer other than the story that has been started. Further, Tabitha notes in the foreword for *Candles Burning* that "the story as I completed it is not the story that Michael set out to tell" (n.p.). In some ways the separation in terms of authorial control and intent can be seen in *Candles Burning*, especially with the last few chapters covering a wide range of material, which suggests a hurried ending, the result of the natural disconnect between the authors. But beyond the issue of effort and Tabitha's noted labor of love in finishing her colleague's novel, this book opens as many doors as it closes.

Candles Burning begins with one of the most dramatic, disturbing, and sympathetic openings in recent fiction. Past the blunt and truthful opening line — "My father died unpleasantly" — the reader is introduced to what initially seems a typical family (King and McDowell 1). But it soon becomes evident that there are several separations and fractures within this unit, which drives the plot towards an ending in the mold of *Survivor*, in that little is really concluded. This novel begins its delineations by way of a brief exploration of family history, with the main characters comprising a family of four — Joe Dakin, Roberta Ann Carrol Dakin, Roberta's son, Ford, and Joe's daughter Calley — which finds a split in that Joe and his daughter Calley are immediately juxtaposed and pitted against the mother, Roberta, and her son Ford, who are decidedly of the Carrol clan. This divide within the family is essential in that the Dakins, or Joe and Calley, are of blue-collar roots, while, as reviewer Ray Olson suggests, "The Carrols fancy themselves Alabama aristocracy and scheme amongst themselves as well as with others to grab the wealth that undergirds the pretense" (38). While summaries are almost never as compelling or revealing as the actual work being summarized, this bare-bones review of *Candles Burning* does seem to do the book quite a bit of justice in that the tale develops into a constant unveiling of dark machinations aimed at securing wealth and position, leaving little else as the focus. This is not to say that *Candles Burning* is without exceptional attempts at creating a full story with the typical inclusions of compelling characters and provocative mystery, which spurs the plot enough for engaged reading. But the suggestive use of the word "attempt" is anything but accidental, in that *Candles Burning* is a well-conceived attempt at completing a novel for a deceased writer, but attempts are never guaranteed any real success.

Taking up the strand of "almost" that best describes *Caretakers*, and mimicking the less than profound ending found in *Survivor*, *Candles Burning* is quite the strange literary entity. Aside from the collaborative elements that both contribute to and detract from the story — any sense of seamless transition between Tabitha and McDowell is celebrated, while any jarring disturbances tend to break the foundations of the story — *Candles Burning* moves from murder-mystery almost into the realm of magical realism, where the supernatural is taken as commonplace and upends the tensions typically connected to the unknown and unseen. Further, *Candles Burning* sees itself moving from traditional Gothic elements of ghosts and specters to the real settings and believable characters placed within the American Southern Gothic that often moves away from the horrors of the supernatural to the real horrors of humanity. Such horror, which is primarily captured by way of Joe Dakin's murder in the early pages of *Candles Burning*, serves as an excellent beginning bookend for the novel: "Stepping on a wasp barefoot — that's unpleasant. A mouthful of sour milk — that's unpleasant. What happened to Daddy was no mere unpleasance. It was murder. And not a cozy one" (King and McDowell 1).

From this passage comes not only the dark promise of exploring and investigating death, but also a commendable ability to create strong imagery through strange comparisons, such as being stung by a wasp as only a minor semblance of what it would feel like to experience the death of Joe Dakin. But before the death of Calley Dakin's father, King and McDowell take time to introduce Calley herself, and not just as the soon-to-be fatherless child deserving of sympathy, but as a strange character with rather strange connections to the world.

Before Joe Dakin is murdered, Calley, who somewhat unsuccessfully narrates the tale, which ultimately focuses on her growth into womanhood, notes in the beginning chapter that she, apparently, is able to hear the voices of the dead: "I was frightened. Not for me. For all those people I couldn't see but whose distant voices under the downpour sang to me not in words but in their terror" (King and McDowell 15). On the one hand, this instance in the plot is a rather muddled look into Calley's character because the distant voices are not explained—these voices can be read as delusions of a troubled child, or even as memories which inundate her psyche. On the other hand, a retrospective look at *Candles Burning* suggests that this brief glimpse into Calley's mind is actually a degree of foreshadowing, in that it is discovered that she does in fact have the ability to hear the dead. However, with what becomes a critical element to a plot concerned with twists expected of a genuine mystery, Calley's supernatural abilities are not discussed again until two-hundred pages of the story have passed. Indeed, the only indication that this story would turn towards, but not necessarily into, a modern ghost tale is the overly blunt foreshadowing that Calley provides when she and her mother move to Florida, and she reflects on her thinly constructed wicked grandmother: "I never saw her again, in life, but we heard from her, Mama and me, and by then she was a ghost for real" (King and McDowell 129). Although this nod towards the supernatural is notably abrupt and seemingly forced into the plot, the backdrop of haunting and clouded pasts that is provided does permeate the text, since mystery and uncertainty is now established as a key component of the plot. At this point in the story, readers have faced the poorly explained yet gruesome death of Joe Dakin, and have also been exposed to the mystery of one million dollars gone missing from a footlocker which once held Joe Dakin's dismembered body. Then there's the suspicion that "Joseph's death had nothing to do with me [Roberta Dakin], that Winston Weems and Deirdre Carroll just found a way to get their hands on Joe Cane Dakin's money" (King and McDowell 124). But as soon as any semblance of clarity is laid out for the reader, obscurity and seemingly unnecessary plot invades the reading experience.

Candles Burning is, by some measures, a rather slow story (aside from the first fifty pages or so which primarily chronicle the murder of Joe Dakin, and the last several pages which briskly conclude the story). From the murder of Joe Cane Dakin to the strange but convincing conclusion which suggests that *all* the events of the novel comprise a well-crafted plan to ensure that Calley

Dakin, and her ability to hear the dead, end up under the care, and control, of one Isobel Mank, *Candles Burning* finds itself a tale with little in the way of solid identity. While this assertion suggests, to a degree, that the collaboration which saw this story to publication is not entirely successful, the claim that the story of Calley Dakin is seemingly incomplete also suggests that the collaborative efforts are also successful, at least in creating *story*. On one hand, although there are many essential threads for a plot that appears to be both convoluted and somewhat simplistic, the story itself mainly turns towards the mundane, as *Candles Burning* largely chronicles Calley growing up. With this focus, it is implied that *Candles Burning* looks towards the minutiae of Calley's personal growth, which can be both interesting to some readers and perhaps boring to others who seek plot over extensive character development or chronicling. In many ways, the story does not extend beyond a seeming fictional biography, as the text mostly follows Calley from her grief as a young girl who has lost her father and the only person who ever seemed to genuinely care for her to a person who discovers that she comes from a lineage of individuals imbued with exceptional abilities.

On the other hand, *Candles Burning* sees its burden of multiple plotlines and exceptional possibility in terms of story (and explanations for the supernatural elements of the story) turn into a blessing of sorts, in that the incompleteness of a story that exceeds 400 pages still warrants more development. As with any story that instigates questions regarding the unanswered, which then tends to lead to the reader's autonomous imaginative speculations as to what explanations might adequately answer the questions left by the text, *Candles Burning* prompts its readers to engage in imaginative introspection. The story of Calley Dakin has several holes, which, while bothersome in some respects, leads to an exceptional interaction between reader and text, as the reader searches his or her imagination for answers and conclusions that a given book may not contain. Or, to say it another way, while *Candles Burning* may be chastised for the noticeable disconnect in its story regarding its dual authorial parentage, the gaps that result, especially concerning the mystical history and genealogy surrounding Calley Dakin, creates a story in which the mysteries of the text remain unresolved, but not necessarily in a problematic way. If the willing reader can take the ambiguities of the text and then use such catalysts to simply imagine his or her own resolutions, then *Candles Burning* takes its place as a text that not only begins with noble intentions, but also concludes well — by asking the reader to function as more than a passive vessel for receiving information, which is, unfortunately, becoming more and more common in contemporary readership.

As with any fast and broad summary of fiction, there is undoubtedly much left to be said concerning *Candles Burning*, from the details behind Calley's grandmother's actual involvement in Joe Cane's murder to Calley's reunion with her brother Ford once all secrets have been revealed. And while the pace of *Candles Burning* allows the complex mystery behind the foregrounded story of Calley's adolescence to ultimately reveal itself, there is an odd sensation that arises at the story's conclusion, one which suggests that a second reading of the text is necessary (but not because of its compelling characters or its subtleties). As previously suggested, the numerous mysteries of *Candles Burning* make the reading experience a rather ambivalent one, but for the individual that approaches the story knowing that the plot will not be spoon-fed, and accepts his or her role as more than just a set of eyes to gloss over the text, the story begins to wrestle itself free of initial critiques based on the tale's obscurities. For example, at one point Calley is told that she is "*the vortex, my darling child, the eye of the storm*" (King and McDowell 271). A first reading of *Candles Burning* might dismiss this rather veiled declaration as an unceremoniously highlighted mystery dropped into the text to create a false sense of tension and suspense. Labeling this particular line as something less than revealing, if not in need of extensive explanation, is quite understandable, especially as the notion is largely forgotten when the next several chapters focus on Calley's daily activities rather than revealing the meaning behind her position as the center of a storm (which can only be assumed to be the numerous disasters that stem from her father's death). But a second reading of *Candles Burning* gives the reader the knowledge that Calley is seen by Isobel Mank as a prize to be gained.

In short, *Candles Burning* essentially comes to the conclusion that Calley Dakin comes from a line of talented individuals, and Calley's particular talent is one that is valuable to the outside party of Isobel Mank. The text takes some time and mild care to reveal that Isobel had known and essentially employed Calley's aunts, but had lost them to Calley's maternal grandmother ("Your mama's sisters had talents. Deirdre [Calley's grandmother Mamadee] tried to kill them"), who is, incidentally, Isobel's sister (King and McDowell 403). This revealed relationship is supplemented by a handful of other revelations relating to how and why Calley and her mother leave Mamadee's home and end up under the care and watchful eye of strangers. Said strangers are ultimately revealed as having a noted stake in, and claim to, Calley who, it is said, needs protection: "You hear what no one else does. It might have driven you insane. I've [Isobel Mank] gone to a great deal of trouble to protect you while you were growing up" (King and McDowell 389). Yet this protection can be seen as more of *investing* in Calley, as Isobel Mank also notes, "I prize talent, special talent. People with special talents have special needs. Their talents need protection" (King and McDowell 402). This suggests that any interest she has in Calley is hardly in the little girl who becomes a young woman throughout the course of the text. To be sure, Isobel Mank is anything but a philanthropist— "I am *owed* Calley. Deirdre promised me. Her stupidity cost me those two girls, Faith and Hope. The two of them weren't half of Calley" (King and McDowell 410). Although Isobel Mank's discussion discloses that Calley's talents eclipse those of individuals who had once been in her employ, the dialogue is almost as ambiguous as it is revealing.

The story of Calley's aunts is one great mystery that has little light shed upon it, as do the pages which follow the unveiling of Isobel Mank's plans to acquire Calley and her talents. The conclusion does not do much beyond providing a smattering of notes in which Calley reunites with her brother, who recounts his general knowledge of Isobel Mank's machinations; a brief accounting of how Calley is given Isobel's fortunes, and that she funnels the money into charitable organizations to enrage Isobel; and that Calley and Ford strangely find their father's skull. In coupling these final plot points with the concluding line—"Out of blinding sun fire came a drawn-out, rude laugh: *uuuuhhhk*"—one sees not just the speed of the conclusion, but how the conclusion is hardly any conclusion at all (King and McDowell 423). The final line, along with the appearance of Joe Cane Dakin's skull, certainly invokes the faint images of the Gothic—the image of death by way of the skull, and the unknown by way of the faceless voice of the concluding line—also bears the problematic aspect of adding no real clarity or purpose to the story. However, as noted, the seeming lack of cohesion that *Candles Burning* carries, especially with the quick conclusion that leaves many questions unanswered and many plotlines untied, can be celebrated for its prompting of the reader to seek answers within him or herself instead of the text.

Perhaps the greatest treasure of *Candles Burning* is not so much Calley Dakin and her development, especially as "some may be disappointed, though, that in the end Calley is much less likable ... than triumphant," but its embedded mysteries, both in terms of plot and the final product which resists any real sense of closure (Olson 38). Without the original author to confirm approval of the text, one can only imagine what *Candles Burning* is missing, whether in terms of Michael McDowell's intents or Tabitha King's adaptation /translation of McDowell's story. But, as suggested, with a little imagination and understanding, *Candles Burning* may prove to be quite the exceptional reading experience for the forgiving and discerning (re)reader.

Composing criticism surrounding the works of Tabitha King is no easy task, especially when considering and celebrating her for being able to do what millions of people are not able to do, which is imagine, create and construct a *story*. But like any author, even with the genuine gems of story and insights that Tabitha provides to her readers, critique does follow. Still, even with many of the heavy critiques which have been provided, Tabitha King stands firm as a writer of great talent and intent. Via some of her stories, like her shorter fictions, and some of the minor elements of her fictions, like the passing descriptions of the speech and dialect within her fiction's settings (as well as the curious linking of her fiction to her husbands), Tabitha King takes great care to connect her reader with fiction and writing that extends well beyond pure make-believe. Like most writers, Tabitha aims at creating not just lasting fictions, both in terms of impression and readership, but also fictions that are founded in achieving a goal of creating lines of *communication*. Tabitha herself suggests, "A writer today continues the social function that has always existed among human beings, of encoding information in such a way that it will be acceptable, it will be rich and it will be passed on and shared with everyone who encounters it" [Shattuck 62].

While it may seem strange for an author to plainly and bluntly note that her work is aimed at communicating key social concerns to her readers, it is also rather admirable for Tabitha to admit her rather lofty goals. Although her readership may not carry the same numbers as, say, her husband, her fiction speaks well for itself. In fact, one of the most amusing yet telling passages from her body of works involves clarifying common misconceptions. In *One on One*, Tabitha uses Sam Styles' literacy development as, essentially, a non-didactic teaching moment for her reader when she narrates, "He [Sam Styles] knows — having read the book under Romney's tutelage — that the movie monster is erroneously known as Frankenstein, who was in fact the scientist who patched him together out of corpses" (T. King, *One on One* 188). While this is not exactly a passage that is essential to the plot of *One on One*, it is interesting to see a writer of fiction comment on how fictional references and knowledge can become distorted; and the larger implication of the erasure of misinformation, even through a minor scene, is but one of many examples in Tabitha King's fiction through which she is able to engage her reader in not just a story, but also concerns that, while captured in fiction, should not be eternally trapped within the pages by disinterested readers or readers that are unable to look beyond the words printed on any given page of fiction.

Tabitha King still writes, and one can only wonder what will be published in the future, or if she will in fact publish any new material. Although she gives the impression that she would like to continue to publish, whatever circumstances may surround a potential end to her writing career are unfortunate. With works such as *The Sky in the Water* and *The Devil's Only Friend* remaining unpublished, the end of Tabitha's career as a writer may be in sight. Further, eager readers may come to discover that Tabitha's early exposure to the public came via an onscreen appearance in George Romero's *Knightriders* (1981), alongside her husband, and that her most recent bridge to the American reading population is as a reader for Stephen King's 2009 audio book *The House on Maple Street: And Other Stories*— all of which indicates that Tabitha will forever be attached, almost literally and most certainly literarily, to her husband. But her presence as an author in her own right remains, and seeks a willing reader who might find her fictions a worthwhile means of occupying the time and eyes of the modern reader.

5

Emerging from the Shadows: Joseph Hillstrom King Becomes Joe Hill

In exploring the fictions of the King Family, labels become not entirely appropriate or necessary for distinguishing each of the writers, but they do tend to form, more or less, on their own. With Owen King it has been suggested that one of the most accurate labels for categorizing him and his fiction is that of both the comedic and semi-dramatic "slice-of-life" writer. Regarding Tabitha King, her gender functions as a conduit to labeling, or pigeon-holing, and she is often considered a writer of the domestic. Concerning Joseph Hillstrom King, or Joe Hill, no one label accurately, or even effectively, captures the essence of his fiction in terms of form, genre, content, or aim. One only need to peruse the pages of his short-story collection *20th Century Ghosts* to see that there is much more to Hill's budding canon than the horrific which is expected of he and his father, Stephen King. While *20th Century Ghosts* does feature tales of the macabre, including the story "Last Breath," which brings readers to a museum of sorts where the proprietor has amassed a collection of dying breaths (and which has also, incidentally, been developed into an online game accessible through Joe Hill's website), Hill also takes his readers to the mundane comforts of the baseball park and the provocative imagined world in which an inflatable child is, like Pinocchio, a real boy. But noting Joe Hill's range as a writer is neither the only way into his fiction nor an easy task.

Of the writers in the King family not named Stephen, Joe Hill most mirrors his father in terms of style and genre. Of course, the generic constraints tend to be burdens placed upon Hill, in that any categorization of his fiction as horror or as Gothic fails to fully capture the range of a writer who, in less than a decade, has shown a literary range that has taken his father a lifetime to explore. While this is not necessarily a critique of Stephen King's first several published works, noting that the early years of Hill's career have seen a level of breadth and experimentation that his father was not afforded suggests several things. First, Hill's range as a writer, accompanied by the success he has found with his published works, suggests that the current market and reading population desires works of fiction that look beyond formulaic plots or common characters and settings. Second, this suggests that the formulas and genres that Stephen King primarily worked with in the late '70s have perhaps run their course. As Edward J. Ingebreston suggests, "Formulas are by definition neither unique nor new; to the contrary, they are familiar, routine, and old. We know the monsters because we know the stories, and we know how they are supposed to turn out" (28). And while the monsters alluded to here tend to take the shape of literal creatures or abnormal individuals who are often aligned with evil, there is more to monstrosity, and expectation, than knowing the stories of well-known creatures. Further, with this sentiment serving as an appropriate backdrop to Joe Hill's fiction, especially as that which can be juxtaposed with the fiction of Stephen King rather than considering the shared blood of these two writers, it indicates that the monstrosities and horrors of the late twentieth-century have, for many readers, become passé and in need of new blood, so to speak. And with Joe Hill's fiction, audiences may be given a glimpse into the horrors and atrocities that undergird Stephen King's canon, but they are also exposed to an accompanying range of concerns and faces of darkness that are both oddly familiar and wonderfully strange. And it is with this sense of newness, this feeling of playfulness joined by a dedication to telling a good story, that Joe Hill has begun to make a name for himself and his craft.

Among the early successes that have met Joe Hill are several awards, notably the Bram Stoker Award for Best Short Story ("Best New Horror"), the same award for Best Fiction Collection (*20th Century Ghosts*), and also the award for Best First Novel (*Heart-Shaped Box*). Additionally, he has been included in numerous recent anthology collections, such as Christopher Golden's *The New Dead*, and his popularity has grown with each passing year. He even maintains a website on which fans are able to blog about his fictions, and Hill maintains a sense of personal contact with his readers by way of the networking tool Twitter. There is little doubt that Joe Hill is plugged-in — in every sense of the clichéd phrase — and with his mass-media connection to his readership, it is hard to deny that Hill's writing career has been anything but successful and fast-paced. Given the speed with which Hill has entered into the world of fiction writing in recent years, while noting that Hill began writing as early as the 1980s (as evidenced by his works found in the Stephen King Special Collections in the Raymond Fogler Library at the University of Maine-Orono, including his already-noted collaboration with his father titled "But Only Darkness Loves Me," along with another short story attributed to him titled "The Bone Men"), there is some wonder as to why Hill has garnered such a large following in recent years. The wonder does not necessarily stem from an overly critical analysis of his work, although he does tend to be safe and predictable with his writing, in that he does not often take a risk with the conclusions (which, incidentally, receives an obtrusive but warranted metafictional analysis in his short story "Best New Horror," which suggests that surprise endings are just as poorly crafted and received as common or flat endings). More than anything, the musings as to Hill's popularity primarily arise while noting that his early efforts as a writer went largely unnoticed — notably the short stories "The Lady Rests" (1997; *Palace Corbie* 7) and "The Collaborators" (1998; *Implosion* 8), not to mention "The Saved" (2001 *Clackamas Literary Review* 5.1), which is the only uncollected early Hill story that is somewhat accessible to the public by way of eBay or interlibrary loan), and the fact that *20th Century Ghosts* was not available in the United States until two years after its 2005 British publication. And while Stephen King, too, endured several years of obscurity and hardship as a fiction writer in the early 1970s, perhaps Hill's similar career path and explosion of popularity indicates that fiction is often subjected to the waves of fate. Then again, when examining Hill's fiction, it clearly seems as if he is indeed a writer for the new millennium, one that is not only knowledgeable of the varied desires and demands of the reading public, but one that is also able and adept enough with his craft to produce fictions that are more than just productions influenced by the market.

A Writer for the Millennium?: "Jude Confronts Global Warming," "The Saved," Gunpowder *and "Twittering from the Circus of the Dead"*

Although Joe Hill first started publishing before the calendar turned to its two-thousandth year, it is somewhat safe to say that his writing is a genuine encapsulation of fiction which stems from and is founded in the concerns of the new millennium. But this is not to say that Hill is a writer cornered by a particular source for his fiction, or even by a single genre. When it comes to the generic elements which surround his father's fiction, Hill notes that despite his visits into the realms of the Gothic and the horrific, he does not do so to merely follow the wave of popularity created for him by other writers: "I figured if I wrote genre fiction as Joseph King, it would look like a grab at my Dad's coattails. Whereas I could write whatever the hell I wanted as Joe Hill. And I did for 10 years" (Patrick 25). However, the journey of a writer who has few connections is not always a fruitful one, and while Hill's purposeful anonymity is quite admirable, struggles marked the first several years of his career:

> Writing under his pseudonym, Hill struggled to get published. After graduating in English from Vassar College, he spent three years toiling on a 900-page fantasy novel entitled *The Fear Tree*, about a young man who discovers he has a rare gift to recognise the secret fears of others. Looking back, he calls the book "a mash-up of John Irving and J. R. R. Tolkien." Nobody would publish it and his mother—

who famously rescued the draft of her husband's first novel, Carrie, from the rubbish—advised him to ditch it. "She said: 'It's time to start the next book'" [Bone 6].

The maturity that Hill displays in his willingness to set aside a work into which he placed much time and effort is quite commendable, especially considering that *The Fear Tree* ultimately transformed into Hill's most recent novel, *Horns*, in which the main character, Iggy Perrish, is able to discover the dark secrets of those around him after a strange visitation to what is best described as the Devil's tree house. Such patience marks Hill's desire to write not necessarily for financial gain, but to tell a good story. And as James Bone notes that Hill has written two other unpublished books, the young adult fantasy called *The Evil Kites of Dr. Lourdes* and *The Briars* ("loosely based on the random killing of two married professors by a pair of teenage boys"), one can only hope that these stories will eventually be published (6). For now, Hill has provided new and old readers alike with enough writing to stir the imagination and obtain a glimpse of the contemporary fiction scene, both that of the horrific and the comedic.

While it is quite unnecessary to belabor the point that genre boundaries serve as restricting limitations for fictions and their authors, it must be noted that Joe Hill, despite his best efforts, has been mostly typecast as a horror writer. And while this is not necessarily a large obstacle for Hill to overcome, especially when some critics carefully note the range of horror in and of itself— "At a minimum, horror fiction is a means of escape, sublimating the very real and often overpowering horrors of everyday life in favor of surreal, exotic, and visionary realms"—others are not so forgiving (Winter 3). Then again, Hill himself suggests that most fictions necessarily fall into the mold of the horrific when he notes "Stories are always examinations of misery. There is no way around it" (Bone 6). Perhaps this is simply the human condition with which writers concern themselves and their fictions, or perhaps this is an oversimplification of the foundation and function of the contemporary story. However, misery, like mystery and drama, serves as an engaging reflection of the world at large, and while writers are often much more than chroniclers of the ages in which they live, it is actually rather telling that misery, in one form or another, seems to be intertwined with contemporary fictions, especially those by Joe Hill. Hill's "Jude Confronts Global Warming," a tale only available online through Subterranean Press (marking just one of Hill's allegiances to a small publisher), takes (as the title indicates) a brief look at the woes facing the contemporary world, as the tale ends by noting, "Jude opened the side door, shaking his head, and stepped out into the Atlantic Ocean" (Hill, "Jude" n.p.). But rather than having a global-scale worry dominate his tale, Hill provides a glimpse into the troubled lives of a seemingly every day couple. The characters, Georgia and Jude, resemble a common couple marked by tension and a certain level of distaste for one another:

Jude flipped the radio over to FUM. They were playing Soundgarden, *Black Hole Sun*. Jude turned it up.

"What the fuck you do that for?" Georgia said.... "I was listening to that, asshole."

"Now you're listening to this," Jude said [Hill, "Jude" n.p.].

More important than this somewhat easy characterization of a miserable couple that seems to find pleasure in purposefully annoying one another is that these characters bear a striking resemblance to the main characters from his novel *Heart-Shaped Box*, which suggests that "Jude Confronts Global Warming" was either an aborted element of the novel that Hill graciously gave to Subterranean Press, or that he lazily crafted a story from one of his existing fictions merely as a favor to this publisher. Either way, "Jude Confronts Global Warming" provides more than just a brief look into the dissentions of everyday life and the purported criticisms of troubled modern life. It is, by and large, a story that shows Hill's humorous side and sets the stage for fictions that are, in many ways, just stories—simple, enjoyable accounts of fictional events with a few reflections of reality put there for a purpose no greater than to be read.

Admittedly, "Jude Confronts Global Warming" is not much of a story. Although fads and trends in fiction have produced "flash fiction," or purposely short tales that attempt to tell an engaging or entertaining story in one or two pages, such conciseness does not always succeed. Much like Stephen King's "flash fiction," which has largely been kept from the mass public (including "Jumper" and "The Killer"), Hill's venture into the excessively short story brings up certain questions, primarily those concerned with understanding Hill's purpose as a writer. In other words, while some fictions are, generally, imaginative yarns with no illusions or delusions of grandeur, some of Hill's fiction reminds readers that even in the new millennium, writers must have a sensitivity to careful and seemingly profound treatments of the human condition that tend to be found in the more serious fictions.

One of Hill's more obscure, or even "lost," stories is titled "The Saved," in which a divorcee struggles through sporadic road work in a time and place resembling depression-era America. Although this story was included in the United Kingdom slipcased printing of *20th Century Ghosts*, which is a later printing of Hill's short-story collection not released in the United States, it remains relatively unavailable to American readers. And while the setting of the story does not necessarily give American readers or publishers any claim to the story in and of itself, it is an interesting comment on the Joe Hill canon that the American-ness of his writing was originally embraced by a British audience, whereas the very people who formed the foundation of the stories, and perhaps for whom Hill intended his writings, received these fictions only after Hill's identity as Stephen King's son was revealed. Regardless of these peculiarities, "The Saved" primarily concerns itself with religious references and imagery against the depression-era backdrop as a metaphor of sorts surrounding the main character, Jubal Scott. Jubal is, in many ways, a lost man who is found wandering aimlessly, to one degree or another, after his separation from his wife. Much of this information is gleaned immediately, as Hill writes, "Linda [Jubal's ex-wife] had gone back to her people in Maine and taken their daughter with her" (Hill, "The Saved" 17). With a single sentence, Hill establishes several key elements of this fiction, ranging from regional clarity (Maine) to a purposely outdated phrasing—"her people"—to further establish not just the scene but also the tensions of the story that rely upon the particular time in which the story takes place to enhance the agony involved in divorce.

On the note of familial separation, both in terms of divorce and the implication that entire families are being pitted against one another, Hill takes great care in the very first page of "The Saved" to create a story that escapes simplistic plotlines that rely upon the invocation of divorce to carry the story. But the tension of Jubal's divorce takes perhaps too much of a back seat, so to speak, as the early plot of the story follows Jubal on the road to Maine where thoughts of his fractured family are put to the side in favor of a rather strange hitchhiker that he picks up along the way. "Strange" may be too strong, or too broad, a term to describe the man who Jubal picks up in the cold northeast weather, in that the hitchhiker merely seems to be a humble, thankful man of God: "I was lost out there and I *prayed* for you, Jubal Scott. I prayed for you to come to me. I was in the snow and the blowin' wind and I prayed for someone to come and lift me out of it and here you are" (Hill, "The Saved" 19). In response, Jubal says, "First time ever I been the answer to someone's prayers," and the mockery of the hitchhiker's faith begins (Hill, "The Saved" 19). The mockery and sarcasm continue as the story itself continues, ultimately resulting in little as far as the plot is concerned. Jubal and the hitchhiker do have a rather heated exchange as they part company, with Jubal actual striking the hitchhiker, which is not simply a moment in which the pent-up feelings Jubal carries from his divorce boils over. Indeed, this scene is reflective of the contemporary attitudes that many Americans possess regarding issues of religion or other ideologies, which tend to result in volatile confrontations rather than intelligent discussions. Consider Hill's description of the aftermath of Jubal's fists speaking not just to his purportedly atheistic beliefs, but also to his stubborn and confrontational persona:

> Jubal had thought he had got the last word in with the man-who-had-a-jacket-from-Jesus, but it turned out he had not. When he came outside, he found a bloody cross fingerpainted on the driver's side window. Another red cross was in the snow on the hood, and over it, in crooked, badly made letters, was a single word: FORGIVE. Jubal wiped it all off with lumps of snow [Hill, "The Saved" 23].

The imagery of this scene, with the blood used as paint, is provocative in its seeming message of hope and redemption. After all, Jubal is traveling to Maine to see his estranged daughter and perhaps make things right with his ex-wife, and the hitchhiker is simply reminding him to shed his arrogances in the hope that he may be able to forgive those he feels have wronged him, as well as seek forgiveness from those he may have wronged. But Hill is careful to ensure that the hitchhiker does not function as the typically convenient *deus ex machina*, perhaps along the literary lines of a Jacob Marley, which prompts Jubal Scott to truly make things right with his daughter and ex-wife. Such convenience would be, one could argue, poor storytelling.

"The Saved" ultimately comes to a close with Jubal Scott arriving at the home of his ex-wife's mother, where his ex-wife and daughter live, and the story takes some rather expected and uneventful turns. Jubal and his ex-wife fight and argue, his daughter does not recognize her own father because of the amount of time that has elapsed between the last time they saw one another, and Jubal then returns to his own home, dissatisfied and defeated. This is not to say that there is little or nothing notable in the last scenes of "The Saved," but the story at this point is so familiar that the reader is left wondering what to make of the tale. While one could focus on the separated family as a common yet notable story for the twenty-first century, or redirect focus back to the treatment of religion as detailed by Jubal's interactions with the hitchhiker, such a wandering perspective or reading of the story seems to mirror the main character, especially as the conclusion of "The Saved" has the audience wandering much in the same manner as Jubal Scott. As Jubal drives his way back to his own home, he envisions his daughter running in front of his truck, leaving tracks in the falling snow, and as Jubal follows this apparition of what appears to be his heart's greatest desire, it would seem that the story would end with this obsessive delusion which Hill takes great care to chronicle:

> He drove following the boot holes she had left behind her in the snow, but was unable to catch sight of her again.... Sometimes he passed little-girl angelshapes made in the snow. No tracks led to them. They appeared to have made themselves ... [and then] there was nothing but the white slopes, and the hiss of snow driven in glittering fans by the wind. He drove on without thought, or any emotion other than desperation, without any true hope of finding where she had gone, out in the snow and pines, alone but for the company of her cold and faceless angels [Hill, "The Saved" 33].

The writing in this passage is notably beautiful, and captures the essence of the tale by having Jubal Scott drive after his daughter in a quixotic and delusional attempt to, at the very least, catch up to his offspring before she is completely beyond his reach. But "The Saved" in many ways lingers a bit, and, beyond the images of an angelic child that is literally and figuratively beyond Jubal Scott's reach, the plot moves Jubal deep into the northeastern woods, off the snowy roads, and into the mercy of nature and complete strangers. By following the apparition of his daughter, closing himself off to the rest of the world, Jubal drives off the road and finds himself lost, stuck, and abandoned, which would seem to be a perfect conclusion for the story. But Hill, it would seem, had further plans, which included drawing out Jubal's desperate and ill-formed attempts at reconstructing a family for no other reason besides a sense of greed and possibly desperation rather than out of a genuine love.

Perhaps one conclusion to draw is that this tale functions in a way similar to that of a religious allegory; Jubal does seem to fulfill the character of a Wandering Jew of sorts, but the underlying meaning, message, or purpose is still rather veiled. And while such a mystery is notable and should be celebrated, in that Hill creates a tale with enough flexibility to be read in multiple ways, there does appear to be a sense of artistic arrogance in that the lack of a clear ending implies that only the truly intelligent or enlightened reader will fully understand what the author intended. Such a conclusion is likely not accurate, but one of the more challenging elements of literature is the level of transparency with which a given story is created. If an author merely writes a story that reads like a lecture or a newscast, then story becomes absent in that there is likely no plotting, character development, or even the symbolism which is generally expected. However, balance needs to be found; composing a story which relies on excessively obscure references or extremely convoluted plotlines that are to be uncoiled by the reader can be problematic. And while "The Saved" may not have much in the way of directing the reader to a clear termination point in terms of the plot's conclusion or the story's intent, Hill does display an ability to strike a balance between leaving some details to the imagination while providing enough to make the chasms between the text and reader manageable when he writes his science fiction novella *Gunpowder*.

Science fiction is, typically, a difficult genre to write, especially when the imagination of the author must find a way to be clearly conveyed to the reader so that questions regarding the plot or any other element do not overwhelm the reading experience. From Isaac Asimov to Arthur C. Clarke to Philip K. Dick, science fiction is one of those genres which has the potential to garner quite the following in terms of fandom and readership, as well as a following which decries the strangeness as well as the uninventive and even clichéd nature of the genre. For example, there were certainly some reservations regarding the latest *Indiana Jones* film, subtitled *The Kingdom of the Crystal Skull*, boiling down to an alien presence on earth and leaving audiences to watch a flying saucer rise from the earth at the film's conclusion. And while this brief review of the film does not contextualize the story beyond the screen, it does imply a sense of dissatisfaction that some moviegoers had with the science fiction turn that the film takes, in that aliens and their science fiction stories seem to have run their course. Although fans of *Battlestar Galactica* and other contemporary science fiction shows would beg to differ with the suggestion that science fiction has, in some ways, developed into a tried and tired genre, Joe Hill's *Gunpowder* indicates that the form can still offer compelling and interesting tales regardless of any issues that readers may have with the recycled themes, creatures and phenomena that generally mark the science fiction genre.

Besides the story itself, *Gunpowder* is a text that was published almost secretly, receiving very little announcement whatsoever, which includes Joe Hill's own personal website where *Gunpowder* is mentioned only in passing. Much like *20th Century Ghosts*, *Gunpowder* was originally published in the United Kingdom in a limited printing that effectively limited access to this work, especially in the United States. Still, as copies are available in many of the usual outlets, such as Amazon.com or eBay, it is still disheartening to see a number of Hill's works poorly disseminated. Perhaps *Gunpowder* merely follows the footsteps Stephen King himself took with his fantasy/science fiction work *The Dark Tower*, and aimed to publish the text with little announcement to see if the book and its story would garner readership on its own merits. The merits of the story are, of course, hard to separate from Hill's increasing popularity as a key factor to consider in terms of readership, but the tale does possess some qualities that suggest it is strong fiction.

From a brief summative standpoint, *Gunpowder* posits that technology has developed to a point where humans can be manufactured in a manner that instills abilities like telepathy, telekinesis, and the ability to literally change the world: "It was a gift that operated at the place where quantum mechanics verged on magic, where the observer could change and remake what was being observed" (Hill, *Gunpowder* 31). The individuals imbued with the gifts to observe the world at large and begin to shape its chemistry, physics and biology are children, and these children are essentially products to be used and consumed: "They had no status as citizens, no rights" (Hill, *Gunpowder* 32). Such information is not given to the reader until about one-third of the way into the tale, where Hill also nods towards his science fiction predecessors in giving even more back story for the children of *Gunpowder* when he notes, "The program that had created the boys—the Leguin Project—was despised and feared" (Hill, *Gunpowder* 32). Hill's accounting of the children as genetically engineered tools that are to be disposed of and cast aside certainly paints a harrowing picture of future developments in terms of environment and the role of the *natural* human. The children created by science, and despised by the larger public, not only create an ostracized group to be explored and exploited in the later pages of *Gunpowder*, but also seem to border on the horrific, which seems to be a complementary generic merging in terms of the story's influences and scope: "The contemporary horror story often utilizes an exaggeration or extrapolation of modern technology as its surrogate for the unknown, operating as a cautionary tale that simultaneously rejects technology while reassuring the reader that things could nevertheless be worse" (Winter 87). *Gunpowder* may not necessarily be a thinly-veiled allegory commenting on the horrors of technology, but it does suggest that the pursuit of power, whether through technology or even children, is rarely ever without victims.

On the thematic of the child, *Gunpowder* provides an amusing and startling examination of the life of the child, specifically the male child, complete with hurtful pranks and the costs of pride and hierarchical positioning. As Lisa Colatrella notes of science and science fiction that "the most progressive innovations might have hidden psychological or moral costs uncomfortable to bear," it could stand to reason that Hill's use of children as victims of technological innovation is simply an easy route to take because children are often vessels that elicit sympathy for no other fact besides their lack of physical development (554). But when considering the extended and layered treatment that children receive in the Stephen King canon, it could also be concluded that Hill shares with his father a sincere concern for the child as a vessel not just for sympathy but as a natural target for the evils of the adult world, and that readers would do well to give attention to the atrocities surrounding these *people*, regardless of their ages and levels of physical or cognitive development. Stephen King's fascination with the innocence of childhood, and the erasure of purity that comes with an engagement or entrance into the corrupt adult world, has been noted by scholars in many of Stephen's novels. And that positioning, the notion that "[Stephen] King's adolescents can also be superior to his adults," finds a firm foothold in Joe Hill's fiction as well (Casebeer 214). For example, the character Charley, who is the least capable of the manufactured children of *Gunpowder* who inhabit the planet with the possibly *Star Wars*–influenced name of R2, finds himself on the wrong end of a cruel prank which leaves him isolated as well as naked. His defense the young boys who tend to treat him as an outsider both justifies and rationalizes their actions by claiming it was all done in jest, that "'it was j-just a g-g-guh-game,' he said. 'A t-t-t-test'" (Hill, *Gunpowder* 19). Perhaps this is merely Charley attempting to win favor by way of essentially forgiving his peers for their transgressions, as it is unsurprising to see a child, fictional or otherwise, almost volunteer him or herself as a target for maliciousness, believing that being a victim is a gateway to acceptance. And as Hill effectively captures the psyche of the outsider, the forgotten and isolated child, with an accuracy that elicits sincere sympathy, he manages to weave a story of the fantastically unbelievable, deftly maneuvering around such images of painful reality that stem from Charley as the Carrie-like figure whose separation from the group suggests major implications for the story.

As previously noted, Charley is set aside from his peers because his is a "void" — "Charley's optical displays were always the same, and required no interpretation. It was **VOID** now and it had been **VOID** since he was eighteen months old" — a child without the talent to form and shape the dead world of R2 into a viable world (Hill, *Gunpowder* 21). As it were, Charley is noted as simply building a rock wall around the main residence as some sort of contribution to the efforts on the alien planet. This scene of a lonely child building with his hands while the other boys of *Gunpowder* are able to build and create with their minds would seem to be just the first instance of drawing attention to Charley's status as an outsider. However, as is the case in Hill's novels, the plotting is drawn up so well that this purportedly minor scene in the beginning pages of the text ends up playing a major role in the story. *Gunpowder* is exceptionally well plotted for being, essentially, a novella consisting of just under ninety pages of text, as evidenced by Charley's rock wall and its critical use in the story's final pages, along with the early descriptions of the planet which Charley and the others inhabit: "The deserts were at least a third sulfur and sodium nitrate, the ingredients of gunpowder. The world was ready to burn; a dangerous place to raise thirty boys" (Hill, *Gunpowder* 8). The reference to the composition of R2, along with the ultimate job of the children on this planet to transform its deadness into liveliness, suggests an eco-critical element to the story. While the eco-critical theme of environmental destruction, along with the surprising ends to which people must go in order to face or repair such damage, is noteworthy, an excessive examination of *Gunpowder*'s environmental message takes way from the story in and of itself, which ultimately takes a turn towards that of the medieval, with the boys facing a challenge to their ways and their family structure. With thirty male children who mostly possess powers that are asked to be tempered by one female mother figure, Elaine, there is nonetheless a certain harmony that this non–traditional family possesses. That is, until one Officer Sheila Jackson comes to R2 so that Elaine can be replaced with a military presence that desires to utilize the children as weapons of mass destruction.

Gunpowder rapidly moves towards its conclusion through threats of force as well as gender. In terms of force, Officer Sheila Jackson, as noted, has come to R2 so that she can use the children as military weapons. But she does not necessarily pose a threat to the children as a military officer, especially when she begins to exert her power and manipulation by creating within the children a desire to become military weapons, and begins her dominance by offering the children war masks. These masks are more than just a manipulative gesture, however; they begin an examination of gender within the story, as Jackson thinks to herself, "Boys didn't want faces. They wanted armor" (Hill, *Gunpowder* 58). By relying on a childish yet presumably *male* predilection to be involved in war and masculine activities associated with battle, Jackson promotes a gender divide in the story. This actually begins with her first visit, in which the character Cutter suggests that even though the mother, Elaine, is female, her femininity, as either a threat or a means of opposition, has been largely negated, as he voices his first impression of Jackson: "'Oh shit,' Cutter said. 'It's got tits'" (Hill, *Gunpowder* 40). This initial reaction to Officer Jackson reflects the lack of gender representation in *Gunpowder*, and also mirrors the realization by the Loser's Club from *It* that Pennywise the Dancing Clown's true form was a *female* spider. But this implied misogyny is more than understandable when the only female presence for the young male children is their mother figure, a nurturing yet firm presence that is completely antithetical to Officer Jackson's military background and demeanor, which perhaps draws inspiration from Hill's character Mallory Grennan from "Thumbprint." Still, the seeming confusion and conflict regarding gender is not entirely a commentary on the socio-cultural constructions of men and women — it is, more than anything, just another tool, or mechanism, of dominance that radiates all throughout the text of *Gunpowder*. Such tools, or power and power-relationships, become the center of attention.

Aside from the gender implications of the war masks that Jackson gifts to the children of R2, the tale turns towards its denouement when it is discovered that the war masks are a means of instigating submission and exercising power. The masks have the capability of rendering the children of R2 powerless, or "zeroing" the children, which is unbeknownst to all the children except Charley, who begins to display certain levels of precognition at this point in the story (implying that he may have some talent after all). In short, the rock wall that Charley constructs in the early pages and which is somewhat forgotten in the middle parts of the tale comes into play when he summons what is assumed to be telekinetic powers and pulls the stones from his rock wall into the castle as missiles aimed at disarming Officer Jackson (which appears to be an obvious reference to Shirley *Jackson* and her novel *The Haunting of Hill House*). This defense, or retaliation, by Charley suggests a particularly plotted plan by Hill, especially as he has the alpha-male of R2 mention early in the story that "you should give Charley a chance to prove himself" (Hill, Gunpowder 17). And in the end, Charley, despite his deficits, which are well documented in the story, does serve a function within the tale, albeit as a saint-figure who is willing to sacrifice himself for the benefit of others. Charley dies while pulling down one of R2's moons (amusingly named "Caliban"— another obvious literary reference to *The Tempest*, and perhaps to *Brave New World* as well) to crush Jackson's military presence. With this, Hill's carefully crafted tale moves towards its conclusion, which returns readers to the theme of the child as only a handful of the children survive the encounter with Jackson and the meteor shower that Charley causes by pulling a moon out of its orbit. And these lonely yet surviving children are left to face not just the deaths of their friends and mother-figure, but the threat of an entire universe that might wish to control them as Jackson had planned to do. To this, one of the boys, Cutter, proclaims, "If they come — when they come — we can make them sorry. We can make them so sorry they won't ever come again. No one can beat us here. Not on our world. Not on Gunpowder" (Hill, *Gunpowder* 81). Whether this is an omen of terrible things to come or a glimmer of hope is left for the reader to decide. Seeing R2, or Gunpowder, left in the hands of children might engender sobering thoughts, but seeing a group of angry and capable children wielding power is no more potentially horrific than ignorant yet capable adults with access to power. And with this layered and endearing tale of survival and power gone awry, Hill adeptly examines the core of fiction — the human condition — and does so within a seemingly repellant genre, ultimately suggesting that even tales of serious fiction can wear varied faces.

As the first decade of the new millennium closed, Hill not only continued to write his graphic novel series *Locke and Key*, as well as publishing his second novel, *Horns*, he also found the time to produce a short piece as a contribution to Christopher Golden's "Zombie Anthology" titled *The New Dead*. Moving right to the heart of this fiction, one which is notably lacking in the sense of profundity that marks *Gunpowder* and, perhaps, "The Saved," it is noted that the short story is written as if it could be a series of web-based personal activity updates delivered on the ever-popular networking tool Twitter. Hill simply titles this story, which is delivered in short "tweets," as "Twittering from the Circus of the Dead." While the progression of the story is necessarily choppy and sporadic, with its look at a teenage girl on a family vacation whose constant escapes to the "Twitterverse" result in the entire story, the experimental delivery that Hill plays with is both wonderfully playful, considering that Hill himself constantly posts personal updates on Twitter, and smartly critical of technology (used at times as an overwhelming crutch). Indeed, as "Twittering" progresses, including the ever-cliché, rationalization for utilizing Twitter — "I'm expressing myself and staying in touch with my friends and she [the mother] hates it" — this look into the constant if not obsessive online interactions of individuals seems to be something which warrants more than just critical examination but a critical revision regarding real-world actions and activities (Hill, "Twittering" 355). Although it is difficult to gauge Hill's intentions here, considering that he, too, "tweets" on Twitter, it is nonetheless difficult to deny Hill's effective capturing of the teen mentality of using communication as a means of self-fulfillment, or "expressing myself," alluding to the old empty rhetoric that teens tend to use without recognizing the ridiculous sentiment that communication within limited circles is somehow a grand manner of creating identity. Hill takes further steps to highlight this irony, as he has his main character chastise her mother for the Luddite approach to electronic communications when the narrator tweets of her mother, "She says the internet is 'life-validation'" (Hill, "Twittering" 353). And it is with this examination of technology and its ability to counterfeit the real world that "Twittering from the Circus of the Dead" really finds its own identity.

Unbelievable and "unsophisticated" fictions generally function as perpetual pathways into horror, and while "Twittering" borders on the amusing more than the enlightening, it still provides some rather entertaining yet critical insights into the online, virtual world that has been created around the populace. With the title of the story instigating expectations of a horror fiction, which is delivered, the theme of death is first discussed and examined not by way of actual loss of life, but rather through the techno-critical mother character. She views the online world as a figurative coffin in which people voluntarily place themselves: "For online people, death doesn't happen. People go online to hide from death and wind up hiding from life. Words right from her lips" (Hill, "Twittering" 353). This sentiment, along with some rather amusing foreshadowing—"my survival skilz would amount to Twittering madly for someone to rescue us"—leads the reader to assume that not only some sort of atrocity awaits the anonymous twitterer, but also that the tale, as noted, takes care to provide an insightful commentary on the nature of web-based communications (Hill, "Twittering" 356). One thought which stems from Hill's commentary on, and allusions to, death, and which is easily on the morbid side, is that one can hardly announce his or her death through the internet—unless such a death is, perhaps, a planned suicide. And as macabre as that thought may be, it is an interesting potential study in terms of the psychological benefits, or ramifications, of creating a semblance of immortality by way of online networking.

As "Twittering" gives the reader an account of a family which wandered into a circus that is, in reality, a gruesome show of death which pulls its victims from the audience (as discussed and described by the "tweeter," who sees the blood and the smell of burning bodies under the circus tent as the writing on the wall). As the reader reads a series of "tweets" in which the traveling family and its chronicler realize that they are not in a normal circus and ultimately are captured so that they can perform for the next unsuspecting audience (who will interpret the cries for help as great acting), the account of a family vacation which ends in death, but which is, essentially, immortalized in the "Twitterverse," reminds the reader that one's death will not immediately erase his or her online presence. Although the Twitter feed which comprises the story ends the tale with an advertisement for the circus, which is wonderfully ambiguous because one does not know whether or not the entire thing is a hoax, the permeating presence of the internet and its various tools of communication and interaction provide an excitingly experimental form and conduit for Hill's imagination.

On a side note which stems from "Twittering," a brief look at Hill's networking with his friend Christopher Golden (author of not only *The New Dead*, in which Hill provides the short story "Twittering from the Circus of the Dead," but also co-author of *The Stephen King Universe* and the name behind the introduction to the 2007 American release of *20th Century Ghosts*) and the small Subterranean Press (which provides online access to Hill's short story "Jude Confronts Global Warming") suggests that access to his fiction will hardly be straightforward. With Hill working with so many presses, including the somewhat infamous Cemetery Dance Press, and within quite the range of mediums, it would be no small feat to acquire copies of all of Hill's writing. This is not highlighted as a nod towards questions of collecting (which has become quite the fancy with the fiction of Hill's father), but questions of *access*, bringing to light the shifting literary scene. Indeed, with online publishing gaining more and more popularity, and with writers contributing to a wide array of small presses to increase sales, the breadth of publication, not to mention the growing costs to the reader (or consumer, depending on the perspective), makes enjoying a single writer more and more difficult.

To be sure, Hill is quite the skilled writer, one who is able to temper his purported roots in horror with a fresh approach to an old genre; but one can only guess as to whether or not Hill will continue to write himself into production corners, or if he will embrace select elements of mainstream publishing — namely, that which opens access to a larger audience. Of course, Stephen King has faced similar circumstances and has even justified the small-press approach that produced some of his earlier fictions, such as *The Gunslinger* and *Cycle of the Werewolf*. And while questions of interest — at least initially — tend to direct an author into one direction or another concerning his or her writing, it is safe to say that Joe Hill has been embraced by the public and has enjoyed a certain demand for his fiction. And while the demands of the reader, or the public, should not necessarily dictate the channels of fiction (especially the creative ones), to listen to the reader and pull the reader into the worlds of one's creation is hardly achieved through constantly limiting access in one way or another. While Joe Hill may feel that some of his lesser-known fictions are not worthy of (re)publication, one would hope that he allows his fiction to take hold within the public forum and public court of judgment. After all, what is fiction that has no reader?

Among Hill's more questionable publishing allegiances is that with Cemetery Dance Publications, a Maryland-based press that has been gaining both favor and notoriety in recent years, especially with its limited release publication of Stephen King's *Blockade Billy*. Further, Cemetery Dance gained much of its popularity by way of its link to Bev Vincent, better known as the author of the largely summative *The Road to the Dark Tower*. With Vincent tapping into a select readership with *The Road to the Dark Tower*, his pre-existing relationship with Cemetery Dance led the way to this press becoming a small niche market, primarily dealing with limited edition publications of popular authors, including Hill's father. The primary issue to take here is not necessarily a particular press gaining popularity by way of a sound business model of fulfilling the public's needs (or desires). Rather, by positioning itself as a publisher that is, in its own words, in the market to produce texts which are largely not for the general public, this press, and Hill (along with his father), are redefining fiction in a manner that has little to do with questions of content or craft. Both Hill and Stephen King, as well as the numerous other authors under the Cemetery Dance umbrella, are contributing to the growth of fiction as a collectible item rather than an artistic product. And although it is hard to argue with the matriarch of the King family, who bluntly asks in *Mid-Life Confidential*, "Would you work for diddly-shit?" there is certainly a difficult line that Hill is negotiating with regard to limited printings of his fiction with a specialty press (T. King, "Paid" 183). Assuredly, such a sentiment is received as humorous when, of course, the point of Tabitha's travels with her and the rest of the Rock Bottom Remainders was not to earn money. But there is quite the difference between working for money and being compensated for one's work. In short, with Hill's emerging popularity, and with a surging public interest in Hill's work, it seems rather irresponsible, if not greedily opportunistic, to perpetually create fiction that comes with an excessive price tag in terms of both the initial costs that readers are asked to pay and the constructed costs of value attached to volumes that are printed in limited quantities.

If Hill (and Stephen King) continues to willingly participate in the production of limited editions that are designed to be collectibles rather than vessels of story, it would be disheartening to say the least, just as it was troubling to see Stephen King first publish his short story "Ur" only through the Amazon Kindle. However, Stephen King suggests in the coda of *Song of Susannah* that

> people are so fucking *spoiled*! They just assume that if there's a book anywhere in the world they *want*, then they have a perfect *right* to that book. This would be news indeed to those folks in the Middle Ages who might have heard *rumors* of books but never actually saw one; paper was valuable ... and books were treasures you protected with your life [393].

While this sentiment is not entirely agreeable in the sense that it essentially commercializes and objectifies books to the point of fetishism, which perhaps fuels the desire for collectable limited editions, it is understandable and commendable to see these writers using their status among the popular reader to promote a small press and to remind larger publishers that there are other pathways open to writers than the mass-market. Still, when the result of aiding a small business is the purposeful creation of limited editions, and various other accoutrements like specialized slip cases to protect not books but *investments*, it serves as a somewhat blunt and crude reminder that reading is being replaced by collecting, and that the admittedly noble intentions of fiction to explore the human condition by way of story is now exploring the human condition not through words or artistry but by way of economics. And while this does distract, if not detract, from the actual fictional creations of Joe Hill (and Stephen King), it also functions as a reminder that beyond the stories Hill writes, his position as a writer that is well connected to the market and the financial side of publishing is a reflection of fiction writing in the new millennium.

Story may be important, but the complexity of fiction now, more so than in previous decades and eras, exists well beyond the twists and turns of the plot contained in a particular work. The fiction of the millennium, then, seems to be concerned with not just craft, but sustained marketability and name recognition. And while it stands to reason, as many academics suggest, that the "best" fiction will always make itself known, it is hard to deny that selective market floods of fiction aided by several different means may not always leave the door open for fair or balanced competition among potential readers. But, then again, perhaps this element of Hill's fiction is essential to viewing the entire context of Hill's career as not just a writer, but a writer in and of the new millennium.

A Comic Flavor: Locke and Key

Comics, or graphic novels, are both a fascinating and frustrating element of the contemporary literary scene. When successful in terms of art and story, the graphic novel serves as an engaging development in storytelling that can aid the imagination and excite the reader with more than mere words. Without doubt, graphic novels provide a new experience when it comes to story: "We interpret a comic by gathering together the successive scenes" (Carrier 55). This idea of interactive reading, one which seems to stem beyond the purportedly passive activity of simply following the words printed on a page within a novel, is key to approaching the graphic novel. But the images that accompany any graphic novel do not eliminate the need for good story and dialogue. Where Hill's father seems to fail with the graphic novel adaptation of *The Dark Tower* (in that story, detail and dialogue become more and more absent as these stories progress), *Locke and Key* adeptly blends the visual elements with the actual *story* contained within the pages. Perhaps Hill's general success with *Locke and Key* when compared to *The Dark Tower* is a matter of originality — Stephen King's graphic novel is an adaptation of a novel, whereas Hill's tale is completely written for the graphic novel medium. However, with reports that *Locke and Key* has been optioned as a television series, it is both exciting and troubling to see Hill's fiction, especially that which is already highly visual, make its way onto the screen.

The excitement for the potential visual adaptations of Hill's stories is exhilarating in the sense that eager audiences are able to become immersed in Hill's fiction and imagination through yet another doorway. But the increasing speed with which fiction is taken from the page to the screen is troubling in that there is always something lost in translation, and it is disheartening to anticipate what might be lost in a visual adaptation of Hill's work. And it is also disheartening to imagine that, potentially, a new reader/viewer will first encounter Hill on the screen and be met with an inferior creation. The word "creation" in this case is purposely substituted for the word "product" because thinking of Hill's fiction as merely another commercial product, no matter how potentially accurate such a term may be, is almost unbearable, especially when considering some of the film failures that his father faced. Still, *Locke and Key*, as it currently stands solely as a graphic novel, is quite the story, despite what initially appears to be an unsurprising introduction to the story and characters with the grisly murder of Rendell Locke by his former student, Sam Lerner.

With the grief witnessed by Rendell's widow and his surviving children, Hill takes the reader, and the family, from California to Massachusetts where the real story of *Locke and Key* begins. Like any good tale, *Locke and Key: Welcome to Lovecraft* has its ample share of set up and plotting to establish its story. Although quite a bit happens early on with the murder of Mr. Locke, the back-and-forth action, along with glimpses of Sam Lerner in prison speaking into a puddle of water, and with Bode discovering a strange skull key in the Locke children's new home, Hill is careful to take his time with his tale, as this first installment of his series also has several panels without any narration or dialogue. Further, as the subtitle for the first series of *Locke and Key* reads "Welcome to Lovecraft," both the reader and the Locke family are brought into the genuinely Gothic house dubbed Keyhouse in the town of Lovecraft, Massachusetts. Aside from the literary reference from which the house takes its namesake, it is immediately made known that the house, although not haunted per se, carries with it several secrets and mysteries, all of which create a literal maze for the stories' characters, and readers, to navigate.

Beyond the initial plotting which sees Rendell Locke murdered and his murderer, Sam Lerner, locked away in a juvenile detention facility, the mysteries of *Locke and Key* commence with a flashback to Rendell discussing his brother, Duncan Locke, and making a strange declaration about Keyhouse: "The house didn't choose me. It chose Duncan" (Hill and Rodriguez, *Welcome to Lovecraft* 16/1). With this statement, the story of *Locke and Key* moves towards its core of purposeful ambiguity, which not only suggests that this series will need several story arcs to fully explain all the mysteries it creates and presents, but also that Hill understands the power and pull of suspense. In many ways, readers are easy to manipulate in terms of their reading experience, in that merely holding back vital information is one way to spur interest — that is, if a given reader has developed a vested interest in the characters, settings, or story in and of itself. To consider suspense as a simple gimmick is inaccurate in the case of *Locke and Key*, especially, as noted, interest in a story must be created in order for any suspense or denial of information to take effect on the reader. And with *Locke and Key*, the murder of Rendell Locke is only the first in a series of events to grip the reader. In fact, murder is only a stepping stone for the continuous elements of the story that pull the reader into the larger story, one that is much more than a slice-of-life tale about a broken and fractured family that is attempting to resume life after the loss of a loved one.

Locke and Key is a graphic novel that is difficult to capture beyond its primary plot of a murder and its rippling effects. Looking backwards, one of the most critical turns that this story takes is the exploration as to why Sam Lerner killed his former guidance counselor. And while the issue of back story and the information it presents for the curious reader is vital to most any tale, the historical elements of *Locke and Key* are, in many ways, aimed towards crafting not just story, but the illustrated story. As Dennis O'Neill, author of *The DC Comics Guide to Writing Comics*, says of the graphic novel, "There must be a major change, development, or reverse in every issue ... something important must happen in every issue" (87). To the satisfaction of O'Neill and the reader, *Locke and Key* admirably succeeds, in that change, and reversal, is constant throughout the story. While *Locke and Key* is anything but piecemeal, it does resemble a broken mirror in some fashion because the story, even through just three installments in the series, has so many purposeful loose ends that each issue of *Locke and Key* must take care to manage the numerous sub-plots that most definitely move the reader and the story back and forth throughout the duration of the building plot. This change, and the reversals between the present of the story and the clouded past, serves as a fulcrum for the tale, as subtly reflected when Sam Lerner, while locked away but still able to communicate with the outside (but supernatural) world, is told that "all doors will be opened" (Hill and Rodriguez, *Welcome to Lovecraft* 34/2). Of course, this particular statement is primarily connected to the story of the Locke children and their imminent adventures in Keyhouse, one of which immediately follows the assurance that the doors of the story will be opened, in that the literal doorways of Keyhouse are shown to be crucial to the plot of *Locke and Key*.

The scene directly following Sam Lerner's revealing discussion with the strange creature who appears in puddles of water in his cell has young Bode Locke using a special key to open and then walk through a previously locked door. He discovers that passage through this door, after being unlocked by the appropriate key, allows the spirit to leave one's body. More importantly, Bode's brief venture into the spiritual world is touchingly connected to the first scenes of the story, as Bode thinks to himself, "If I showed Kinsey [sister] and Tyler [brother] about how fun it is to be a ghost, they wouldn't feel so bad about what happened to our father" (Hill and Rodriguez, *Welcome to Lovecraft* 45/4). And while Bode's seemingly accidental exposure to one of Keyhouse's secrets opens the story to a perpetual series of discoveries for the reader and the Locke children, *Locke and Key* is more than just a tale with Hill's mind functioning as an imaginative toolbox from which the story can and will draw particular developments.

Returning to the first scene in which Keyhouse is firmly revealed as more than just a constructed dwelling (when Bode Locke discovers a way to separate his soul from his body), readers find more than just a fantastical gimmick or plot device. While the idea that separating body from soul is important to the plot of *Locke and Key*, and also pushes the story towards the generic classification of fantasy, Bode's first adventure into the realm of death establishes a foundation of duality for the story in that each scene of fantastical or magical imagination or occurrence has a serious element to it. Again, with Bode's discovery of, essentially, the joy of being dead, and suggesting that such knowledge would help his siblings cope with the loss of their father, Hill opens the story not just to the potential of Keyhouse — which sees shadows unleashed upon the unsuspecting Locke children, as well as Tyler Locke transformed into a giant — but suggests a particularly critical and serious concern that is attached to what some might merely look at as spectacle. For instance, in the third installment of the story, *Crown of Shadows*, Tyler Locke finds a key which turns him into a giant, and while his size in this transformation reflects a literal spectacle in terms of grandiosity, one would do well to note that Tyler's role as a giant is also a manifestation of his self-imposed role as protector of the Locke family (as prompted by his father's death). Additionally, Tyler's consuming guilt, in that he believes he is responsible for his father's death (it is revealed that Tyler knew Sam Lerner before Rendell Locke is murdered, and that Tyler's frustrations with his father at the time prompted him to say to Sam, who also struggles with his relationship with his own father, "You ever decide to kill your dad, do me a favor and kill mine while you're at it"), supplements the serious examination of his character by way of a single key and its transformative powers (Hill and Rodriguez, *Welcome to Lovecraft* 97/2). Indeed, seriousness, as well as spectacle, has its place in *Locke and Key*, especially in terms of misdirection and veiled meaning that contributes to the development of the story — in stages — as well as the development of the reader's interest.

In very basic terms, *Locke and Key* is a tale of mystery and cunningly crafted circumstance which takes the Locke family from San Francisco to Massachusetts and into the mysterious childhood home of the murdered Rendell Locke. Here, the youngest of the Locke children discovers a strange creature apparently trapped in a well house. The creature's discussion with Bode opens many threads to the tale when it says, "My names are Legion, Bode. But I'll tell you what. In a place called once upon-a-time, your daddy would've done anything to make me happy" (Hill and Rodriguez, *Welcome to Lovecraft* 116/6). The mystery inherent in this scene seems to be quite the simplistic construction in denying information to the reader in terms of the creature's actual identity and its relationship to Bode's father, although it is later revealed that Sam Lerner is a tool of this Legion — or Echo/Dodge/Zack, of which the third name becomes a façade that the Locke children ultimately befriend (as they have no knowledge of its role with their father's murder). And this lack of information, which is just one of many veiled elements of the story that remain hidden for both the reader and the characters, propels the story into the numerous purposeful unknowns that mark *Locke and Key*.

While ambiguity is a necessary component of suspense, there are times when it becomes almost overwhelming in *Locke and Key*. Moreover, attempting to explain and summarize the story itself is difficult, in that it would take more words to describe the story than there are actual words used within these graphic novels. Of course, the illustrations in *Locke and Key* tell much of the story, which is not to say that the dialogue is substandard, unrealistic or lacking; the story stands very well on its own, with all the elements of the tale working together to form quite the cohesive and enjoyable whole — which is not always the case with graphic novels (Stephen King's graphic novelization of *The Dark Tower* included). But grasping *Locke and Key* in its entirety is all but impossible, even with the unity to be found between the visual and the written elements. But with only three story arcs completed, and no clear termination point in sight for the story, the clandestine nature of *Locke and Key* is more intriguing than it is problematic. Amusingly, Hill admits that his story of Keyhouse and the Locke children can be difficult to follow. Echo/Dodge/Zack says, in a metafictional bit of dialogue to both Bode and the reader, that, regarding the vagueness which clouds the story, "You can't understand. Because you're reading the last chapter of something without having read the first chapters" (Hill and Rodriguez, *Welcome to Lovecraft* 140/1). With this statement, Hill creates two key components to the growing story of *Locke and Key*. First, he purposefully reminds his readers that there is quite a bit of missing information, and that in order to learn more, the audience will have to keep reading. And while one could interpret that as being a cheap maneuver to gain readership through transparent tension and mystery, one could just as easily see this as another doorway within the story, and that behind this door is the story that readers have been pushed to yearn for.

Setting aside the obscured plot elements that Hill will undoubtedly unveil as *Locke and Key* moves further and further towards some sort of resolution regarding the mysteries of Keyhouse and, perhaps, the evil designs of Echo/Dodge/Zack, there are quite a number of subtleties in the text, as well as the artwork — like seeing a forgotten key laying atop a grandfather clock — that Hill (and his illustrator, Gabriel Rodriguez) weave into a text already constructed with an immense amount of indirectness. While the term "subtlety" suggests even more obscurity in an already clouded tale, the subtleties with which readers would do well to concern themselves include the larger themes that Hill develops, including the identity of the child. As the first installment of *Locke and Key* primarily involves Sam Lerner's murder of Rendell Locke, as well as Lerner's escape and ultimate flight to Keyhouse in search of the many keys that Echo/Dodge/Zack seeks, Lerner notes that his errands are hindered by adults, but not in the sense that Lerner is still an adolescent and adults thereby function as authoritative obstacles. Rather, as Sam Lerner breaches Keyhouse and takes widow Locke hostage in the hopes that threats against her life will help him find the keys he seeks, he notes that her adult mindset and memory are an obstacle: "Dodge said you might not remember. Dodge said grown-ups don't believe" (Hill and Rodriguez, *Welcome to Lovecraft*

103/3). While this establishes even more mystery for the reader in terms of how the many keys to be discovered and used in Keyhouse seemingly depend on imagination and a genuine belief in magic to function, Sam Lerner's knowledge that the adult mind is closed to many of the perspectives and beliefs of the child is almost hidden in *Locke and Key*, at least as to how the child figure seems to be necessarily distanced from the adult and the adult world, which mirrors the treatment of children and childhood innocence in Stephen King's canon.

With the character Rufus, the mentally challenged son of Ellie Whedon (who, incidentally, has a strange connection to the demon known as Echo/Dodge/Zack), Hill creates a character whose only real connection to the world is by speaking to and through his Army action figures, almost as if he exhibits a certain type of autism. But, for a point of comparison between Hill and his father, as well as a look beyond mere mental debilitation, Rufus' indulgence in fantasy and the pleasures of the television seems to be almost a mirror of Seth Garin, the autistic boy who defeats the demon Tak in Stephen King's *The Regulators*, which suggests that the child, or this character in particular, has what is perceived to be a real handicap by the adults in his life, but which seems to serve him in a way that logic and the adult mind cannot comprehend. As the final pages of the second installment, titled "Head Games," progress, in which a specific key is able to literally open character's heads, Zack attempts to open Rufus' head, but to no avail — whereas all characters before this instance are shown to have some sort of keyhole in the back of their heads which allows whoever possesses the Head Key access into other people's minds and memories, for some unexplained reason Rufus has no keyhole in his cranium. At this point in *Locke and Key*, all that readers have to work with is speculation (as well as the connections to Stephen King's fictional children who also face mental deficiencies, including Duddits from *Dreamcatcher*) and Rufus' declaration that he senses something amiss regarding Echo/Dodge/Zack: "We must be on our guard. The Replicant could be the greatest enemy we've ever faced. His capacity for cruelty is immeasurable" (Hill and Rodriguez, *Head Games* 143/4). Such an insight, which is only surmised by a few select characters in the story, as well as the reader, suggests more than just connections to Stephen King's fiction, whether one is thinking of Richard Bachman's hero or the unassuming savior of *Dreamcatcher*, or even the entire cast of the Loser's Club from *It* and their need for a child's clear imagination to achieve victory in their fight against evil. Rufus' awareness (coupled with the few selections which suggest that imagination and memory are a far cry from the debilitations of time and cynicism as often found in the adult mind and in the adult world) is a critical subtlety of *Locke and Key* that is anything but a gimmick, and necessitates further exploration and explanation in later issues.

To end an exploration of *Locke and Key* without looking at the various keys which are discovered throughout the text — from a key that facilitates changes in gender to a key that is able to literally open people's heads—is certainly not desirable. Neither is selectively dismissing the growing cast and Hill's critically keen eye for character development and engaging the sympathies of the reader, especially through the gay character Duncan Locke and his struggles with contemporary ignorance and bigotry: "I'm old enough to remember what this town was like before it turned into cocksucker paradise every summer. Best thing about the fall is seein' the queers go home" (Hill and Rodriguez, *Head Games* 86/1). But perhaps these omissions, alongside the actual mysteries from within the text, will serve as a prompting of sorts for readers who have yet to visit Keyhouse, a push towards the vivid imagination of Joe Hill. And even as this imagination is adeptly transferred from Hill's mind onto the pages of his graphic novel series, *Locke and Key* may not be taken seriously because of its graphic form. However, it is, perhaps, the best example of Joe Hill's imagination and storytelling ability. Such a statement is undoubtedly premature, in that Hill's career has, quite possibly, only just begun. And perhaps such a sentiment is slanted as well, in that the fantastical nature of *Locke and Key* necessitates an imagination dependent upon the wide possibilities that the supernatural, magical and inexplicable afford. But with many new keys and doorways to be discovered, Hill has not only crafted a tale that has unlimited growth potential, he has also created a story with glimpses into the realities of loss, grief, ignorance, and revenge—elements that populate so many other fictions, and with which his readers can easily identify and explore, accompanied by the engrossing magic of *story*.

An English Flair? 20th Century Ghosts

As Joe Hill has primarily been discovered through his novels *Heart-Shaped Box* and *Horns*, the preceding discussion reveals that Hill is immersed in the world of story, no matter its length. And with *20th Century Ghosts*, Hill provides numerous new doorways into his imagination via a wide selection of short stories, ranging from kidnappings with supernatural overtures to a seemingly haunted typewriter (which resonates with a sense of his father's short story "The Word Processor of the Gods"). But one of the most interesting, or problematic, elements of *20th Century Ghosts* involves its national and geographic connections—while the characters and settings appear to be largely American, this collection was first published in the United Kingdom: "No American publisher took a chance on Hill's story collection, *20th Century Ghosts*. Published by PS, a British publisher, in 2005, it won awards and a cult following, but only 2,000 copies are in print" (Minzesheimer 1D). Of course, attempting to account for the national split in initial interest in Joe Hill is entirely a matter for speculation, and perhaps one believable supposition is that the American public simply no longer has an interest in the short story form. Stephen King scholar Tony Magistrale, however, champions the form, stating, "The short story has one great advantage over the novel: its forced concision creates an intensified effect. Because it can be read in one sitting rather than over a series of days or weeks, the short story leaves a more powerful imprint on the mind" (*Second Decade* 88). With this said, it would seem that Hill's first major venture into the fiction market would have found a welcome embrace by the American public, which often seems to face and desire literary experiences, whether profound or innocuous, with extreme brevity. However, even the short story form, for all of its benefits and potential for quick and easy reading, has its difficulty in becoming situated within a contemporary public, no matter how compelling or entertaining such fictions may be.

If it stands to reason that modern audiences, especially of the American kind, tend to have had their reading tastes and practices shaped so that even short readings are less than desirable, this clarifies why Hill's early efforts went largely unnoticed. But in assuming that the other end of the writing spectrum — the novel — stands more of a chance of being published and read by the public, one would be mistaken, even though in Hill's case it was his first novel that jumpstarted his career. Still, with this increase in popularity and awareness by the public regarding the fiction of Joe Hill, it is not only appropriate but also revealing to look at his first major publication, *20th Century Ghosts*, to see that even good writing and engaging stories do not always garner attention or praise. *20th Century Ghosts*, by its title alone, might suggest a particular brand of horror which seeks to illuminate the dark recesses of recent history, perhaps providing a sense of discomfort that many readers would likely wish to avoid. Of course, the nature of horror is that it asks the reader to confront familiar grotesqueness as well as clear truths which tend to be unflattering. Still, the invocation of horror that the single word "ghosts" brings is misleading when considering the bulk of Hill's writing in this collection. Ghosts are, in many ways, simple reflections of nostalgia that have been forgotten or lost, and within *20th Century Ghosts* the specters of memory both haunt and uplift the characters Hill creates. But even by reading Hill's fiction as an accurate and somewhat anthropological series of literary snapshots of the variety of ghosts that haunt the modern social-scape, the shadow of genre looms large over his fiction, adding another layer to the speculations surrounding the lack of immediate acceptance that his collection received.

As a final prefatory and critical note on *20th Century Ghosts* (which, when removed from the lenses of popularity and genre, functions as an exceptional literary convergence of stories that resist definition and boundaries), it must be observed that this collection faces many of the issues that other stories of the "dark" or "macabre" face in the form of generic classification by way of the Gothic. To once again reiterate the problems that the Gothic genre poses not just for Hill but for any writer who ventures into a realm of purportedly formulaic markers and thematics of the Gothic, it must be noted, as Thomas J. Roberts suggests, that "the word *genre* is not a synonym for words like *class* and *set* and *category*. A genre is a tradition" (201). Roberts' declaration is critical in looking at the Gothic as anything other than a stock set of symbols and tropes that create particular expectations among readers. In other words, as "*20th Century Ghosts* … displays consummate skill in a variety of genres," one would do well to consider that, at the very least, Hill and many of his fellow contemporary writers cannot necessarily be read solely through one particular lens, although such simplistic approaches to writing and reading appear to be all too commonplace (Barnes 4D). As popular novelist Dean Koontz advises young writers that "your path to success in any genre will be shorter if you walk the known trail and leave the exploration of new territory for later," the clear impression left is one of simplicity on behalf of not just the pandering author seeding a ready-made audience, but also a reader that has neither the desire nor the inclination to engage in a text with any semblance of layering, development, or perhaps even insight (151). Although using Dean Koontz as a scapegoat of sorts for the speculation that readers have developed an almost reverse literacy is a touch over the top, it is nonetheless revealing that, in some cases, contemporary readers have developed as passive vessels that resist depth and variety.

Moving into the actual text that comprises *20th Century Ghosts*, while keeping in mind that this collection faced quite the selection of obstacles (as well as fortunate circumstances regarding its ultimate publication within the United States), the 2007 publication of this collection marks the first time that most American eyes were laid upon the pages, beginning with Hill's colleague, Christopher Golden, who introduces American readers to this collection. The reason that Golden's introduction is notable is that he immediately tells readers that they will be entering into a collection that is anything but pure gore and titillation, that Hill has attempted to create more than just consumable fiction. Golden depicts Hill's writing as largely within the genre of horror, but he carefully notes that typical conceptions of horror are inapplicable to Hill: "Most horror is not often subtle. Most of those who practice the art of the unsettling far too often go for the jugular, forgetting that the best predators are stealthy" (xi). And it can be said with surety that Hill tends to be rather "stealthy" with his horror, avoiding basic plots splattered with blood merely to paint a gory picture that is nothing less than disturbing. Hill does, however, not shy away from some of the darker sides of the world, as is the case with the opening story of *20th Century Ghosts*.

Leading with his best foot forward, Hill begins his collection with a tale examining the current state of horror fiction while also considering its close link to reality. Titled "Best New Horror," this story, perhaps in an exaggerated manner, reminds the reader that horror fiction is not completely made-up, and resonates with the assertion that "if we could safely keep the horror within the pages of a text, we would live in a society which has no need of horror fiction" (Holland-Toll 251). The tale begins innocuously enough by focusing on the character of Eddie Carroll, who serves as editor of the journal *America's Best New Horror*. And as Christopher Golden suggests in his introduction to *20th Century Ghosts* that many modern horror writers are out of touch with the subtleties of horror, Hill reflects upon this state of affairs by noting that Eddie Carroll's editorial duties were not always enjoyable: "He didn't finish most of the stories he started anymore, couldn't bear to. He felt weak at the thought of reading another story about vampires having sex with other vampires" (Hill, "Best New Horror" 1). While this sentiment could be construed as an attack on the burgeoning field of vampire tales exemplified by Stephenie Meyers' *Twilight*, this metafictional commentary makes for an excellent duality within this story. Seeking to be more than just another indistinguishable fiction, this tale is so self-aware that Eddie Carroll's knowledge as an editor — "a surprise ending (no matter how well executed) was the mark of childish, commercial fiction and bad TV"— resonates so strongly through the story that readers are almost invited to critique Hill through the literary critiques that he himself provides (Hill, "Best New Horror" 7). To that end, "Best New Horror" examines the market of fiction, noting the troubles in the literary and public market regarding a story titled "Buttonboy," about the kidnapping of a woman named Cate, who is imprisoned with a young boy named Jim who has had buttons pinned to his eyelids. Further, Cate and Jim are forced into sexual acts by their captors, and Cate is ultimately disfigured because her kidnapper fails to become aroused at their coercions. And although Cate escapes, she is haunted by the nightmares of her captivity until she is recaptured. But this simple summary of the story that serves as the core of Hill's own story hardly captures the key horrors of "Best New Horror."

Within the story in "Best New Horror," Hill notes that many of the horrors surrounding horror fiction include the inability to read beyond images of destitution and despair: "The story lingered on images of female degradation, and the heroine had been written as a somewhat willing accomplice to her own emotional, sexual and spiritual mistreatment. This was bad ... but Joyce Carol Oates wrote stories like it ... and won awards for them" (Hill, "Best New Horror" 7). Indeed, comparing the fiction of Joyce Carol Oates to the fictional story of "Buttonboy" may be difficult for some literary critics to embrace, but such juxtaposition is rather fair. Just as Hill's father can be favorably compared to his "literary" contemporaries like Toni Morrison or Don DeLillo (depending on the particular comparison), invoking the fiction of an accepted author despite her less than wholesome content in an effort to justify a reading of a rather depraved story like "Buttonboy" is easily within the realm of fairness. But the point to be made here is that approaches to particular fictional treatments, especially those based on images and conceptions surrounding a text by way of established public acceptance through generic classification, or based upon the author's established public image, are rather inconsistent. And this inconsistency in literary judgment, where a reader or critic chides one story while celebrating another, stemming from arbitrary standards of taste or immediate reactions with little to no context (or willingness to investigate a text beyond the words printed on the page), serves Hill rather well for the first fiction in his collection.

To say it another way, "Best New Horror" takes on the status of a story that is not just a story to be chastised for its often lackadaisical efforts at traditional elements of story (including the lackluster attempt to create a back story for the main character in which passing commentary notes an affair), but one that functions as the backbone for a collection of fictions that ask readers to alter their conceptions of reading and the reading experience. It asks readers to not simply judge tales on their purported genres or the basic events of their respective plots. Yet to consider *20th Century Ghosts* as just a thinly-veiled metaphor seeking to challenge readers and their reading practices is to reduce the collection to something that it is not. While this collection and its initial story establish a critical foundation for reading practices, it nonetheless keeps within the boundaries of fiction and provides quite the selection of tales, suggesting that fiction may have its serious side; but to be entirely in one camp or the other (i.e. serious/literary versus popular/spectacle) is also detrimental to the reading experience.

"Best New Horror" takes care to avoid the pitfalls of exceeding the boundaries of fiction by transforming into an extensively didactic tale seeking to change common reading practices by providing a *story*, which remains as the basic yet universal tag line for the fictions of the King family. With "Best New Horror," beyond the metafictional commentary, readers are taken to the home of one Peter Kilrue, author of the disturbing "Buttonboy," in which Eddie Carroll sees a glimpse of Peter's real world, which, frighteningly, mirrors the fictional world of his creation. Among Eddie's descriptions of Peter's home include Peter's brother: "This guy was — I don't want to be insensitive — but I would say he was disturbingly fat. And tattooed. Disturbingly tattooed. On his stomach there was a windmill, with rotted corpses hanging from it. On his back, there was a fetus with — scribbled-over eyes. And a scalpel in one fist. And fangs" (Hill, "Best New Horror" 10). From this menacing individual, to Peter Kilrue's discussion of his original designs of his story ("The way I wrote it at first, the giant is strangling her, and just as she's passing out, she can feel the other one using buttons to pin her twat shut. But I lost my nerve and cut it out") Hill creates a truly horrific tale that slowly builds to the likely realization that Peter Kilrue based "Buttonboy" on his own life (Hill, "Best New Horror" 19). Consequently, Eddie attempts to flee the Kilrue residence, taking the story towards a somewhat formulaic ending. Eddie flees through the surrounding woods and thinks to himself that his own life story is coming to resemble, more and more, a fictional construction: "He knew better than anyone how these stories went, and if anyone could find their way out of these woods, it was him" (Hill, "Best New Horror" 23). In short, the discovery of Peter Kilrue's disturbing nature and reality, along with Eddie's necessitated escape, suggests the "twist ending" that Hill notes is not always well received, at least by the literary elite. More to the point, what Hill does here is create a story in which the twist ending slowly creeps upon the reader not so much to shock and engage through a cheap tactic, but rather to show how a well-executed gimmick can work in fiction. The ending is, in a way, a mockery of both convention and criticism, suggesting that writers need not avoid twist endings because they can engage the audience, and that writing a twist ending even in the face of imminent criticism is a move to ask critics to reconsider their often fruitless efforts to direct and manufacture fiction from afar.

With "Best New Horror" primarily functioning as a critical cornerstone regarding convention and reception, Hill establishes *20th Century Ghosts* as a collection of stories that seek to be more than just fictions. To that end, the second tale of this collection, "20th Century Ghost," continues to form the larger framework of the collection in that this story is presented almost like a documentary, which seems to inventively borrow cinematic approaches for fiction (as a noted inversion of written fiction often being translated for the screen). But, as tends to be the case with several of the fictions in *20th Century Ghosts*, this story carries with it much potential for development well beyond what is provided, but also seems to resonate with a sense of limitation. To say that "20th Century Ghost" is limited ignores exceptional criticisms which examine minute elements of the story and suggest that they grow much larger when read beyond the pages, including the declaration that the ghosts of which Hill writes are more than mere specters, that they are, according to Hill, "a metaphor for the way the past leaps into the present" (Bone 6). This notion that ghosts are more than phantasms expected to function as horrific images of the past as they exist in the present suggests that the ghosts of this story, primarily one Imogene Gilchrist, serves as a connection among diverse times, bringing people closer to a forgotten history, from eras of war to times of struggle and even moments of pure ecstasy.

To say it another way, Joe Hill's re-positioning of the ghost figure certainly combats conceptions of the Gothic one might erroneously place upon Hill and his fiction, as Hill creates for "20th Century Ghost" a story in which a movie house becomes haunted and then transforms into a spectacle of wonderment rather than a location of fright. To be sure, there are numerous pathways into reading this story as a critique of modern cinema, which includes nothing close to the experiences of the motion pictures from the 1940s through the 1970s; hence Hill's use of Imogene Gilchrist's ghost as a connection to the forgotten pleasure of early cinema. However, as the story progresses, the plot diverges and removes the power of Imogene's ghost as a vessel for reliving old, treasured and lost experiences, and turns her into a spectacle, as moviegoers begin to flock to the aptly named Rosebud theater simply for the opportunity to see a ghost rather than to connect to a classic era of American history: "People were happy to pay for the opportunity to experience a little terror in the dark — if they weren't, there wouldn't be any business in horror pictures" (Hill, "20th Century Ghost" 39). This critique of how the cinema, much like the trajectory of the short story, has become a shadow of its former self among audiences suggests not just a move from the generally traditional form of story to which "Best New Horror" tends to adhere, but also that much work is to be done among the contemporary scene of those who interact with art. In seeing a ghost that carries with it the potential to make money off its own constructed gimmickry as a haunting presence rather than a creature of endearing nostalgia is, perhaps, the most horrific element of "20th Century Ghost." This subtle horror is more unnerving and engaging than the actual story itself, which is, of course, not to demean or reduce the story to a single image or reading. Rather, by focusing on subtlety and a movement from tradition, one can then begin to read Joe Hill effectively as an author who seems to be helping to usher in a new wave of fiction that seeks to revive interest in sadly waning readership and understanding of fictions beyond the basics.

With the first two stories of Hill's collection displaying a noticeable yet subtle divergence in terms of style and content, the third story of this collection takes readers into a starkly contrasted direction, in that the horrors observed in the first two stories take on the shape of the fantastically imaginative in "Pop Art." While the title perhaps serves as a nod towards *popular artistry* and the range that is seemingly necessary to find any success in the contemporary literary marketplace, "Pot Art" is a tale of childhood and wonderment — and the complete suspension of disbelief, in that the main character is an inflatable boy named Arthur Roth. To use the words "cute" or "quaint" in reference to this story is nothing short of disrespectful, especially to the imagination that runs throughout this tale and which Hill and his fiction celebrate. From the amusing discussions as to how it would be difficult to circumcise a plastic boy to the foundational premises of the story ("*I* talked — Art couldn't. He didn't have a mouth. When he had something to say, he wrote it down"), "Pop Art" is still one of several stories in *20th Century Ghosts* which simply follows a small cast of characters through one obstacle towards a conclusion that is not always climactic, at least in the dramatic sense (Hill, "Pop Art" 47). But, as is always the case when reading a given fiction with more than a cursory glance, "Pop Art" turns the mundane of everyday life among adolescent boys into, among other things, an imaginative adventure. Although the power of imagination seems to be at the heart of this tale, in which readers willingly suspend disbelief in a living inflatable child, the tale also comes with a sense of ambiguity that creates some doubt as to what the author is hoping to accomplish. In many ways, issues of imagination dominate the story, as the ultimate adventure of Arthur Roth is to float into the sky. He says (or, rather, writes), "I want to see if it's true. If the sky opens up at the top" (Hill, "Pop Art" 53). As it were, Art does find the answers he seeks, which is more than can be said for the reader.

From the standpoint of the plot surrounding "Pop Art," Arthur Roth lives a fragile life, constantly threatened by heat, animal bites, and sharp office supplies, and he is given a funeral of sorts in the tale's penultimate scene, as he is tied to a bundle of balloons and floats into the atmosphere. In many respects, this scene is sad because the narrator loses his only friend, a good listener who understands the trials and tribulations of the young male's teenage life. But in terms of resolution, the only real conclusion that is given suggests that, eventually, the narrator is able to escape the bonds of his turbulent home life and attend college, where he meets yet another inflatable person. This time around, one Ruth Goldman enters as a wholly imagined character, and as one that largely fulfills the same role as Arthur Roth—companion. Among the brief glimpse into the life of Ruth Goldman, which warrants little exploration (as her life as an inflatable person is inevitably similar to that of Arthur Roth), readers are shown Ruth's literary tastes in juxtaposition to the narrators: "We were both English majors. Her favorite was Kafka—because he understood the absurd. My favorite writer was Malamud—because he understood loneliness" (Hill, "Pop Art" 68). This not only leads into the next story of *20th Century Ghosts*, in which the main character wakes up as an insect, but also attempts to close "Pop Art" with a semblance of genuine closure. The narrator has a friend, as well as a potential love interest, and the emotions invoked concerning friendship, death and love actually seem to be highlighted because of the mixture of characters both real and impossible. Perhaps ending "Pop Art" with the loss of the main character but with the promise of the narrator rediscovering his childhood happiness is a conclusion exceptionally clear, one that is realistic in its treatment of common human conditions regardless of the unreal people that populate the story. It is with this focus on emotion for things which do not commonly receive any emotion or attachment in purportedly normal situations, instead of imagining, say, how one human and one inflatable girl might be able to consummate a relationship, that Hill's own imagination takes on a life which escapes the common boundaries that see imagination as mere experimentation. Hill's inflatable boy ultimately turns out to be more than just a character that is "creative" or "imaginative" or even a successful experimentation in that Hill makes his readers believe that an inflatable boy can and does think and feel emotions. Arthur Roth, it turns out, functions as an exceptional catalyst to analyzing human emotion and the lasting effects that relationships with anyone or any*thing* inherently possess.

Following the reference to Kafka at the end of "Pop Art," *20th Century Ghosts* follows one tale of the fantastic with another in which a teen experiences a metamorphosis into a locust. The premise of the story seems simple enough (borrowed from, but in homage to, the aforementioned writer and his tale *The Metamorphosis*), and the story begins simply enough: "Francis Kay woke from dreams that were not uneasy, but exultant, and found himself an insect" (Hill, "Locust" 69). Just as Arthur Roth from "Pop Art" or even Imogene Gilchrist from "20th Century Ghost" can be read as more than just imagined and non–human characters, Francis Kay and his status as a locust, as an *other*, opens the text of "You Will Hear the Locust Sing" to quite the array of criticism, readings and interpretations. The theme of the outsider, as well as the victim, which stems from the first several tales of *20th Century Ghosts* opens the text to numerous standard literary criticisms of the outsider to be found in, say, black studies or post–colonial theory. Yet, even with this undeniable possibility for a theory-informed reading, "You Will Hear the Locus Sing" also resists an overly theorized analysis regarding the status of marginal citizens, whether they be full of air or in the literal guise of an insect. As far as Francis Kay is concerned, and perhaps his author Joe Hill, this particular yarn can be read as that which does not necessarily go beyond the grotesque and the darkly ironic. In short, as Francis Kay comes from a broken home and finds himself a despised yet empowered figure after his transformation, he finds his new form to be a catalyst for both nostalgia and revenge against his father:

> Once he and his father had gone to the dump together, with the shotgun, and took turns with it, picking off cans, rats, seagulls. "Imagine the fuckin' krauts are coming," his father said. Francis didn't know what German soldiers looked like, so he pretended he was shooting the kids at school instead. The memory of that day in the dump made him a little sentimental for his father—they had some good times together, and Buddy had made a decent meal in the end. Really, what else could you ask for from a parent? [Hill, "Locust" 87].

Without any need for false suspense, Francis does, in fact, eat his father before fleeing to the local school, where he begins a showdown with an impending military force. And at this point the story concludes abruptly but appropriately with another purposeful lack of building up cheap and easy tension by way of drawing out the imminent confrontation between Francis and the armed forces. The quick move to end a story that is largely familiar to most readers and which does not necessarily pose any great insights aside from those imposed upon the text by theory-burdened critics is important in that Hill seemingly suggests that this story needs no extensive denouement or excessive detail beyond Francis' lone good memory of time spent with this father.

The purposeful simplicity of "You Will Hear the Locust Sing" serves as another lesson in reading fiction, especially Hill's fiction, in that there are times when a short story, familiar or outlandish, simplistic or complex, asks for little else besides being read. Again, this is not to say that Hill is simplistic in his writing or that his tales are devoid of sincere thought and insight that can be gleaned with careful and discerning reading. Rather, "You Will Hear the Locust

Sing" completes a general treatise of reading in which convention is considered, tradition is revered, imagination is championed, and story is highlighted above all else. Indeed, it is more than refreshing to read "You Will Hear the Locust Sing" as just a story, as a tale that can and should be read without the urge and pull to find some great universal truth hidden in the trash heaps that Francis explores during his childhood and early hours of his transformation, or in the lonely and quiet hallways of the school that will likely serve as Francis' grave.

It is after "You Will Hear the Locust Sing" that Hill's collection further embarks on myriad wanderings in the world of fiction beyond the horrific (real and cinematic) and the fantastical, almost instigating a litmus test of sorts to test Hill's explorations of reading and readership that are found in the first four stories of *20th Century Ghosts*. Hill's tales revisit scenes of traditional horror, and the frightening tensions woven into such texts, but also takes readers into the slice-of-life fictions that are generally the cornerstone of Owen King's collection of writings, as well as those which are so fantastically strange that their appeal does not necessarily lay within the writing but perhaps more so in the sense of alien content. "The Black Phone," for example, is more of a mainstream horror story, containing abduction, dreadful isolation, and the supernatural. Beyond the foundation of the story, which focuses on a kidnapper known as the Galesburg Grabber and his latest abduction, a young boy named John Finney, "The Black Phone" highlights elements of horror which are somewhat sporadic in *20th Century Ghosts*. But this particular tale does not solely focus on potentially real and disturbing horrors which are found in "Best New Horror." Rather, as the title of "The Black Phone" suggests, the main object of focus for this story is a lone yet disconnected phone in John's basement prison, an object that taunts him with images of a connection to the outside world—"'I was in here and it rang once,' Al [the Galesburg Grabber] said. 'Creepiest thing'"—but also ultimately perpetuates the conviction that he will die because he cannot reach out for help (Hill, "The Black Phone" 143). Such a mental trapping can be said to resonate with allusions to the early foundations of the Gothic, especially as John's imprisonment is stretched out for several days when the Galesburg Grabber's drugged-up brother comes to stay at his house for a while, which not only prevents the Grabber from carrying out his planned murder of John, but also pushes John into the realm of madness which stems from the excessive anticipation of his own death. However, as it has been repeatedly claimed that singular or overarching labeling of the fictions within the King family is inaccurate and misleading, this holds quite true for "The Black Phone."

Despite its drawn-out psychological drama which witnesses John actually hearing voices of the Grabber's other victims, as well as voices on the dead and disconnected black phone—"None of us heard it. It rang, but none of us heard. Just you. A person has to stay here a while, before you learn how to hear it. You're the only one to last this long"—Hill is quite careful to avoid a complete reliance upon convention and formula by focusing on more than just psychological disturbances and instability (Hill, "The Black Phone" 151). Although the voices which John hears seem to be in the vein of the supernatural as well as the Gothic, their function extends beyond a mere inexplicable inclusion, as they not only provide John a way out of his predicament—he is told to fill the receiver of the black phone with sand from the floor of his prison and then use it as a blunt striking instrument to disable the Grabber—but they also further establish a genuine sense of tension for the *reader* that is oftentimes difficult to achieve. At this juncture in the story, readers are placed in a real situation of suspense because the Grabber is still very much a threat to John; and although John is seemingly equipped with knowledge and a tool for escape, uncertainty overshadows the story and the reading experience. Even when the story ends, as the Grabber, Al, kills his brother, Frank, and proceeds to carry out his designs of killing John, there is a startling but fascinating lack of clear resolution.

In short, John, equipped with the weighted phone receiver, attacks his kidnapper and, as far as the reader knows, kills him, as suggested by the cheesy yet appropriate ending which has the story concluding with the black phone ringing and John telling Al, "It's for you" (Hill, "The Black Phone" 155). On the one hand, the pseudo cliff-hanger ending creates a mild sense of obscurity and opaqueness which pulls the reader further into the story despite it being finished—while the reader can assume a particular ending, there are no definitive answers, which is certainly Gothic by some standards. On the other hand, any adaptation or appropriation of literary convention is wonderfully undercut by the tale's concluding line, which establishes not just a contemporary backdrop for the story but also situates it as a story that does not take itself too seriously, as a story which selectively borrows from numerous genres (mystery, horror, and the Gothic) and ultimately creates a pleasurable reading experience which finds a true climax not in the plot, but in the reader's laughter.

Although it may seem rather strange, and perhaps even disturbing, to create a story of kidnapping and murder with an ending aimed at amusement, Hill appears to be rather comfortable with approaching death in not a disrespectful way, but through alternative perspectives that allow for humor. Case in point: "Last Breath," one of the better stories in *20th Century Ghosts* in terms of its originality and its ability to create an exceptional amount of story in only nine pages, brings readers into the realm of death through a museum of death which proudly displays a collection of jars filled with the last breaths people take before they die. Perhaps the novelty of a collection of dying breaths is somewhat mitigated by the oddities that have been placed for auction on the internet in recent years (or in Hill's first novel, *Heart-Shaped Box*, in which a ghost is auctioned), in addition to "Last Breath" being presented in game-form on the internet through Hill's personal website. But this premise for the story is quite compelling in its inventiveness, even though the museum's curator and collector, Alinger, notes that the technology to collect dying breaths "has been around since the beginning of the nineteenth century" (Hill, "Last Breath" 199). Among the technology and the somewhat macabre curiosity surrounding Alinger's "museum of *silence*" and the amusingly labeled tool known as the "deathoscope" with which visitors can listen to the breaths Alinger has collected, one notes that this story has much more to it than a general theme of death (Hill, "Last Breath," 196). As a nameless family enters Alinger's museum, the mother is found to be quite distanced and displeased with the museum and the curator, who explains that his training as a doctor has not only nurtured his fascination with death but also has allowed him to develop a machine with which he captures the last exhalations that comprise his collection.

Hardly enthralled with Alinger's innovation, and ultimately exasperated with the museum and the doctor's strangeness, the mother leaves the free exhibit, only to be run down in traffic. Answering pleas for help, the doctor starts out the door. Here, Hill ends his story with a genuinely chilling ending to parallel the purposefully cold pragmatism of the doctor himself:

> "Your bag," the boy said. "You might need something in it."
> Alinger smiled fondly, went back up the steps, took it from the boy's cold fingers.
> "Thank you," he said. "I just might" [Hill, "Last Breath" 203].

The varied impressions of this ending serve Hill well in that his ability to produce subtlety is cherished as something more than a gimmick or an accidental outcome of one's reading of Hill's texts. With the nameless boy, a child, looking to Alinger with the doctor's bag in hand, some may see the boy as a deranged and distanced child who simply wishes to aid the doctor in adding to his collection. Then again, with the doctor's bag serving as a symbol of hope, regardless of its limited contents (i.e. the machine which collects last breaths), the boy bringing the bag to Alinger can be perceived as an action of innocence and purity that has the child only seeing the doctor's bag as a symbol of hope. But with the varied readings of the child in "Last Breath," it is hard to deny that a certain sense of humor or amusement is attached to Alinger, as the mother dies and he sees not death but an opportunity to collect. This alternative perspective surrounding death, complete with an ambiance of detachment and fascination which is darkly comical, shows not just Hill's desire and ability to engage in subjects that remain somewhat unspoken or taboo, but also reminds readers of his range. And while this range is laudable, there are instances in *20th Century Ghosts* when Hill's wide sweep of fiction can be considered problematic.

As *20th Century Ghosts* moves past the first several stories, many of the remaining ten selections seem to take on the role of mere stories, or rather events and or ideas simply written down and presented for the public to read. While the idea of *story* undoubtedly varies from author to author, reader to reader and even critic to critic, it is both refreshing and disheartening to look upon a story as if it were a rescued Polaroid — a forgotten snapshot that has some allure to it but no real place or meaning beyond its actual existence. Conceiving of a story as just a collection of words appearing on a page is not exactly laudatory or generous, but some tales within *20th Century Ghosts*, regardless of authorial intent, simply fall flat. With the short story "Dead Wood," for example, Hill explores the possibility of spirituality within trees, as he claims, "It has been argued even trees may appear as ghosts" (205). Beyond the interesting oddity of this declaration, the notion which ultimately follows suggests an almost paradoxical existence for a tree — to be in possession of a soul and consciousness — as Hill says, "Somehow it's easier to imagine the ghost of a tree than it is the ghost of a man.... Something that doesn't know it's alive obviously can't be expected to know when it's dead" (Hill, "Dead Wood" 206). While this statement is intriguing, it is hard to determine the purpose behind the words beyond their mild philosophical bent, especially as "Dead Wood" does little else besides offer what appears to be a selection of random musings on nature. Of course, it is unfair to think of "Dead Wood" as a limited story because of its brevity (it is only two pages long) and its complete resistance to any sort of story form concerning character, conflict or even climax. And perhaps while "Dead Wood," as well as a handful of slice-of-life stories to be found in *20th Century Ghosts*, may not be complex or overtly profound, there is something to be said for a story that is focused and elegantly simple.

To use the term "simple" when exploring fiction seems to create a sense of distaste and dismissal, but this is hardly the intended use of the term as it pertains to four particular stories in *20th Century Ghosts*: "In the Rundown," "Better Than Home," "The Widow's Breakfast" and "Bobby Conroy Comes Back from the Dead." These stories, scattered throughout the last half of *20th Century Ghosts*, can be read as simple tales which primarily focus on a single character and his/her daily routines and reflections surrounding a specific and critical life moment. These mentioned fictions do display moments of the mundane and inconsequential, from, say, smoking cigarettes to taking a walk or engaging in general reminiscence. But each one of these stories, in their seemingly purposeful and elegant simplicity, provide exceptional and familiar snapshots of life that perhaps show a new trend in fiction which takes readers away from heavy-handed and excessively burdensome forgings of tension, suspense and developments of both plot and character.

With "In the Rundown," the story can, in some ways, be reduced to a brief exploration of a callow youth recently fired from his job at a video store who finds solace in memories of his days playing little league baseball. The recovery of both lost memory and lost potential — "He never got a chance to find out what he could do in high school. He didn't play in a single game, was always on academic or disciplinary probation"—may be all but forgotten as the story progresses to its last scenes in which a young mother is discovered with a bleeding child that she has presumably wounded by cutting the child's throat (Hill, "In the Rundown" 158). But the horror of attempted infanticide gives way to the nostalgic memories of baseball when the young man, Wyatt, seeks to save the life of the bleeding child, thinking to himself and praying to an unseen presence, "Please make me fast. Make me fast again. Make me fast like I was" (Hill, "In the Rundown" 171). Much like with "The Black Phone," no clear resolution is provided, but there is really no need for an actual conclusion. The simplicity of memory merging with the present, just like in "20th Century Ghost," gives the story its main focus, a focus on a particular theme rather than the full development and divulgence of a plot that would, if carried out, undercut the aesthetic of a character lost in his own life finding a pathway out of his life's quagmire by reconnecting to a happier past.

Just as "In the Rundown" focuses on the theme of memory, with baseball as a backdrop, "Better Than Home" follows in much the same mold, with a young child, Homer, taking the reader through a rather innocuous series of moments from his life as the child of one Ernie Feltz, the manager of the Detroit Tigers. Homer's life is primarily marked by his relationship with his father, from various travels with the team to the distanced but not disconnected viewing of the Tigers on television. This relationship between father and son, especially the memories surrounding specific moments at the ballpark and memories of his father, including viewing his father's outbursts on national television, tend to dominate a story which seeks to explore Homer beyond his relationship to baseball, which can be problematic considering his namesake. Still, for the attention given to Homer's anxiety and eventual mental breakdown, as well as his seemingly exceptional mental capabilities and the examinations offered concerning Ernie Feltz, it is the theme of memory that stands out above all else in "Better Than Home." The final pages take the reader to the ballpark, looking down at the field through Homer's eyes and relishing in the simplicity of watching his father work.

Of course, to consider managing a baseball team as common work or drudgery is to take away from the profound experience of spending time at Tiger Stadium as, in essence, a member of the team, a family of sorts that supplements rather than subtracts from the biological connection between Homer and Ernie. And concerning the recollections of childhood and bonding, Homer says it best when he recounts watching his father prepare for a game, while also thinking of scavenger hunts his father had set up in the stadium, as well as striking images of a seagull floating down into the stadium: "It's a nice memory to have in your head. Everyone should have a memory just like it" (Hill, "Better Than Home" 133). Such a basic sentiment concerning a seemingly minor part of Homer's life is beautiful in its simplicity and its implication that even a single positive experience is nothing short of ecstasy. And while it is not exactly proper to reduce "Better Than Home" to a story that makes a memory for the reader by commenting on the comforts and pleasures of memory as manifested in a fictional character who only shares a few moments of his childhood, it must be noted that Hill is quite clever in moving a simple story to a single profound moment that perfectly captures the essence of a story that has numerous threads. Said threads are bound together with a strongly simple scene rather than an overly elaborate or falsely philosophical climax that reeks of an arrogant writer.

"Better Than Home" finds itself situated among other short stories that insist upon the joys of reading and attaching oneself to a single and often simple image or thought. And to Hill's credit, the risk that he takes in creating stories that are largely dependent upon a single image or consideration which serves as the crux of a story often results in success. While some writers will take a scattershot approach to fiction and aim at capturing a reader through numerous layers of complexity, symbolism and obscurity, some of Hill's fiction marks an interesting turn to the microcosmic rather than a wider picture. It is with this smaller focus, that which asks author and reader alike to exercise a sense of patience that is becoming lost in a culture where multiplicity and speed are becoming more and more accepted and expected, that "The Widow's Breakfast" as well as "Bobby Conroy Comes Back from the Dead" find their respective foundations.

Two tales loosely gathered under the umbrella of slice-of-life stories, "The Widow's Breakfast" and "Bobby Conroy Comes Back from the Dead," further illustrate Hill's patient and careful writing with smaller scenes and limited casts of characters. While it has been noted that Hill runs a calculated risk in writing stories that tend to culminate in a single or simple image, and that he does find some success with this approach, there are instances in his writing when these types of stories do not always find a ready embrace from the reader. With "The Widow's Breakfast," Hill revisits a familiar temporal landscape similar to that in which "The Saved" is situated, and this time around Hill follows a hobo named Killian. Killian, unlike Jubal Scott, does not negotiate issues of religion and family, but, similar to Jubal Scott, he is concerned with survival. And this theme, enhanced by Killian's status as a hobo, leads the story to its key scene in which Killian falls into the favor of a widow whose husband had died in an automobile wreck, taking five others with him. As the widow comments, "The only good thing about his death is he doesn't have to walk around with that guilt on him" (Hill, "The Widow's Breakfast" 214). Conversely, it appears that the widow carries much of her husband's guilt; and she attempts to erase some of this transferred blame by purging memories of her husband. To this end she gives her dead husband's clothes to Killian. This charity, however, alongside the widow's apparent desire to clear her husband's tainted memory (or mitigate it by facilitating his erasure by removing physical reminders of his existence), becomes negligible when considering the ending.

As Killian has acquired the dead husband's clothes and then leaves the widow's home, he is stopped just outside of the house and is asked to play "Funeral" with the widow's daughters. At this prospect, Killian says, "I don't believe this is my kind of game. I don't want to be the dead person" (Hill, "The Widow's Breakfast" 217). In response, and to end the story, the eldest child says to Killian, "Why not? ... You're dressed the part" (Hill, "The Widow's Breakfast" 217). While the ending is amusing, if not perhaps revealing of the daughter's indifference to her father's death (which might suggest that the father's shame has cast a shadow on the entire family), one must wonder if there is more to take than a mere chuckle stemming from ten pages of setup for such a punch-line — like the themes of memory, charity and survival. Yet, "The Widow's Breakfast," like any text, can be picked and pulled apart so that its parts can be isolated and then examined rather than read in unity and harmony. But it is as a whole that this story finds its voice as yet another example of fiction from a contemporary writer who pushes his readers to consider that fiction is changing, and that even a short story that ultimately results in a mild guffaw is nonetheless a story, albeit a somewhat unconventional one.

Completing the quartet of slice-of-life fictions in *20th Century Ghosts*, "Bobby Conroy Comes Back from the Dead" not only serves as a mild homage to George Romero (as the story takes place on the set of *Dawn of the Dead*), but also continues Hill's trend to write stories concerned with purposefully abbreviated plots. This story is primarily a love story. Even among its entertaining and sentimental moments, it is also rather unique in that it utilizes the set of a zombie film to reunite two lovers, Bobby Conroy and Harriet Rutherford, who have lost contact over the years and have gone their separate ways. In this way, "Bobby Conroy Comes Back from the Dead" finds its only real departure from most any other love story in that the catalyst for bringing him back to his former lover is not pangs of regret or sadness, but circumstance and a chance meeting at a rather unusual place. More to the point, the locale of a film set allows Hill to close the story with the anticipated reunion of Bobby and Harriet as the two shoot a close-up scene together. At this, Hill's non-fictional character George Romero, as the director of the film and as the director (or apparent *deus ex machina*) who prompts the reunion between Bobby and Harriet, sets up the story's conclusion by asking, "What do you two kids say? Either one of you feel like a do-over?" (Hill, "Bobby Conroy" 239). Of course, Romero is referring to the scene that Bobby and Harriet have just completed, and the reply from Bobby — "I guess it's unanimous.... Everyone wants a do-over"—certainly comes as no surprise (Hill, "Bobby Conroy" 239). The declaration that a "do-over" is desired is hardly surprising and provides the tale with a convenient if not abrupt ending, almost negating any real sense of love or compassion that might be (re)developing between Bobby and Harriet.

However, avoiding an extensive look into the psyches of Bobby and Harriet, or their libidos, is quite the bold and successful maneuver for Hill.

Although one might critique Hill for composing a love story that is admittedly limited in the examination of love and the exploration of the reunion beyond the set of *Dawn of the Dead*, one must also remember that, again, lack of development or completion is not necessarily a mark of poor fiction or a hack writer. With "Bobby Conroy Comes Back from the Dead," the issues of love and second chances may be the bedrock of the story, but there is more to this short yarn than two lovers finding each other again, especially in terms of the humor which serves as the main current for compatibility between Bobby and Harriet. And while Hill does not fully explore the typical avenues of love, romance and reunion, he does subtly tell his readers that humor can function as a key pathway to love, as implied by Bobby's and Harriet's recollections. For Harriet, her fondest memory of her and Bobby involves a phallic joke: "Remember we got two weeks after the cooking show skit? You had a cucumber carved like a dick. You said you needed it to stew for a hour and you stuck it in your pants. It was the finest moment in the history of the Die Laughing Comedy Collective" (Hill, "Bobby Conroy" 220). For Bobby, his fondest memory involves Harriet's breasts: "*I love to watch you in the shower. I hope that's not obscene. But when I see you soap your boobs, I get sticky in my jeans!*" (Hill, "Bobby Conroy" 220). With these memories, readers see that there is a functional combination of sexuality and humor between Bobby and Harriet, which seems to provide a certain synthesis for the story. By combining humor and sexuality, while avoiding the tired and clichéd elements of love (like destiny or other mystical and inexplicable means of bringing two people together), Hill suggests that, just like a work of fiction, love can be beautifully simple, that even something as seemingly innocuous as a shared sense of what is funny is just as believable, if not more so, as a prompt for love than chance meetings or infatuation stemming from a single glance.

Moving from the tales of the somewhat realistic and purposefully limited in terms of scope and content, one finds in *20th Century Ghosts* several other stories which take readers back to the early pages of the collection in which the inexplicable and the supernatural serve as key elements. But this is not to say that the tales titled "The Cape," "My Father's Mask," and "Voluntary Committal" are overwhelmed by images of the horrific or grotesque, suggesting a leaning towards the genres of horror or the Gothic. This set of stories may be less in the vein of reality-based fictions than the previously discussed quartet, but they do not move completely into realms of fiction separated from the everyday. Further, "magical realism" is not exactly the correct term to apply to this new subset of stories in *20th Century Ghosts*, even if they do follow in the mold of "Pop Art" and take uncommon occurrences within a real-world setting as commonplace or not entirely surprising. Perhaps it is best to consider these stories as yet another example of Hill writing "simple" stories, tales with small-scale scopes yet which utilize elements of the magical and the surreal to not just propel the story, but also to capture the reader not by way of gimmickry but by imagination.

For example, "The Cape" tells the story of two brothers, Nicky and Eric, and while this story looks at these individuals and provides glimpses into their adult lives (complete with adult problems like failed relationships and alcohol abuse), it is the tale's bookend discussion of the childhood dream of flying which not only becomes a reality in this story, but also provides the story and the reader with a pure sense of imaginative pleasure. As the story begins, a single image is given, depicting two young children at play and arriving at a moment of immediate danger: "We were little. I was the Red Bolt and I went up the dead elm in the corner of our yard to get away from my brother, who wasn't anyone, just himself.... He was too old to play superheroes. It had happened all of a sudden, with no warning" (Hill, "The Cape" 173). Beyond this general introduction in which Eric ultimately falls from his perch and is saved by his magic cape, which, incidentally, "didn't fly again for ten years," the story merely chronicles Eric's troubled life and leads up to the day when he finally flies again (Hill, "The Cape" 177). Although a brief look at a fictional individual's life alongside the genuine magic of flying seems to be somewhat limited, one can easily find instances in which the story itself is interrupted by Hill approaching fiction in the same manner as his brother, Owen, in that there are times when Hill simply drops somewhat random thoughts or witticisms into the story. Case in point: in "The Cape," Hill isolates two short sentences from the narrator as an entire section of the story that is separated from the rest of the tale, almost like a minute chapter. These lines read, "Whenever my brother and I played superheroes, he always made me be the bad guy. Someone has to be," which serves as more than the narrator, Eric, remembering a mild disconnect between he and his brother while growing up (Hill, "The Cape" 193). The notion that the world is inundated with both "good" and "evil" individuals is really not an original insight, nor it is completely necessary to the story of a young man and his magic cape, but it does suggest that Hill takes great care to craft fiction that manages more than just events accounted for and then relayed to the reader.

Just as "The Cape" mainly focuses on a single item of childhood fascination which also possesses a particular magic, "My Father's Mask" takes readers into the strange memory of a young boy escaping with his parents to a lakeside cabin where, as the title indicates, a particular mask belonging to the father becomes a central object of charming mystery and fascination. About this cabin the mother notes, "In this place it's always Halloween. It's called Masquerade House. That's our secret name for it. It's one of the rules of the cottage: While you're staying here you have to wear a mask. It's always been that way.'" This establishes the initial focus on masquerade and illusion, which is essential to the family's flight to the isolated dwelling (Hill, "My Father's Mask" 250).

But as much as this story plays with the themes of identity and family as they pertain to the growth of the young boy taken into a realm of extreme mystery which surrounds the family cabin, "My Father's Mask" also moves well beyond a story of family, childhood innocence and strife into a story that is, in many ways, quite difficult to sort out.

The sway and pull of imagination as it concerns the child, which is quite well-developed in *Locke and Key* as well as *Gunpowder*, seems to be critical to the story of "My Father's Mask," especially as the young boy begins to navigate his unfamiliar surroundings and is warned by his mother that they are, it seems, in a land that does not follow the rules of the real world. To clarify, Masquerade House is firmly situated in the wilderness, surrounded by a forest that looks to be almost separated from reality but still accessible to the child by way of its imagination, as indicated by the mother: "Grown-ups can't go into the forest at all. Not even the trail is safe for someone my age. I can't even see the trail. Once you get as old as me it disappears from sight. I only know about it because your father and I used to take walks on it, when we came up here as teenagers" (Hill, "My Father's Mask" 252). The suggestion that only the unclouded mind of the child can find and navigate the surrounding woods does more than link "My Father's Mask" to fictions within the King family that champion the child above the adult—it firmly situates the story in a realm of imagination, which may not necessarily offer much explanation for the rest of the story and the few glimpses into a world of reality, but which ultimately allows the reader to become enraptured by the unfamiliarity that surrounds the tale. This sweep of the imaginative ultimately places the young boy in a game of cards with two unknown children in the mystical woods, a game which is not just odd, but potentially deadly:

> I deal five cards to each player, face up. When I'm done, whoever has the best poker hand wins. That probably sounds too simple, but then there are a lot of funny little house rules. If you smile during the game, the player sitting to your left can swap one of his cards for one of yours. If you can build a house with the first three cards you get dealt, and if the other players can't blow it down in one breath, you get to look through the deck and pick out whatever you want for your fourth card. If you draw a black forfeit, the other players throw stones at you until you're dead. If you have any questions, keep them to yourself. Only the winner gets to ask questions. Anyone who asks a question while the game is in play loses instantly [Hill, "My Father's Mask" 257].

The description of the potentially lethal card game may not be the crux of "My Father's Mask," nor does it even begin to provide any clear insight into the tale's purpose, but it does create a keen sense of intrigue. Part of this intrigue involves seeing the game played out, and seeing if all who play will survive, which they do. But even a wonderfully strange game does not fully sustain the story or interest on the reader's behalf. In short, while part of the joy in reading is discovery, there is something to be said for some semblance of clarity, and as "My Father's Mask" seems to revel in what one assumes is a purposeful lack of clarity, the reader does not necessarily find a similar pleasure instigated by chaos. However, perhaps the key consideration to take from "My Father's Mask" is that while ambiguity carries with it a high level of risk in terms of reader response and engagement, sometimes all that remain are questions rather than answers.

Answers are often difficult to ascertain when it comes to reading fiction, as well as writing about it, and Joe Hill utilizes this lack of absolutism and definitiveness as a critical element of his story "Voluntary Committal." Immediately, a sense of disconnectedness is provided when the narrator, Nolan, states, "I don't know who I am writing this for, can't say who I expect to read it" (Hill, "Voluntary Committal" 263). Aside from the narrator's apologetic opening, "Voluntary Committal" manages two particular plotlines, and brings them together as the story concludes, only then to have the story unravel once again and move towards a lack of closure and resolution. In short, "Voluntary Committal" concerns itself with the disappearance of Eddie Prior, Nolan's friend of convenience who manipulates the narrator into dropping a brick from an overpass into traffic, resulting in an accident. Aside from the sympathies that result from this incident on behalf of the reader—including sympathies for the mother and child who were injured by the dropped brick, as well as for Nolan for finding himself responsible for an act of pain and destruction—it is the keen understanding of Nolan's brother Morris regarding Nolan's poor choice of friends that takes precedence and propels the story towards its strange and supernatural conclusion. Of course, fast-forwarding through so much of "Voluntary Committal" just to look towards the conclusion eliminates many key components of the story, especially learning of Eddie's troubled background, as he tells Nolan that he will do everything in his power to avoid taking blame for the overpass incident: "I'm not going to Juvie over some stupid accident that wasn't even my fault. No one's going to turn me homo. I already had something like that happen to me once" (Hill, "Voluntary Committal" 286). While this lends some sympathy to Eddie, if not some context to his delinquent ways, he is nonetheless characterized as an individual who is almost devoid of any conscience or empathy for others. And although Eddie deserves some sympathy for what he has endured, his complex character, as both a friend and an enemy to Nolan, is ultimately reduced to that of a threat, which Morris Lerner observes and plots to rectify.

As is the case with many of Hill's other tales, "Voluntary Committal" takes its time exploring the daily workings of the characters, especially the children. Aside from Eddie's turbulent yet ambivalent persona, Nolan's character is primarily explored through his school life, which consists of common struggles to complete homework by any means necessary and listening to the exaggerated stories of sexuality from his peers. These avenues of exploring Nolan can easily be seen as more than a means of moving the plot forward, but it might be difficult to do so when looking to his brother, the presumably autistic Morris Lerner. Morris, at least according to Nolan, is a troubled character: "I thought there was a good chance, then, that Morris had suffered a minor break with reality.... Only a year before, he had taken to painting his hands red, because he said it helped him to *feel* sounds" (Hill, "Voluntary Committal" 271). But Morris displays quite the acumen when he observes Eddie's influence on Nolan, as well as quite the architectural ability—at the heart of "Voluntary Committal" and Morris' love for his brother is an expansive network of cardboard boxes that have been put together in the Lerners' basement. Inside "Morris's cardboard kraken" reality and fantasy converge, as these tunnels actually lead into other dimensions (Hill, "Voluntary Committal" 279). Inside these cardboard tunnels, one hears the sound of bells, or wind-chimes, which, if one is familiar with Stephen King's *Dark Tower* series, resembles the sounds of *todash*, which is the elder King's term referring to travel between worlds and times. How Morris is imbued with the ability to construct doorways between worlds, dimensions and realities is uncertain, but his intentions are crystal clear. As noted, Morris, despite his perceived handicap, acknowledges that his brother is essentially trapped by Eddie, and Morris is able to lure Eddie into the cardboard maze, never to be seen again.

Although it seems that Eddie Prior's disappearance, and Nolan's recollection of this occurrence, forms the core of "Voluntary Committal," one must look back to the Lerner children for clarity and closure. As noted, it is Morris' love rather than a sense of vengeance or experimentation that prompts him to construct his cardboard maze and rid the world of Eddie Prior. In Morris' words, "I wanted to help. You [Nolan] said he [Eddie] wouldn't go away, so I *made* him go away" (Hill, "Voluntary Committal" 298). And what is perhaps even more emotive is that this brotherly love seems to be the only real positive that each of the Lerner children possess. Both Nolan and Morris are characters whose only tether to the world looks to be one another, and as Morris becomes more and more disconnected from the world, ultimately committing himself to the Wellbrook Progressive Mental Health Center, he then builds a new labyrinth in the basement and disappears. Nolan, who seems to fancy himself an outsider like his brother, thinks that perhaps it would be best if he, too, simply stepped away from the world: "If it's still standing there in the basement, I could always climb in someday, and pull the flaps shut behind me. There is always that. Anything can run in families. Even disappearing" (Hill, "Voluntary Committal" 311). What Nolan and his brother will find is debatable, which returns readers to the issue of seeking, and likely not finding, answers. In many ways, enough answers have been provided in "Voluntary Committal" in that Eddie Prior is known to have disappeared, which provides some relief for Nolan, even though he finds himself facing Eddie's disappearance many years later. Still, among the mysteries of "Voluntary Committal," and unanswered questions, especially as to Nolan's decision to either escape into his brother's labyrinth or to remain grounded in the world surrounding him, mark this story as another example of an imaginative tapestry that asks the reader to do more than passively follow events. To that end, reader engagement, as well as a working knowledge of classical literature, is essential for approaching the one tale within *20th Century Ghosts* that has yet to be considered.

As Hill moves from stories of the seemingly everyday to the horrific and to the outright fantastical, *20th Century Ghosts* is, in many ways, mildly undistinguished because of the multiple story forms and concerns presented. Admittedly, the variety to be found in *20th Century Ghosts* suggests many things, among them that Hill approaches fiction in the same way a bird hunter approaches his hobby — with a wide, scattered approach. Sometimes such an approach misses with its breadth, but when Hill is on his mark, the reader instantly knows it. In terms of originality, *Locke and Key* should be seen as Hill's strongest fiction, but this is not to say that his fictions which find origins elsewhere are innately weak. Although "You Will Hear the Locust Sing" does little with the springboard that Franz Kafka provides, the one story from *20th Century Ghosts* to yet be discussed, "Abraham's Boys," borrows its plotline from a familiar and established source, and is crafted well enough so that Hill's adaptive appropriation is acknowledged as more than just a writer seeking a starting point in established fiction — it establishes Hill's ability to, more than anything, create a story. By the title alone, it is not clear what "Abraham's Boys" is concerned with, but the moment the first reference to vampires is made, it becomes clear that Hill has situated this fiction, and his own career, in a shared spotlight with Bram Stoker and his masterpiece *Dracula*. But just as, for example, Jean Rhys takes Bertha Mason from Charlotte Brontë's *Jane Eyre* and creates a stand-alone story, *Wide Sargasso Sea*, Hill also takes the vampire story which Stoker penned but creates a story that not only stands alone, but which is careful to avoid categorization as "coat-tailing."

One of the better tales of this collection, "Abraham's Boys" is particularly engaging not just for its treatment of children and the pains of losing innocence that seeps into several of Hill's other stories, but because of the back story that Hill relies upon for the tale to work. In other words, "Abraham's Boys" is a bit of a revisionist tale which examines the life of famed vampire hunter Abraham Van Helsing several years after the conclusion of Bram Stoker's *Dracula*. Hill's own take on the story is that Van Helsing had fathered two children, Maximilian and Rudolf, and that their mother is none other than Mina Harker, who marries Van Helsing after Jonathan Harker passes away. Yet beyond Hill's take on the story outside of Stoker's foundational text on the vampire and vampire lore, "Abraham's Boys" transforms into a story that is decidedly a Joe Hill story with its treatment of the child. As Christopher Golden notes, "'Abraham's Boys' [is] a chilling, textured examination of children who have begun to realize — as all children do — that their father is imperfect" (xii). Golden accurately directs the reader's attention to the troubled relationship that Max and Rudy Van Helsing have with their (in)famous father, and while some might read "Abraham's Boys" for its exceptional adaptation of and addition to the *Dracula* story, it is indeed the children that make the story a fiction which is more than that of mere appropriation.

One of the primary obstacles facing Abraham Van Helsing and his children is their inability to agree as to what is real and important. Of course, this separation between parent and child is not uncommon, and it has its amusing moments, such as Rudy comments on the vampire figure in which his father wholeheartedly believes: "I think it's all bullshit. *Bullll*-shit" (Hill, "Abraham's Boys" 101). Language issues aside, assuming that "bullshit" as an expression of disbelief was hardly popular in the early years of the twentieth century, the Van Helsing boys are nonetheless curious about their father's secrets, even though they have professed disbelief. And it is with their discovery that their father is, in essence, a murderer, that the Van Helsing boys are forcibly asked to grow up as well as take over their father's self-imposed duties as a vampire hunter. As it were, Abraham has captured a vampire in the basement of his house, and he then teaches his sons how to kill — but when it comes to killing the vampire, especially with the traumatic removal of the vampire's head, Abraham's children do not envision themselves as heroes or *vampire* slayers. They have become killers, plain and simple, as Max kills his father at the end of a struggle to break free from his father's domineering and myopic designs for his children: "He put the tip of the stake where his father had showed him and struck the hilt with the mallet. It turned out it was all true, what the old man had told him in the basement. There was wailing and a frantic struggle to get away, but it was over soon enough" (Hill, "Abraham's Boys" 111). There is, of course, a certain irony in that Abraham Van Helsing's death finds root in his insistence that his children carry on his work. Further, there is a particular commentary in "Abraham's Boys" on the pressures that children face from parents whose teachings and ideologies are so parochial and demanding that some sort of backlash is likely to result. But Hill is careful to abstain from didacticism, and while this story points towards the woes of generational conflict in the hope that awareness through strife might lead to resolution in the world outside of the text's pages, actual answers and conclusions remain, as expected, hidden.

Assuredly, "Abraham's Boys" serves as a continuation of the development of vampirism beyond the creatures of the night, equating Van Helsing's obsessive dedication to a literal drain on his family. But one wonders if Max, with the taste of killing, will continue his father's work. This unanswered question, as one of many to be found in *20th Century Ghosts*, reminds readers that each and every one of these stories asks, if not demands, for additional readings, interpretations, criticisms and analyses. Such is certainly the case with the tale embedded in the conclusion of *20th Century Ghosts*, as Hill rewards the reader with one additional story in the form of the supernatural situated among the purportedly real, titled "Scheherazade's Typewriter." With the reference to the narrator of the expansive *One Thousand and One Nights,* Hill follows the allusion with a story that looks towards a typewriter haunted by a dead writer.

In only three pages the story suggests that this haunted typewriter is responsible for a real collection of stories written by the deceased writer, about which the narrator, the dead man's daughter Elena, says, "The ghost in the machine wrote about the dead with great authority" (Hill, "Scheherazade's Typewriter" 315). Perhaps the words of the dead are simply meant to function as a frightening prospect, adding to the surreal and dark ambiance of Hill's final fictional correspondence with the reader. Perhaps conceiving of a collection of fictions actually written by the dead is meant to simply be an entertaining prospect aimed at leaving the reader with an amusing and entertaining story. No one can say for sure. But one conclusion, or connection, to be drawn is that, like the possessed typewriter containing the promise of thousands of stories, Joe Hill has worlds of imagination waiting to see the light of day and waiting to grace the eyes of readers. While the intentions and purposes may remain unclear at times, one might do well to consider that contemporary fiction just might find resurgence by simply providing, again, *story.*

Great, and Gothic, Expectations: Heart-Shaped Box

First impressions, as the cliché suggests, can only be made once. And with Joe Hill's first major impression on the American literary scene being made with his first novel, *Heart-Shaped Box,* the results, like the stories from *20th Century Ghosts,* are mixed. Perhaps it is unfair to immediately mark Hill's first novel as one which reaches no consensus in terms of its appeal and craft, but with the surrounding scene of *Heart-Shaped Box* including the (un)timely revelation of Hill's identity, it is more than fair to deem his first novel a text of mixed impressions because of the author's own life story. But setting aside the media's treatment of *Heart-Shaped Box,* readers are introduced to an interestingly ambiguous protagonist, Judas Coyne, who is an aging rock star with an obsession for all things taboo and stereotypical of a Gothic rocker, including his possession and occasional viewing of a snuff film. Coyne is an anti–hero of sorts, as his adopted namesake (his real name is Justin Cowzynski) is a purposeful reference to the betrayal of Jesus Christ by way of Judas taking money (Coyne=coin, or silver), and this allusion which places this main character into a position of ambivalence for the reader is just one of many twisting constructions within *Heart-Shaped Box.* As Hill dedicates the novel to his father — "For my dad, one of the good ones"— he is careful to keep names hidden and further cloak the story with a strange sense of secrecy that, incidentally, runs throughout the novel, which comes to resemble a suspense thriller more than a genuine horror. Then again, as Hill has developed fictions of horror that cannot be limited to just a single categorical label, perhaps it is unnecessary to highlight the maze-like narration that marks this text, especially as such a description would further complicate conceptions of this book, in that convoluted navigations invoke erroneous images of the Gothic.

Beyond initial impressions of *Heart-Shaped Box* as informed by Hill's identity or the text's reported allegiance to contemporary horror and Gothic models, the story in and of itself is one that takes care to move right into the plot rather than slowly building up to any semblance of action. *Heart-Shaped Box* begins with an uncanny speed which immediately introduces the primary vehicle for the plot — Judas Coyne buys a ghost on the internet from an advertisement that reads: "I will 'sell' my stepfather's ghost to the highest bidder. Of course a soul cannot really be sold, but I believe he will come to your home and abide with you if you put out the welcome mat" (Hill, *Heart-Shaped Box* 7). The pace with which the novel begins is maintained throughout the book, yet this pace does not eliminate any real character development. As the introductory chapter sets the strangely familiar contemporary scene of shopping online (which is a social presence that Hill embraces in his fiction as more than just a temporal point of reference), readers are primarily introduced to the main character not through common means of pure physical description or selective examinations of the character's psyche by the omniscient narrator. Rather, with the online auction and, more important, its ultimately successful attempt to sell a ghost, the character of Judas Coyne is primarily developed by his tastes. But such tastes are not necessarily informed by Judas himself, but rather by individuals he does not even know — the mass public.

Judas Coyne, as a rock star, is a character that is mainly subjected to the whims and desires of his audience, which could easily be seen as a critique of the publishing industry in which writers and publishers are often at the mercy of the reading public's desires. However, Judas does not necessarily mind the spotlight of his position and appears to be pleased at the prospect of further constructing his identity through his purchase of a ghost: "He thought it might be good publicity: *Judas Coyne buys a poltergeist*. The fans ate up stories like that" (Hill, *Heart-Shaped Box* 8). With this sentiment, in which Judas contemplates how his acquisition of a ghost will affect not himself but his fans, Hill suggests that the scope of the novel (which originally "was conceived as a short story, tentatively titled *The Private Collection*") ultimately exceeds mere eccentricity captured on the page for the purpose of spectacle (Bone 6). In many ways, Judas Coyne's collection, which includes a snuff film, drawings by John Wayne Gacy, a skull, a used noose, and occultist Aleister Crowley's chessboard, serves as more than just a starting point or a backdrop for *Heart-Shaped Box*. It serves as a point of troublesome identity construction. While the narrator suggests, "When he [Judas Coyne] was home, he wanted to be himself, not a trademark," Judas' collection becomes merely another extension of himself for the public to examine and analyze to the point of exhaustion (Hill, *Heart-Shaped Box* 5). Of course, with the cogitation surrounding Judas' identity and the influence of his audience, Hill establishes a certain sympathy for Judas early on, despite the generalizations and images that are attached to this aging rock star who sees band mates pass away, deals with his own addictions, and routinely beds young women (as if anything else were unexpected).

But such sympathy is all but removed when examining Judas' collection; while it is private, or at least privately owned, the growing public awareness of it suggests a contemporary reflection for individuals to become defined by what they have or through particular connections to people, places, or things. As James Clifford notes, "The inclusions in all collections reflect wider cultural rules— of rational taxonomy, of gender, of aesthetics. An excessive, sometimes even rapacious need to *have* is transformed into rule-governed, meaningful desire" (60). While Clifford's statement seems almost too obvious to warrant mention, what people have tends to define who they are or how they are perceived by the outside world. With the nature of collecting serving as a foundation for the book and Judas' seemingly coincidental purchase of Craddock McDermott's ghost, it makes sense to reiterate the cultural sway of *possession*, no pun intended. Building and projecting identity is, of course, more than just the catalyst for Judas Coyne's purchase of the specter that chases him from New York to Georgia and into Louisiana throughout the duration of the text— the notion of image, as it pertains to the actual text, is also important in how one reads *Heart-Shaped Box* as a whole.

In one sense, *Heart-Shaped Box* is simply a ghost story, and the possibilities of the spiritual realm, especially with the possibilities of technology— speaking in-sync with the radio, speaking through a television, sending e-mails from beyond the grave—serve Hill well in terms of originality (even though this idea of the dead communicating with the living through concrete means is explored by Hill in his short story "Twittering from the Circus of the Dead," as is also the case with his father's short story "The New York Times at Special Bargain Rates"). But *Heart-Shaped Box* does not stop with the basic idea of the dead speaking with, or haunting, the living. Hill provides a remarkably provocative stamp on his use of the ghost figure with his conceptions and descriptions as to how ghosts interact with the living beyond speech, in that his descriptions of Craddock's ghost gives *Heart-Shaped Box* a particular stamp of originality. First and foremost, the eyes of Craddock are described "as if a child had taken a Magic Marker—a truly magic marker, one that could draw right on the air—and had desperately tried to ink over them" (Hill, *Heart-Shaped Box* 56). Further, as Hill draws attention to, and perhaps invokes a sense of symbolism with, the destruction of Craddock's ghostly eyes, he also notes the ghost's movement: "Craddock McDermott moved in stop motion, a series of life-size still photographs" (Hill, *Heart-Shaped Box* 88). This literally haunting image of a specter moving almost at random, and providing a constant threat because its movements cannot ever be fully anticipated, is a noted departure from the typical or quintessential ghost. This is important in that Hill is always careful to depart from established conventions and norms within his fiction, even concerning monstrous figures and presences. This springboard of sorts, much like Hill's connection to the Gothic, takes *Heart-Shaped Box* from familiar footing into arenas of discomfort and oddity with which readers are able to find a genuinely unique reading experience composed by an author who is quite aware of his roots and literary predecessors, but who also is careful to forge an autonomous path for himself and his fiction.

As previously noted, *Heart-Shaped Box* both captures and challenges categorical definitions with its multiple generic invocations, primarily with its presumably Gothic snapshots in terms of Judas' collection and the presence of literal and figurative ghosts throughout the story. However, as is the case with schoolyard children who don black dusters and utilize black lipstick, among other purportedly Gothic means of identity construction which is little more than ill-informed decoration and adornment, it is critical to consider that "'Gothic' is a borrowed term in contemporary art" (G. Williams 12). And when Joe Hill describes Georgia, Judas Coyne's girlfriend, who also has multiple names (Marybeth Kimball and Morphine), as a girl who dresses in a Gothic manner, he may be alluding to common conceptions and images associated with the term "Gothic." However, when it comes to accuracy, it is hardly appropriate to consider dark clothes and black fingernails as representations of Gothicism. Although Hill's commentary on the Gothic seems, at times, to reflect a humorous criticism —"When you were a Goth, it was important to at least imply the possibility you might burst into flames in direct sunlight"— one must wonder if some readers will identify such passages as sarcastic, or as a means of insightful connection to the purported contemporary Gothic experience (Hill, *Heart-Shaped Box* 153). (Mis)conceptions aside, the use and invocation of the Gothic is perhaps that of a catalyst, especially as the early Gothic novels examined more than just darkness in terms of atmosphere and death. With the taboo functioning as one of the primary foundations of the Gothic, including incest, *Heart-Shaped Box* and its ultimate plot revelation — that Craddock McDermott had molested his step-daughter Anna — is brought into the story with a certain level of ease by way of the purportedly Gothic backdrop.

When Judas deduces that Craddock McDermott had molested his step-daughters—"I get the picture you [Jessica McDermott] and him were pretty close. Least until Anna was old enough and he started fucking her instead of you"—the horrors which lie at the heart of the McDermott family, and the plot of *Heart-Shaped Box*, bleed out into the rest of the story, but not unexpectedly so (Hill, *Heart-Shaped Box* 260). The conversation regarding personal violation largely begins with Georgia, Judas' current girlfriend, who initiates the examination of molestation when she recalls that, as a teen, she let one George Ruger "fuck me for shoe money" (Hill, *Heart-Shaped Box* 100). Without delving too deeply into Georgia's woes and the effects of her stunted growth as an individual, harsh, unloving and violent relationships sweep all through the text, from Judas and his father (as well as his mother — "Jude and his mother had never helped each other. When they needed it most, they had never dared") to Jessica McDermott agreeing to not just help her step-father murder Judas but also offering her own daughter, Reese, to Craddock for sex (Hill, *Heart-Shaped Box* 124). Although Reese, as well as Judas and Georgia, survives the varied and hypnotic onslaughts of Craddock McDermott, *Heart-Shaped Box* ultimately concerns itself with ghosts of the past and the forgotten yet harmful memories that tend to be a fixture in most people's lives. It is with this idea of the looming threat of disaster that Judas Coyne suggests, "If you think our story ends 'and they lived happily ever after,' then you've got the wrong fuckin' fairy tale" (Hill, *Heart-Shaped Box* 102). With this statement, alongside the noted yet mildly anticlimactic survival of Judas, Georgia and Reese, Hill seems to follow a pattern established by his father, as David Punter suggests that "many of [Stephen] King's protagonists conclude their stories by leaving us with a sense that there is nowhere very much to go from here: the sheer strength required in the struggle to suppress the problem of the past means that nothing is left over" (Punter 79). *Heart-Shaped Box* may end with Judas, Georgia and Reese all surviving Craddock's assaults, but there is little to be said or gained for their endurance. Perhaps such a conclusion is, as Judas states, a far cry from a fairy-tale ending, or even an ending with any glimmer or potential for hope in any shape. But the truth, and horror, of Hill's fiction is that sometimes with no hope, no answers, readers can see the world more clearly through these images of despair than through the rose-colored glasses of redemption.

Conclusion — A Devilish Delight?: Horns *and Beyond*

Joe Hill's popularity has only been alluded to thus far, but his growing reputation, especially as it relates to his second novel, *Horns*, must be considered when examining this text and Hill's future as a contributor to the contemporary fiction landscape. In short, with Hill's identity becoming largely known when his first novel was published in February of 2007, his popularity has grown immensely, as has his canon. And one of the most noticeable outcomes of this popularity is the anticipation that Hill's novel *Horns* received. Of course, measuring the "buzz" surrounding any given work of fiction or film is anything but an exact science, but when noting that *Horns* was optioned as a movie before its February 2010 release, it is hard to deny that there is quite a high level of real and expected popularity concerning *Horns*. On the one hand, it is a testament to Hill's capabilities as a writer that a book, a work of *written* fiction, can be conceived of as a cinematic production even before the public is able to *read* and *imagine* the story for itself. On the other hand, it is troubling to see Hill's written work be prepared for a "reading public [that] has gradually become a watching public," which suggests that Hill and his exceptional ability to create a story is preferred by readers to be reduced to ninety minutes of devilish images and fiery action rather than several hours or days of actual reading and engagement with the subtleties of characterization and plot development that find difficulty within cinematic restraints (Demarinis 7). Nonetheless, *Horns* marks a crossroads of sorts for Hill's growing career, and not just because of its general popularity among the public, but because of its popularity for the author.

Horns looks to be quite popular for Hill as an author, who notes on his website that *Horns* is essentially a reworking of two previously unpublished works, *The Fear Tree* and *The Surrealist's Glass*, which suggests that the text — along with its manipulative satanic figure that, like Milton's Satan, functions as a hero of sorts — is something that he could not let go. Much like "Abraham's Boys," in which Hill looks towards Bram Stoker for a touch of inspiration, Hill's likely look towards John Milton and *Paradise Lost* marks Hill as not just a writer knowledgeable of the classics, but also one who is confident in his ability to build upon the literary foundations that his predecessors have established. This is important in that many contemporary authors who situate themselves in pre-existing stories (think of the *Star Wars* universe and its multitude of fictions that add to but more often than not detract from the primary story conceived by George Lucas) find themselves unable to escape the core tale and are, consequentially, unable to create a particular voice and identity for themselves or their writing. Hill's playfulness, as evidenced in the Morse code message found in the inside cover of *Horns*—which reads "Pleased to meet you, hope you guess my name," (a nod towards "Sympathy for the Devil" by the Rolling Stones)—reminds readers that he is a writer for the new millennium who is not just knowledgeable of his field and his surrounding culture, but that he knows his own authorial voice. And that voice, although it may eventually be lost when *Horns* reaches the big screen, is one which has developed a confidence in Hill that brought a once-abandoned novel to the reading public, much to their delight.

From a technical standpoint, *Horns* follows upon the advice that "every good book starts at a moment of threat" (Bickham 11). The immediate conflict of *Horns*—"Ignatius Martin Perrish spent the night drunk and doing terrible things. He woke the next morning with a headache, put his hands to his temples, and felt something unfamiliar, a pair of knobby pointed protuberances"— not only takes the text right to the point of the ensuing plot, but displays a careful authorial and editorial hand on Hill's part (Hill, *Horns* 3). Just as *Heart-Shaped Box* takes care to not burden the reader with a drawn-out introduction that takes multiple pages to arrive at any moment of real interest or importance, *Horns* immediately immerses readers in the primary story of one Ignatius Perrish transforming into a devil whose demonic horns turn out to be a means of opening people up to their evil. These horns allow Ig to hear people's desires and see into their mind's most hidden recesses—"when her skin brushed his, Ig knew that her name was Allie Letterworth and that for the last four months she'd been sleeping with her golf instructor, meeting him at a motel down the road from the links"—and even allow him to push individuals towards their unpleasant inclinations (Hill, *Horns* 13). The frightful clarity with which Ig Perrish is able to see the darker side of his peers is more than just a result of his alteration and a recurrence throughout the text, which constantly reminds readers of the objectionable thoughts that people carry within their minds. It is a strong marker of Hill's fiction and his fearlessness that he writes of the honest yet unsavory, especially when the uncouth effectively and accurately captures the venomous attitudes of fictional characters that may portray non–fictional thoughts.

Horns and its author find a particularly engaging voice through the direct and unforgiving presentations of thoughts that tend to remain unspoken, which both Ig and the reader must confront throughout the duration of the story. With *Horns* concerning itself with Ig's fall, as precipitated by the rape-murder of his girlfriend, Merrin Williams, which Ig is thought to have perpetrated, the entire Maine town of Gideon makes some rather scathing judgments towards Ig as well as some disrespectful remembrances of a woman that the entire town liked. Among the most telling and darkly comedic (depending on one's point of view) revelations within the early pages of *Horns* that Ig is able to hear because of his newfound powers is one Father Mould's recollection of Merrin's death, of which the priest says, "I think about Merrin Williams all the time. Usually when I'm balling her mother" (Hill, *Horns* 35). Although one could easily look at this passage and think that Hill is simply providing an implied critique on the clergy, one must consider that *Horns* not only finds much of its story grounded in secrecy, regardless of the individual and his or her position in the community, but that sexual (mis)conduct drives the story. One only needs to look towards Lee Tourneau to recall the power and sway of sex as the critical pulse of the story.

As noted, *Horns* continues its necessarily unapologetic examination of the taboo with its movement into the heavy sexual elements of the story, as Ig's ultimate nemesis, Lee Tourneau, is given the spotlight, which includes the unabashed pornographic and explicit mental cogitations of the teenage male. What is striking, however, is how the delusional fantasies and obsessions about sex stay with Lee Tourneau, a young man who, on the surface, is a God-fearing individual with exceptional commitment to his community, yet reveals much about his character when he bluntly and surprisingly asks Ig, "You like pictures of snatch?" (Hill, *Horns* 91). Lee's obsessive and oppressive view of the woman as an object of sex and desire to be mastered serves, in one way, as the malformed impetus for him to pursue Ig's girlfriend, Merrin. This pursuit, which culminates after Merrin breaks off her relationship with Ig (as she has discovered she has cancer and does not wish to burden Ig with her impending death), is not only disturbing because it results in the rape and murder of Merrin by Lee, but also because it is a startlingly accurate examination of the male psyche and its delusional constructions concerning the female. For Lee, Merrin's breakup with Ig can have no other explanation besides her realization that, according to Lee's slanted mental constructions, she holds a desire for Lee that must finally be realized: "That's what you think? That I broke up with him ... so I could fuck *you*?" (Hill, *Horns* 291). Lee may not be fully aware that he is a creature of delusion, as he rationalizes his actions—"It wasn't rape ... she *wanted* me to fuck her. She was coming on to me for months. Sending me messages. Playing little word games. She had this whole cocktease business going on behind your back"—but this is no excuse for his actions, nor does this establish Lee as a straw-man enemy for Ig to confront and ultimately defeat so that Hill can establish his devil as a genuine protagonist (Hill, *Horns* 165). Ig may be set up as a character in utter contrast to the demon-figure he is transformed into (as evidenced by the constant push and pull that he experiences, and by the good deeds he attempts even after realizing that he is a devil of sorts), but his relationship with Lee is anything but a clear-cut case of black and white, of good versus evil. Such would be too easy and a mark of fiction that shows no originality or ability on behalf of the writer.

As Hill carefully and even humorously addresses the issue of Ig's dual personality by briefly touching upon the actual nature of the Devil by way of suggesting that the Devil is not the divine adversary he is reported to be, he is careful to consider that "the writer has to act as if the available novelistic methods are continually about to turn into mere convention" (Wood 247). Although he may not necessarily be on to something new in observing that "Satan turns up in a lot of other religions as the good guy. He's usually the guy who tricks the fertility goddess into bed, and after a bit of fiddling around they bring the world into being," one sees Hill constantly attempting to forge his own path as a writer all throughout *Horns*, and in the rest of his canon (Hill, *Horns* 313). One such example is Hill's exceptional word play. The title alone recalls not just Ig's supernatural protuberances but also the musical instrument which brings wealth and fame to the Perrish family (as Ig's father and brother are famous trumpeters), as well the horns that are to be sounded when the seals of the Apocalypse are broken. Further, the spelling of "Perrish" seems to functions as a double-entendre with its multiple misspellings—one for "perish," linking the themes and images of death in the book to the main character, and the second being a misspelling of "parish," or a church, which connects the issues of faith, or at least perished faith, to Ig. Beyond engaging with the flexibility of language and the difficult subject of religious examination, Hill further experiments with his writing by beginning the construction of a fictional universe which links his writings as a familiar reference: "*fucking Judas Coyne on the jukebox,*" links *Horns* to *Heart-Shaped Box* (Hill, *Horns* 195). But even with excursions into rather difficult subject matter, as well as playful language and inter–textual references, what can Hill hope to accomplish?

When an author is faced with the open sea of expectation and taste, sometimes the only thing he or she can do is throw as much to the audience as possible and see what is embraced. In the case of Joe Hill, the general consensus regarding his efforts and experimentations seems to concur with reviewer Lucy Sussex's claim that "regardless of pedigree, he is a remarkable writer" (22). Robert Crais mirrors this sentiment in his introduction to Hill's first hardbound installment of *Locke and Key* when he says, "If Joe Hill was only one thing, it would be this: An amazing storyteller" (5). Even the stories within Hill's stories, like Ig Perrish's "fire sermon," are written with a skill and passion that warrants recognition as exceptional crafting and portraying of ideas:

> Satan has long been known as the Adversary, but God fears women more than He fears the devil—and is right to. *She,* with her power to bring life into the world, was truly made in the image of the Creator, not man, and in all ways has proved Herself a more deserving object of man's worship than Christ, that unshaven fanatic who lusted for the end of the world. God saves—but not now, and not here. His salvation is on layaway. Like all grafters, He asks you to pay now and take it on faith that you will receive later. Whereas women offer a different sort of salvation, more immediate and fulfilling. They don't put off their love for a distant, ill-defined eternity but make a gift of it in the here and now, frequently to those who deserve it least. So it was in my case. So it is for many. The devil and woman have been allies against God from the beginning, ever since Satan came to the first man in the form of a snake and whispered to Adam that true happiness was not to be found in prayer but in Eve's cunt" [Hill, *Horns* 216].

More than anything, regardless what colleagues and critics say of Hill, and despite the broad examinations of his fiction that occur here and elsewhere, it can be safely said that the reader of Joe Hill will, at the very least, find fictions with a thankful author. When Hill says at the conclusion of *20th Century Ghosts*, "How about a little thanks for you, the reader, for picking up this book and giving me the chance to whisper in your ear for a few hours?" he establishes more than a sense of humility that serves as but one additional doorway into his fiction (Hill, *20th Century Ghosts* 314). He creates an open embrace for the contemporary reader that may not always enjoy what is placed before his or her eyes, but will find, with Hill, stories that attempt to bridge the growing gap between artist and observer, a gap that may be widening with each passing day, but which finds hope in the words and imagination of writers like Joe Hill.

Conclusion

The problem with a comprehensive examination of a writer's entire body of work, or even an entire family's corpus, is that potential or alternative discussions of the works in question, as well as theorized readings of the fictions, tend to be necessarily limited. While this statement can be considered as either obvious or as a cop-out of sorts concerning the content of his book, it merely serves as a reminder that the function of this text is to establish a working foundation for reading and studying the fictions of the King family beyond those penned by the patriarch. For example, when Stephen King biographer Lisa Rogak notes that "Steve [Stephen King] passed *Small World* to his editor, George Walsh, at Viking, who later told Tabby [Tabitha King] that he grudgingly decided to read it as a favor to her husband," some of the nepotistic concerns which shadow Tabitha King's writing are foregrounded and open the debate as to whether or not she and her craft are responsible for her fiction being published (110). Whether or not this issue will be answered any time soon remains to be seen, just as it remains to be seen if the fictions of Owen King, Tabitha King and Joe Hill will find sustained readership in the coming years and decades. If one had to speculate, however, the resulting picture, unfortunately, looks rather grim.

Any future debates and discussions surrounding the fictions of Tabitha King and her sons, Owen King and Joe Hill, face quite the uphill battle, but not necessarily because of controversial content or lackluster writing. More than anything, contemporary fiction seems to find itself quite clouded and hidden from the public eye, as volumes of fiction are published each year with only a handful gaining any status beyond largely forgotten. For the one King who has remained primarily outside of the discussion at hand, Naomi, the only writing that she has been attributed with besides her award-winning sermons, which are not designed as fictions and are thus not intended for mere readership or consumption, is locked away in the Stephen King Special Collections at the University of Maine-Orono's Raymond Fogler library, along with two of Joe Hill's unpublished works, "The Bone Men" and "But Only Darkness Loves Me." Owen King's fiction, although less in number when compared to his brother, but which is more abundant than his sister's lone fictional creation, has all been accounted for, as well as a handful of non–fiction pieces, including the essay "Spit It Out! The Top Ten Stutter Songs" in the book *Hang the DJ: An Alternative Book of Music Lists*, edited by Angus Cargill (2008).

These works, along with Hill's first two published stories, which have all but disappeared from not just the public eye but also public *access*—"The Lady Rests" and "The Collaborators"—are mostly noted (along with Hill's recent graphic novel creations "Kodiak" and adaptation of his short story "The Cape," not to mention his short story "The Devil on the Staircase") in order to provide at least a mildly complete snapshot of each writer's canon, as all known works are mentioned at least once in this book. To wit: Tabitha King wrote an episode of *Kingdom Hospital*—"The Passion of Reverend Jimmy"—and a short story that has recently surfaced under the title "The Woman's Room" (2002). Many of these works are, to say the least, not well-advertised and are mostly left untouched and, moreover, unread. In the case of Tabitha and "The Woman's Room," which tells the tale of an alcoholic woman, Mary Dorr, who finds herself trapped in an office building and being hunted down by a mysterious murderer, the general plot of mystery and pursuit, coupled with dull descriptions (including one observation of a dead female who was covered in "so much blood, she appeared to be wearing underpants somehow made of it"), one might surmise that many of the published works by the King family simply do not warrant the attention of modern readers, especially if the plots and descriptions are familiar or otherwise seemingly boring (T. King, "The Woman's Room" 9). This appears to place responsibility on the writer to adapt and adjust to new times and their new scenes and concerns, and to do so through new means of fiction and through never-before-seen characters or literary forms. It seems to follow, then, that originality, in addition to spectacle, rather than attempts at profound philosophical insights or identifiable and believable characters whose obstacles and foibles are easily recognized and embraced by the reader, looks to remain the key element in winning over readers.

While originality is certainly desirable in an author and his or her fiction, numerous scholars and critics have pointed towards the ever-changing reader as one of the primary factors in what appears to be a massive dwindling in readership and enjoyment in the written word. As Alvin Kernan bluntly states, "Reading of all kinds is becoming a lost skill" (147). The nostalgic yearnings of Kernan suggest, among other things, that readers have lost their *intimacy* with reading and replaced it with *immediacy*, a sense that instant gratification is to be had and that such can only be attained with original and perhaps startling writing that is exceptionally clear. Indeed, the commentary provided here concerning Joe Hill's supernatural fictions, namely "My Father's Mask" and "Voluntary Committal," suggests that these fictions fail in some ways because of their excessive obscurity and lack of clarity. Yet the curiosity that these stories instigates, whether out of anger or out of a genuine desire to revisit the texts and attempt a better understanding of the content and the purpose, is praiseworthy. Just as Hill's father prompts a genuine investment in his fictions, especially with *The Dark Tower* and its circular plot, which necessitates at least one careful re-reading of the entire 3,000-plus page series, Joe Hill's complex and mystifying fictions ask that contemporary readers reconsider how they approach fiction and ask that readers actually *read* what is written on the page rather than merely observe the words printed.

With the call of authors like Joe Hill for readers to, essentially, retrain themselves to become better and more engaged readers, there nonetheless remains much resistance. One of the main misconceptions about literature founded in contemporary readership is that it is inert and inactive, or, at best, catalytic or cathartic — a means of escape or solace that holds no sway beyond the temporary and fleeting emotive state of a given reader. And when a contemporary reader approaches literature, especially contemporary writings like those of the King family, one notices a disconnect between the reader and the author which warrants some sort of explanation; and the simplest answer is often suggested as that of inept writing. But even if, in some cases, poor writing leads to a general disinterest in literature, one must remember that times have indeed changed, and not just in terms of the changing focus regarding literary content. When Gerald Graff says that "literary culture was [once] a flourishing part of the extracurricular life of the college and general community," he reminds readers and critics that literature does not necessarily serve the same purposes that it once did, and that contemporary culture has essentially marginalized fiction (19). Harriet Hawkins mirrors this sentiment when she suggests that the study of literature in a culture that does not treasure the written word only perpetuates the separation between author and reader: "The surest way to destroy ... any given work might well be to put it on the syllabus and thus create an instant hostility to it on the part of the unwilling student" (109). In sum, when one considers the future of fiction, in general sense and for the King family, it would appear that there are more obstacles than there are open doors concerning readership. With a society moving further and further away from the written word, and then often resisting fiction and literature even in an academic setting, fiction looks to be withering rather than growing.

Even in the face of numerous pressures and an overwhelming sensation that reading in and of itself is struggling to gain a stable foothold among contemporary audiences, this does not stop authors from writing, publishing, and advertising their fictions. But even the best efforts to gain, at the least, exposure do not always find success. As Daniel Grassian asks, "How can an author promote his or her work, when the 'normal' modes of mass communication, such as television, film and radio, rarely concern themselves with literary fiction?" (174). Although the one technology not mentioned by Grassian, the Internet, has been appropriated by much of the population to promote his or her own agendas, publishing or otherwise, one must consider that even exposure and awareness does not always result in interest or desire. Still, like Stephen, Tabitha, Owen and Joe each have their own websites, further marking a movement towards awareness of writing awareness. However, simply creating and maintaining a website does not guarantee exposure or even access to, say, a writer's fiction. As is the case with Stephen King's website, both Joe and Owen make note of their lesser-known fictions, providing and even prompting a curiosity and perhaps a demand for the writings that have not reached a large public forum and have, to an extent, been forgotten. For those within academia, access to a number of Owen and Joe's stories is more open than to those outside the hallowed halls of the extensive and generous library network among colleges and universities in the United States, but approaching these fictions solely through an academic lens is likely not the aspiration or intention by these authors. Yet in observing that access, awareness and desire for fiction currently faces numerous fractured avenues, what can be reasonably expected from the King family in terms of future readership?

Early indications as to the futures of Owen King, Tabitha King and Joe Hill tend to point towards the conclusion that only Hill has a chance of enduring much beyond the next several years if trends continue. One reason for this conclusion stems from a brief analysis of library holdings across the United States, as provided by WorldCat.org. As a benchmark, most of Stephen King's novels and collections are shown to be held in over 2,000 libraries worldwide. When this measurement of relative success is used as a point of comparison for Owen King, Tabitha King and Joe Hill, only Hill's major works appear, on average, in over 1,000 libraries worldwide, with Owen's works averaging placement in roughly 400 libraries and Tabitha's works averaging placement in roughly 800 libraries. Interpretations of these numbers can vary to the point that several conclusions can be drawn, especially as Janice Radway notes that "bourgeoning sales do not necessarily imply increasing demand or need" (45). While Hill looks to stand the best chance of enduring as a writer, even his growing popularity may not position him as anything but a *known* writer. When Stephen King critic Don Herron admits, "Except for his persistent appearance on the bestseller lists, I would never have read a Stephen King novel," he suggests that any footing as a known, read and/or popular writer is a tenuous position at best (62). While exposure is necessary, as this book seeks to at least start opening the doors of the Family King that have remained mostly closed, even a clear, open road to an author does not guarantee any acceptance or readership.

According to Stephen King, "Readable, interesting novels don't begin with a desire to teach but a desire to please" ("Typhoid Stevie" 14). But how does this assertion hold up under scrutiny? Rather, how does this notion apply to the reading tastes and desires of the reading public? In an attempt to take Stephen King's views on writing as being aimed at pleasing an audience, a survey of sorts was given to the students of a recent Contemporary Literature class I taught. I asked that the students read and discuss a selection of short stories by the King family: "Last Breath" by Joe Hill, "I Swear I'll Jump" by Owen King, and "Djinn and Tonic" by Tabitha King. Of course, a single group of students gathered in the southeast suburbs of Minneapolis hardly serves as a representative selection of readers across the entire United States. As Richard Miller adds,

> There are limits to having students "investigate" popular literate practices in an academic setting, of course. First of all, there's the problem of determining the status of the students' own responses to the novel in this context, since it goes without saying that the way students read a book for class differs considerably from the way they read a book on their own [131].

My students' observations and opinions, despite Miller's cautions, are nonetheless helpful when looking towards the horizons of literature and the fiction of the King family, with the most interesting result being that their general response, at least within the isolated case of my recent Contemporary Fiction course, was rather tepid. Among the broad sweep of reactions and readings of the King family by my students, Tabitha King was viewed as an author with something to prove and with an off-putting vocabulary (think of terms corresponding to genitalia); Owen King was seen as mildly predictable and with writing that was not entirely engaging because of its common reality; and Joe Hill, by contrast, seemed to receive the best response, partly due to the brevity of the story assigned and the sense of curiosity elicited by the tale's strangeness and morbidity. With this brief overview of the discussions, certain speculations arise, including the aforementioned prediction that Joe Hill stands the best chance of becoming a fixture in the contemporary literature scene.

Based on the small samples of stories that my students were asked to read, it seemed that entertainment, above all else, was the key to preference, and that the strange unfamiliarity in Hill's story, as opposed to purportedly common and mundane tales of sibling rivalry and a genie, functioned as the most successful means of engaging these readers. This conclusion that I have drawn — that entertainment is the primary desire for contemporary readers — may be countered by many means, especially by my own admission stemming from the observation that many of my students found Toni Morrison's *The Bluest Eye* to be an engaging work of fiction even without the overt humor or eccentricity found in Hill's writing. But *The Bluest Eye*, it could be said, has an advantage over the fictions of the King family in that its place in the literary world has established a reputation that often precedes it, and while reputation is not exactly equitable to entertainment value, there is something to be said for the myriad outside factors which affect the way in which an individual approaches fiction.

Ultimately, the face of fiction in the contemporary social scene seems to be that which is subjected to the whims of the market, that which may not necessarily govern taste but which severely limits certain tastes while aiding others. This is not to say that fiction writers are to give up their dreams or that their fiction will inevitably become appropriated by corporate interests for the sake of merely making money. But what the current picture of fiction writing does suggest is that the channels of fiction writing — and more importantly, fiction *publishing*— remain rather limited. Janice Radway says, "The principal problem facing the publisher in a heterogeneous, modern society is finding an audience for each new book and developing a method for getting that book to its potential readers," implying that constructing an audience first is becoming more of a common practice than creating fiction to be dispersed and left to the whims of the public (32). Removing risk in terms of appealing to an audience rather than promoting literary expression and experimentation with less emphasis on sales is, and has been for some time, the new norm with which readers and writers have engaged literature. Moreover, with writers often seeking either the big break, which has been undoubtedly mythologized through both the Stephen King story as well as the success of J. K. Rowling and Stephenie Meyer, such occurrences of immediate success, or even sustained success in terms of either readership or financial gain, are quite rare. And with the rarity of major success as either a popular novelist or as a writer of any other categorical ilk, writers are often left to publish in mediums like the small literary journal, those publications which are often known only within select circles of writers and which rarely ever go beyond the shelves of the libraries closest to the presses which produce such works.

There is no easy way to conclude the discussion on contemporary readers and the fiction of the King family because the conversation is only beginning. Still, as reading taste and reading practices change and develop over the next several years and decades, the wide net of the King family is sure to ensnare and engage readers. Even so, when fictions that approach the tried and tested core of fiction in the form of exploring the human condition are, in many ways, chastised for such purportedly "common" content, it suggests quite a shift in readership and expectation. Even when a story is little more than an account of a strange occurrence stemming from the author's imagination answering a simple question of "what would happen if..." such tales are, too, deemed as common. This looks to be the case even within the King family, as Stephen King says, "I read Joe's stuff and I relate to it because it's plot-driven and high conflict.... Owen writes more like Bret Easton Ellis, flavor-of-the-month New York relationships" (Rogak 228). Of course, this is only one opinion as to why certain fictions are more appealing than others, which is not to say that Owen King is a fledgling writer or that his own father does not care for his fiction. Rather, this simply serves as a reminder of the miasma surrounding contemporary fiction, with its unnerving and exceedingly puzzling status and readership. And since the futures of Owen King, Tabitha King and Joe Hill have no clear projection, there is something refreshing about not seeing answers form or even beginning to form. As Joe Hill might suggest, an absence of answers makes for quite the interesting tale. Therefore, perhaps simply watching the journey, and the story, of the King family unfold is all that one is able, or can be asked, to do.

Works Cited

Adams, Jon Robert. *Male Armor: The Soldier-Hero in Contemporary American Fiction*. Charlottesville: University of Virginia Press, 2008.

Barnes, Ken. "Believe in 'Ghosts' and Hill's Range." *USA Today*, November 15, 2007: 4D.

Bass, Judy. "Review of *Caretakers*, by Tabitha King." *New York Times*, October 23, 1983: BR27.

Bickham, Jack M. *The 38 Most Common Fiction Writing Mistakes (and How to Avoid Them)*. Cincinnati, OH: Writer's Digest Books, 1992.

Bloch, Robert. "Monsters in Our Midst." *Kingdom of Fear: The World of Stephen King*. Tim Underwood and Chuck Miller (eds.). New York: Signet, 1987, pp. 23–28.

Block, Marylaine. "Review of *Survivor*, by Tabitha King." *Library Journal*, 121.19 (November 15, 1996): 89.

Blodgett, Jan. "Review of *One on One*, by Tabitha King." *Library Journal*, 118.3 (February 15, 1993): 192.

Bloom, Harold. *How to Read and Why*. New York: Scribner, 2000.

Blue, Tyson. *The Unseen King*. Mercer Island, WA: Starmont, 1989.

Boerman-Cornell, William. "The Five Humors." *The English Journal*, 88.4 (March 1999): 66–69.

Bone, James. "They're So Alike, It's Scary." *The Times* (London), March 10, 2007: 6 (Section-Features; Books).

Botting, Fred. *The Gothic*. New York: Routledge, 1996.

Carrier, David. *The Aesthetics of Comics*. University Park: Penn State University Press, 2000.

Casebeer, Edwin F. "The Art of Balance: Stephen King's Canon." *Bloom's Modern Critical Views: Stephen King*. Harold Bloom (ed.). Philadelphia: Chelsea House, 1998, pp. 207–218.

Clifford, James. "On Collecting Art and Culture." *The Cultural Studies Reader, Second Edition*. Simon During (ed.). New York: Routledge, 1999, pp. 57–76.

Cocchiarale, Michael, and Scott Emmert. "Introduction: Sports and American Literature." *Upon Further Review: Sports in American Literature*. Michael Cocchiarale and Scott Emmert (eds.). Westport, CT: Praeger, 2004, pp. xv–xxiv.

Colatrella, Carol. "Science Fiction in the Information Age." *American Literary History*, 11.3 (Autumn 1999): 554–65.

Crais, Robert. "Welcome to Hill's House." *Lock and Key: Welcome to Lovecraft #1–6*, by Joe Hill et al. San Diego: IDW, 2008, pp. 4–5.

Davis, Jonathan P. *Stephen King's America*. Bowling Green, OH: Bowling Green State University Popular Press, 1994.

Davis, William A. "The Literary Realism of Maine's Other King." *The Boston Globe*, 18 (December 1994): B1.

Demarinis, Rick. *The Art & Craft of the Short Story*. Cincinnati: Story Press, 2000.

Dyson, Cindy. "Biography of Stephen King." *Bloom's Bio Critiques: Stephen King*. Harold Bloom (ed.). Philadelphia: Chelsea House, 2002, pp. 3–47.

Eagleton, Mary. *The Woman Author in Contemporary Fiction*. New York: Palgrave Macmillan, 2005.

Figliola, Samantha. "Reading King Darkly: Issues of Race in Stephen King's Novels." *Into Darkness Peering: Race and Color in the Fantastic*. Elisabeth Anne Leonard (ed.). Westport, CT: Greenwood, 1997, pp. 143–158.

Gallagher, Bernard J. "Reading Between the Lines: Stephen King and Allegory." *The Gothic World of Stephen King: Landscapes and Nightmares*. Ray B. Browne and Gary Hoppenstand (eds.). Madison, WI: Bowling Green State University Popular Press, 1987, pp. 37–48.

Gallop, Jane. *Thinking Through the Body*. New York: Columbia University Press, 1988.

Golden, Christopher. "Introduction." *20th Century Ghosts*, by Joe Hill. New York: William and Morrow, 2007, pp. xi–xiv.

Graff, Gerald. *Professing Literature: An Institutional History*. Chicago: University of Chicago Press, 1987.

Grassian, Daniel. *Hybrid Fictions: American Literature and Generation X*. Jefferson, NC: McFarland, 2003.

Gunn, James. "Toward a Definition of Science Fiction." *Speculation on Speculation*. James Gunn and Matthew Candelaria (eds.). Lanham, MD: Scarecrow Press, Inc., 2005, pp. 5–12.

Hand, Elizabeth. "Small-Town Love and Ambition." *The Washington Post* (December 11, 1988): X8.

Hawkins, Harriet. *Classics and Trash: Traditions and Taboos in High Literature and Popular Modern Genres*. Toronto: University of Toronto Press, 1990.

Hendin, Josephine G. *Heartbreakers: Women and Violence in Contemporary Culture and Literature*. New York: Palgrave, 2004.

Herron, Don. "Horror Springs in the Fiction of Stephen King." *Fear Itself: The Horror Fiction of Stephen King*. Tim Underwood and Chuck Miller (eds.). San Francisco: Underwood-Miller, 1982, pp. 57–82.

Hill, Joe. "Abraham's Boys." *20th Century Ghosts*. New York: William Morrow, 2007, pp. 91–111.

_____. "Best New Horror." *20th Century Ghosts*. New York: William Morrow, 2007, pp. 1–23.

_____. "Better Than Home." *20th Century Ghosts*. New York: William Morrow, 2007, pp. 113–133.

_____. "The Black Phone." *20th Century Ghosts*. New York: William Morrow, 2007, pp. 135–154.

_____. "Bobby Conroy Comes Back from the Dead." *20th Century Ghosts*. New York: William Morrow, 2007, pp. 219–239.

_____. "The Cape." *20th Century Ghosts*. New York: William Morrow, 2007, pp. 173–194.

_____. "Dead Wood." *20th Century Ghosts*. New York: William Morrow, 2007, pp. 205–6.

_____. *Gunpowder*. Hornsea, UK: PS Publishing, 2008.

_____. *Heart-Shaped Box*. New York: William Morrow, 2007.

_____. *Horns*. New York: William and Morrow, 2010.

_____. "In the Rundown." *20th Century Ghosts*. New York: William Morrow, 2007, pp. 155–171.

_____. "Jude Confronts Global Warming." *Subterraneanpress*. Subterranean Press, 2007 (Web, April 5, 2009).

_____. "Last Breath." *20th Century Ghosts*. New York: William Morrow, 2007, pp. 195–203.

_____. "My Father's Mask." *20th Century Ghosts*. New York: William Morrow, 2007, pp. 241–262.

_____. "Pop Art." *20th Century Ghosts*. New York: William Morrow, 2007, pp. 47–68.

_____. "The Saved." *Clackamas Literary Review*, 5.1 (Spring/Summer 2001): 17–33.

_____. "Scheherazade's Typewriter." *20th Century Ghosts*. New York: William Morrow, 2007, pp. 314–316.

_____. "Thumbprint." *Postscripts*, 10 (2007): 225–244.

_____. "20th Century Ghost." *20th Century Ghosts*. New York: William Morrow, 2007, pp. 25–45.

_____. "Twittering from the Circus of the Dead." *The New Dead: A Zombie Anthology*. Christopher Golden (ed.). New York: St. Martin's Griffin, 2010, pp. 351–378.

_____. "Voluntary Committal." *20th Century Ghosts*. New York: William Morrow, 2007, pp. 263–311.
_____. "The Widow's Breakfast." *20th Century Ghosts*. New York: William Morrow, 2007, pp. 207–217.
_____. "You Will Hear the Locust Sing." *20th Century Ghosts*. New York: William Morrow, 2007, pp. 69–89.
Hill, Joe (w), Gabriel Rodriguez (i), Jay Fotos (c) and Robbie Robbins (l). *Locke and Key: Head Games* #1–6. San Diego: IDW, 2009.
_____, _____, _____, and _____. *Locke and Key: Welcome to Lovecraft* #1–6. San Diego: IDW, 2008.
Hill, Joe, et al. "Fanboyz." *Spiderman Unlimited* #8 (May 2005). Tom Brevoort (ed.). New York: Marvel, 2005, pp. 2–16.
Holland-Toll, Linda J. *As American as Mom, Baseball, and Apple Pie: Constructing Community in Contemporary Horror Fiction*. Bowling Green, OH: Bowling Green State University Popular Press, 2001.
Hoppenstand, Gary. "Interview with Gary Hoppenstand." Interviewed by Jonathan Davis. *Stephen King's America*, by Jonathan Davis. Bowling Green, OH: Bowling Green State University Popular Press, 1994, pp. 161–176.
Houston, Gail Turley. *From Dickens to Dracula: Gothic Economics and Victorian Fiction*. Cambridge, MA: Cambridge University Press, 2005.
Ingebreston, Edward J. "Monster Making: A Politics of Persuasion." *Journal of American Culture*, 21.2 (Summer 1998): 25–34.
Johnson, Samuel. "Preface to Shakespeare." *The Norton Anthology of Theory and Criticism*. Vincent B. Leitch (ed.). New York: W.W. Norton, 2001, pp. 468–482.
Joshi, S.T. *The Modern Weird Tale*. Jefferson, NC: McFarland, 2001.
Kernan, Alvin. *The Death of Literature*. New Haven, CT: Yale University Press, 1990.
King, Owen. "The Cure." *One Story*, 85 (December 20, 2006): 1–34.
_____. "Frozen Animals." *We're All in This Together*. New York: Bloomsbury, 2006, pp. 137–156.
_____. "I Swear I'll Jump." *The Dickinson Review*, 14 (2000): 7–23.
_____. "The Meerkat." *Who Can Save Us Now? Brand-New Superheroes and Their Amazing (Short) Stories*. Owen King and John McNally (eds.). New York: Free Press, 2008, pp. 122–157.
_____. "My Second Wife." *We're All in This Together*. New York: Bloomsbury, 2006, pp. 199–223.
_____. "Nothing Is in Bad Taste." *Subtropics*, 5 (Winter/Spring 2008): 50–63.
_____. "Snake." *We're All in This Together*. New York: Bloomsbury, 2006, pp. 179–197.
_____. "Sports." *When I Was a Loser: Stories of (Barely) Surviving High School*. John McNally (ed.). New York: Free Press, 2007, pp. 182–200.
_____. "We're All in This Together." *We're All in This Together*. New York: Bloomsbury, 2006, pp. 1–135.
_____. "Wonders." *We're All in This Together*. New York: Bloomsbury, 2006, pp. 157–178.
King, Owen, and John McNally. "Introduction." *Who Can Save Us Now? Brand-New Superheroes and Their Amazing (Short) Stories*. Owen King and John McNally (eds.). New York: Free Press, 2008, pp. xi–xiii.
King, Stephen. *Danse Macabre*. London: Time Warner, 1981.
_____. "I Want to Be Typhoid Stevie." *Reading Stephen King: Issues of Censorship, Student Choice, and Popular Literature*. Brenda Miller Power, Jeffrey D. Wilhelm, and Kelly Chandler (eds.). Urbana, IL: National Council of Teachers of English, 1997, pp. 13–21.
_____. "Interview with Stephen King." Interviewed by Mat Schaffer, reprinted in *Bare Bones: Conversations on Terror with Stephen King*. Tim Underwood and Chuck Miller (eds.). New York: McGraw-Hill, 1988, pp. 111–116.
_____. "Introduction." *The Best American Short Stories: 2007*. Stephen King and Heidi Pitlor (eds.). Boston: Houghton Mifflin, 2007, pp. xiii–xviii.

_____. "The Man in the Black Suit." *Everything's Eventual*. New York: Pocket Books, 2003, pp. 35–68.

_____. "Man with a Belly." *Gent*, 20.10 (November/December 1979): 20–25.

_____. "Morality." *Esquire*, 152.1 (July 2009): 57–67, 110–111.

_____. "*Penthouse* Interview: Stephen King." Interviewed by Bob Spitz, reprinted in *Bare Bones: Conversations on Terror with Stephen King*. Tim Underwood and Chuck Miller (eds.). New York: McGraw-Hill, 1988, pp. 181–191.

_____. "*Playboy* Interview: Stephen King." Interviewed by Eric Norden, reprinted in *Bare Bones: Conversations on Terror with Stephen King*. Tim Underwood and Chuck Miller (eds.). New York: McGraw-Hill, 1988, pp. 24–56.

_____. *Song of Susannah*. New York: Scribner, 2005.

_____. "Stephen King: The Art of Fiction No. 189." *The Paris Review*, 48.178 (Fall 2006): 66–101.

_____. "Steve's Take: An Interview with Stephen King." *Hollywood's Stephen King*, by Tony Magistrale. New York: Palgrave Macmillan, 2003, pp. 1–20.

_____. *Under the Dome*. New York: Scribner, 2009.

King, Stephen, and Joe Hill. "Throttle." *He Is Legend: An Anthology Celebrating Richard Matheson*. Christopher Conlon (ed.). Colorado Springs: Gauntlet, 2009, pp. 17–53.

King, Tabitha. "The Blue Chair." *Shadows 4*. Charles L. Grant (ed.). New York: Berkley, 1985, pp. 93–111. Print.

_____. *The Book of Reuben*. New York: Signet, 1995.

_____. *Caretakers*. New York: Signet, 1984.

_____. "Djinn & Tonic." *The Best of the Best: 18 New Stories by America's Leading Authors*. Elaine Koster and Joseph Pittman (eds.). New York: Signet, 1998, pp. 213–226.

_____. "Dump on Vulgarity." *Maledicta*, 10 (1988–1989): 5–13.

_____. "I Didn't Get Paid Enough." *Mid-Life Confidential: The Rock Bottom Remainders Tour America with Three Chords of Attitude*. Dave Marsh (ed.). New York: Viking, 1994, pp. 183–193.

_____. "Living with the Bogeyman." *Murderess Ink: The Better Half of the Mystery*. Dilys Wynn (ed.). New York: Workman, 1979.

_____. *One on One*. New York: Signet, 1994.

_____. *Pearl*. New York: Signet, 1989.

_____. *Playing Like a Girl: Cindy Blodgett and the Lawrence Bulldogs Season of '93–'94*. (No City Named): Dendrite, 1994.

_____. *Small World*. New York: Signet, 1982.

_____. *Survivor*. New York: Signet, 1998.

_____. *The Trap*. New York: Macmillan, 1985.

_____. "The Woman's Room." *Stranger: Dark Tales of Eerie Encounters*. Michele Slung (ed.). New York: Perennial, 2002, pp. 1–20.

King, Tabitha, and Michael McDowell. *Candles Burning*. New York: Berkley, 2006.

Koontz, Dean R. *Writing Popular Fiction*. Cincinnati, OH: Writer's Digest, 1972.

Labrie, Aimee. "Stephen King: Exorcising the Demons." *Bloom's Bio Critiques: Stephen King*. Harold Bloom (ed.). Philadelphia: Chelsea House, 2002, pp. 49–61.

Lant, Kathleen, and Theresa Thompson. "Imagining the Worst: Stephen King and the Representation of Women." *Imagining the Worst: Stephen King and the Representation of Women*. Kathleen Lant and Theresa Thompson (eds.). Westport, CT: Greenwood, 1998, pp. 3–8.

Lundie, Catherine A. "Introduction." *Restless Spirits: Ghost Stories by American Women, 1872–1926*. Catherine A. Lundie (ed.). Amherst: University of Massachusetts Press, 1996, pp. 1–24.

Magistrale, Tony. *Stephen King: The Second Decade, Danse Macabre to The Dark Half*. New York: Twayne, 1992.

McGee, Celia. "Shining Alone." *New York Daily News*, June 19, 2005: 22 (Sunday Now).

McIntyre, Clara F. "Were the 'Gothic

Novels' Gothic?" *PMLA*, 36.4 (December 1921): 644–667.

Miller, Richard E. "Schooling Misery: The Ominous Threat and Eminent Promise of the Popular Reader." *Teaching Literature: A Companion*. Tanya Agathocleous, Ann C. Dean, and George Levine (eds.). Basingstoke, UK: Palgrave Macmillan, 2003, pp. 125–138.

Minzesheimer, Bob. "Unwritten Publishing Secret out of the 'Box.'" *USA Today*, February 12, 2007: 1D.

Morrison, Jago. *Contemporary Fiction*. New York: Routledge, 2003.

Oates, Joyce Carol. "Beginnings: 'The Origins and Art of the Short Story.'" *The Tales We Tell: Perspectives on the Short Story*. Barbara Lounsberry, et al. (eds.). Westport, CT: Greenwood, 1998, pp. 47–52.

Olson, Ray. "Review of *Candles Burning*, by Tabitha King and Malcolm McDowell." *Booklist*, 102.18 (May 15, 2006): 38.

O'Neill, Dennis. *The DC Comics Guide to Writing Comics*. New York: Watson-Guptil, 2001.

Parker, Barbara. "Review of *Caretakers*, by Tabitha King." *Library Journal*, 108.14 (August 1, 1983): 1503.

Patrick, Bethanne. "Family Resemblance." *Publisher's Weekly*, December 4, 2006: 2 4–5.

Pearl, Nancy. "Review of *The Book of Reuben*, by Tabitha King." *Library Journal*, 119.3 (August 1, 1994): 130.

Punter, David. "Stephen King: Problems of Recollection and Construction." *Literary Interpretation Theory*, 5.1 (1994): 67–82.

Radway, Janice. *Reading the Romance: Women, Patriarchy and Popular Literature*. Chapel Hill: University of North Carolina Press, 1984.

Reino, Joseph. *Stephen King: The First Decade, Carrie to Pet Sematary*. Boston: Twayne, 1988.

Roberts, Thomas J. *An Aesthetics of Junk Fiction*. Athens: University of Georgia Press, 1990.

Rogak, Lisa. *Haunted Heart: The Life and Times of Stephen King*. New York: Thomas Dunne, 2008.

Romines, Ann. *The Home Plot: Women, Writing & Domestic Ritual*. Amherst: University of Massachusetts Press, 1992.

Sachs, Andrea. "Galley Girl: The Son Also Rises." *Time.com. Time*, July 7, 2005 (Web., May 4, 2009).

Schweitzer, Darrell. "Collecting Stephen King." *Discovering Stephen King*. Darrell Schweitzer (ed.). San Bernardino, CA: Borgo, 1987, pp. 153–164.

Shattuck, Kathryn. "Tabitha King: An Oeuvre of Her Own." *Publisher's Weekly*, February 10, 1997: 61–2.

Shoard, Catherine. "As I See It." *Sunday Telegraph*, May 21, 2006: 21 (Section Seven).

Siegel, Ben. "Introduction: Poets, Novelists, and Professors—A Bittersweet Mix." *The American Writer and the University*. Ben Siegel (ed.). Newark, NJ: University of Delaware Press, 1984, pp. 9–35.

Spender, Dale. *The Writer or the Sex? Or, Why You Don't Have to Read Women's Writing to Know It's No Good*. New York: Pergamon, 1989.

Spooner, Catherine. *Contemporary Gothic*. London: Reaktion, 2006.

Sussex, Lucy. "Horror Has a New Dark Prince, Born of a King." *The Age* (Australia), June 9, 2007: 22 (Section-A2; Books).

Talbot, Mary M. *Fictions at Work: Language and Social Practice in Fiction*. London: Longman, 1995.

Thompson, Bob. "The Kings of Fiction: Stephen, Tabitha and Owen Offer a Family-Style Look at the Literary Life." *Washington Post*, April 7, 2008, suburban ed.: C01.

Vicarel, JoAnn. "Review of *The Trap*, by Tabitha King." *Library Journal*, 110.6 (April 1, 1985): 158.

_____. "Review of *Pearl*, by Tabitha King." *Library Journal*, 113.19 (November 15, 1988): 85.

Warren, Bill. "The Movies and Stephen King: Part II." *Reign of Fear: The Fiction and Films of Stephen King*. Don Herron (ed.). Lancaster, PA: Underwood-Miller, 1992, 123–147.

Weinstock, Jeffrey Andrew. *Scare Tactics:*

Supernatural Fiction by American Women. New York: Fordham University Press, 2008.

Williams, Amy. "Review of *We're All in This Together: A Novella and Other Stories*. *Publishers Weekly*, 252.19 (May 9, 2005): 40, 42.

Williams, Gilda. "Introduction." *The Gothic: Documents of Contemporary Art*. Gilda Williams (ed.). London: White Chapel, 2007, pp. 12–19.

Winter, Douglass. *Stephen King: The Art of Darkness*. New York: New American Library, 1984.

Wisker, Gina. *Horror Fiction: An Introduction*. New York: Continuum, 2005.

Wood, James. *How Fiction Works*. New York: Farrar, Straus and Giroux, 2008.

Yamamoto, Judith T. "Review of *Small World*, by Tabitha King." *Library Journal*, 106.7 (April 1, 1981): 814.

Yarbro, Chelsea Quinn. "Cinderalla's Revenge: Twists on Fairy Tale and Mythic Themes in the Work of Stephen King." *Fear Itself: The Horror Fiction of Stephen King*. Tim Underwood and Chuck Miller (eds.). San Francisco: Underwood-Miller, 1982, pp. 45–55.

Young, James N. *101 Plots: Used and Abused*. Boston: The Writer, 1945.

Zobenica, Jon. "At the End of Wretch Lane." *The New York Times*, July 24, 2005: F19.

Index

Abe ("The Cure") 34–36
"Abraham's Boys" 170–171, 177
Abu Ghraib (prison) 38, 39
AC/DC (band) 48
Ackerly, Frank 64–66
Ackerly, Ken 64
Adamson, John "Race" 18
Adamson, Vince 17–19
Alden, Helen 91–92
Alinger ("Last Breath") 160
Apocalypse 179
Asimov, Isaac 134
The Awakening 119

Bachman, Richard 148
Backwards Man 61
"Bad Karma Girl Wins at Bingo" 46
Barry, Dave 75
Battlestar Galactica 134
Beetlejuice 74
Bellingham Review 46
"Best New Horror" 128–129, 151–155, 158
Beth ("The Blue Chair") 1, 30–31
"Better Than Home" 161–163
Black House 16
Black Mansion 61–62
"The Black Phone" 158–159, 162
Blockade Billy 141
Blodgett, Cindy 75–76
"The Blue Chair" 1, 29–32
The Bluest Eye 185
"Bobby Conroy Comes Back from the Dead" 161, 163–165
"The Body" 114
"The Bone Men" 128, 181
Book Magazine 46
The Book of Reuben 98, 108–113
Boston Red Sox 10, 102
Bottom of the Ninth 46
Bracken, John 24–25
Braffet, Kelly 11, 46
Brave New World 138
The Briars 136

Brontë, Charlotte 170
Brower, Ray 114
Browning, Elizabeth 9
Browning, Robert 9
Buckner, Bill 102
Burke, Mike 116, 118–119
Burlingame, Jesse 77
Burnham, Cleatus "Woodpecker" 61–62
Bush, George W. 43, 55, 58
"But Only Darkness Loves Me" 128, 181
"Buttonboy" 152–153

Callahan, Chad 26–27
Callahan, Donald 26
Callahan, Nora 26–27
Candles Burning 16, 74, 120–125
"The Cape" 165–166, 182
Captain Kirk 80
Caretakers 81–82, 84–90, 98–99, 111, 114, 121
Cargill, Angus 182
Carmody ("Thumbprint") 39–40
Carrie 12, 18, 72, 130, 136
Carroll, Eddie 152–154
Castle Rock 108, 114
Cavalier 25
Cell 116
Cemetery Dance Press 37, 138, 140
Chapin, J. C. 105
Charlie (*Gunpowder*) 136–138
Cheryl ("Nothing is in Bad Taste") 50–53
children 135–137, 147–148, 167, 170–171
"Children of Tomorrow" 13
Chopin, Kate 119
Christopher, David 98–101, 109–112
Christopher, India 88–89, 91, 100–101, 111–112
Christopher, Torrie 81, 84–90, 98, 109–112
Clackamas Literary Review 129
Claiborne, George 54–58
Clarke, Arthur C. 78, 134

Clarke, Dean 17
Clootie, Bernadette "Bernie" 118
Clootie, Junior 116–119
Coffey, John 97
"The Collaborators" 37, 129, 182
collecting 38, 159–160, 173–174
Coney Island Wonders 61
Conroy, Bobby 164–165
Correzente, Norma 24–25
Correzente, Vito 24–25
Coyne, Judas (Justin Cowzynski) 1, 172–176, 180
Creepshow 10
Cross, Nadine 94
Crowley, Aleister 173
Crowther, Peter 36–37
The Crying of Lot 49 86
"The Cure" 33–36, 49
Cutter (*Gunpowder*) 137–138
Cycle of the Werewolf 141

Dakin, Calley 74, 121–125
Dakin, Ford Carrol 121
Dakin, Joe Cane 121–123, 125
Dakin, Roberta Ann Carrol 121–122
Danse Macabre 23
"The Dark Man" 72
The Dark Tower 20, 29, 114, 135, 143, 147, 169, 182–183
Dawn of the Dead 164–165
"Dead Wood" 161
death 15, 17, 18, 20, 47–50, 52, 70, 74, 83–85, 88–89, 100–101, 110–111, 114, 116, 119, 121–122, 125, 138–140, 145–146, 156, 158–161, 163–164, 171–172, 179
DeLillo, Don 152
Denver Drovers 117
Desjardins, Gil 55–58
Detroit Tigers 102
deus ex machina 133, 164
"The Devil on the Staircase" 182
The Devil's Only Friend 126
The Devil's Wine 72
Dick, Philip K. 134
Dickenson, Pearl 88, 96–101, 103, 108–109, 113
"Djinn & Tonic" 29–30, 32–33, 184
"Donovan's Brain" 72
Douglass, Dorothy "Dolly" Hardesty 79–81
Dracula 170–171
The Drawing of the Three 25
Dreamcatcher 148
Duddits (*Dreamcatcher*) 148
"Duel" 16
"Dump on Vulgarity" 117
Dynah (*Survivor*) 118

Eckstein ("Wonders") 61–64
Edgecombe, Paul 97
Elaine (*Gunpowder*) 137
"Elegy for Ike" 72
Elena ("Scheherazade's Typewriter") 172
Eric ("The Cape") 166
Ernst, Dorothy 34–36
ethnicity 54, 61, 88, 96–97
The Eyes of the Dragon 10, 29

"Fadeaway" 16
Faithful 102
family 9, 18, 23, 31, 54, 63–64, 74, 91, 92–93, 98, 101, 104–105, 107, 109, 111, 119, 121, 132–133, 137–138, 140, 144, 146, 160, 162–164, 166–167, 171
"Fanboyz" 36–37
The Fear Tree 129, 130, 177
Federicci, Jimmy "Leatherneck" 65–66
Feltz, Ernie 162
Feltz, Homer 162
Finney, John 158–159
Firefight 92
Flagg, Randall 29, 94
"For Owen" 10
Frankenstein 82–83
"Freddie Wertham Goes to Hell" 37
"Frozen Animals" 46, 59–60, 65
"Fuck High School" 46

Gacy, John Wayne 173
Galesburg Grabber, The (Al) 158–159
Garin, Seth 148
Gary ("The Man in the Black Suit") 29
Gaunt, Leland 108
Gauthier, Deanie "The Mutant" 82, 102–107, 113
Gauthier, Judy 106
gender 15, 38–39, 54, 61, 67, 73, 83, 89, 96, 99–100, 104, 115, 127, 137–138, 149
Gent 25
Georgia ("Jude Confronts Global Warming") 130–131
Georgia (Marybeth Kimball and/or Morphine; *Heart-Shaped Box*) 175–176
Gerald's Game 10, 77
Gibbon, Francine "Frankie" 46–49
Gibbon, Roger 47–49
Gilchrist, Imogene 154–155, 157
The Godfather 25
Golden, Christopher 3, 128, 139, 140, 151–152, 170–171
Gore, Al 43, 53–57
Gothic 11–12, 14, 28–29, 31, 62, 74, 82–4, 121, 125, 127, 129, 144, 150–151, 154, 158–159, 165, 172–173, 175
"A Gradual Canticle for Augustine" 72

Gravity's Rainbow 35–36
The Green Mile 97
Greenan, Diane 116
Grennan, Mallory 38–40
Gretzky, Wayne 117
Gulf War 98
Gunpowder 129, 133–139, 167
The Gunslinger 14

Haggerty, Laura 109–110, 112–114
Halloran, Dick 97
Hanes, Wade 69–70
Hang the DJ 182
Hardesty, Michael 78
Harker, Jonathan 170
Harker, Mina 170
Harpur Palate 46
Harry Potter and the Half-Blood Prince 45
The Haunting of Hill House 138
Hawthorne, Nathaniel 28–29
Heart-Shaped Box 1, 13, 36, 128, 131, 149, 159, 172–176, 178, 180
Hillstrom, Joseph 54
Horns 1, 116, 130, 139, 149, 176–180
horror 12, 13, 23, 28, 46, 75, 83, 94, 121, 127, 130, 135, 139, 141, 150–153, 155, 158–159, 165, 173
The House on Maple Street 126
Houston, James 116, 118
humor 26, 32, 35, 37, 43–44, 46–47, 49–53, 56, 59, 65–70, 98, 118, 131, 159–160, 165, 175, 179, 185

"I Didn't Get Paid Enough" 75
"I Swear I'll Jump" 45–49, 51, 184
Implosion 37, 128
"In the Rundown" 161–162
Indiana Jones and the Kingdom of the Crystal Skull 134
Inside the Dark Tower Series 7
Iraq (war) 17, 39
It 86, 137, 148

Jackass 36
Jackson, Sheila 137
Jackson, Shirley 138
Jane Eyre 170
Jay ("The Blue Chair") 1, 30–31
The Jerry Springer Show 68, 118
Jesse ("My Second Wife") 1, 68
Jones, Stephen 38
Josie and Jack 46
Jude ("Jude Confronts Global Warming") 130–131
"Jude Confronts Global Warming" 37, 129–131, 140
"Jumper" 131

Kafka, Franz 156, 170
Kay, Francis 157–158
"The Killer" 131
Killian ("The Widow's Breakfast") 163–164
Kilrue, Peter 153
King, Naomi 5, 6, 10, 12, 13, 181
Kingdom Hospital 182
Knightriders 126
"Kodiak" 182
Koontz, Dean 151
Kosskoff ("Frozen Animals") 59–60
Kravitz, Heidi 32–33
Kravitz, Scott 32–33
Krimsky, Doris 70

"The Lady Rests" 37, 129, 182
"Last Breath" 127, 159–161, 184
Last Seen Leaving 46
Laughlin, Jackie 17–19
Leonard ("Nothing Is in Bad Taste") 52–53
Lerner, Morris 168–170
Lerner, Nolan 168–170
Lerner, Sam 144–149
Lillian ("Wonders") 61–63
Lisey's Story 52, 120
"Living with the Bogeyman" 13
Locke, Bode 144–147
Locke, Duncan 144, 147
Locke, Rendell 144–149
Locke, Tyler 145–146
Locke and Key 1, 13, 37, 139, 143–149, 167, 170
Loser's Club 137, 148
Lovecraft, H.P. 27
Lucas, George 177
Lunt, Joyce 112
Lunt, Sonny 112

The Magnificent Seven 20
Maine 14–15, 75–76, 79, 81, 83, 98, 102–103, 114–115, 132, 178
The Mammoth Book of Best New Horror 38
"The Man in the Black Suit" 23, 28–29, 32
"Man with a Belly" 23–27, 93
Mank, Isobel 123–125
Marley, Jacob 133
Márquez, Gabriel García 80
Mason, Bertha 170
Matheson, Richard 16
McDermott, Anna 175
McDermott, Craddock 1, 174–176
McDermott, Jessica *see* Price, Jessica McDermott

McDowell, Michael 16, 74, 170–175
McGlaughlin, Henry 54–58
McKenzie, Walter 91, 96
McNally, John 23–24, 46
McQueen, Steve 20
"The Meerkat" 69–70
Mellors, Kissy 98, 115–120
Melville, Herman 23
The Metamorphosis 157
Meyer, Stephenie 45, 186
Mid-Life Confidential 75, 141
Milton, John 176
Moore, Melinda 97
"Morality" 23, 26–27
Morrison, Toni 23, 117–118, 152, 185
Moth 72
"My Father's Mask" 165–168, 182
"My Second Wife" 1, 19–20, 46, 66–69

Nader, Ralph 56–57
Needful Things 108, 114
Nevars, Cora 87, 89, 111
Nevars, Joe 81–82, 84–91, 96
The New Dead 3, 128, 139–140
"The New York Times at Special Bargain Rates" 174
Nighswander, Rand 91, 93–95
Nighswander, Ricky 91, 93–95
9/11 37
1986 World Series 102
Nodd's Ridge 89–114
"Nonsong" 72
"Note I from Herodotus" 72
"Nothing is in Bad Taste" 45, 49–53

Oates, Joyce Carol 22, 152
O'Connor, Flannery 23
On Writing 72
O'Nan, Stewart 102
One Hundred Years of Solitude 86
One on One 82, 98, 101–109, 113–115, 126
One Thousand and One Nights 172

Palace Corbie 37, 128
Paradise Lost 176
"The Passion of Reverend Jimmy" 182
Paula ("My Second Wife") 68
Peaceful Ivan 69
Pearl 88, 96–101, 103, 108–111, 113
Pendergast, Virgil 68
Pendergast, Yolanda 68
Pennywise the Dancing Clown (*It*) 137
Perrish, Ignatius (also "Iggy" or "Ig") 1, 130, 176–180
Pinet ("Frozen Animals") 59–60
Pinocchio 127
Playing Like a Girl 75–76, 102

Poe, Edgar Allen 27
"Pop Art" 155–157, 165
Prashker, Ruth 116
Price, Jessica McDermott 175–176
Price, Reese 176
Prior, Eddie 168–170
Purple Girl 61
Puzo, Mario 25
Pynchon, Thomas 35–36, 86

"Quitters, Inc." 25

rape 24–25, 27, 85, 87, 93–96, 99, 106, 118, 178, 179
The Regulators 148
Rhys, Jean 170
The Road to the Dark Tower 141
Rolling Stones, The 177
Romero, George 126, 164
Roth, Arthur "Art" 155–156
Rowling, J.K. 186
Ruger, George 176
Russell, Olivia "Liv" 91–96
Russell, Pat 91–94
Russell, Sarah 91
Russell, Travis 91–92, 95
"Rustle" 37
Rutherford, Harriet 164–165

'Salem's Lot 26
Sartoris, Leighton 79
"The Saved" 129, 131–134, 163
"Scheherazade's Typewriter" 172
science fiction 29, 73, 76–83, 134–138
Scott, Jubal 131–134, 163
Seduction of the Innocent 37
sex 27, 31, 63, 68, 77, 80, 88–89, 93–94, 98–100, 103, 105–107, 109–112, 116–119, 175–176, 178–180
Shaw, Leyna 79–81
Shawshank (prison) 96
Shelley, Mary 82
The Shining 97
"Silence" 72
The Sky in the Water 126
Small World 19, 72–73, 75–81, 83, 93, 181
"Snake" 64–66
Song of Susannah 142
"Spit it Out!" 182
"Sports" 44–45
The Stand 29, 48, 94
"Stand by this Faith" 13
Stanley "Stan" ("My Second Wife") 1, 66–68
Star Trek 80
Star Wars 136, 177
The Stephen King Universe 140

Stoker, Bram 170, 177
Straub, Ben 10
Straub, Peter 10, 16
Styles, Frank 98
Styles, India 103
Styles, Karen 98–99
Styles, Reuben 86, 98–100, 103, 107–114
Styles, Sam "Sammy" 98, 102–107, 113, 126
Subterranean Press 37, 130, 131, 140
Sugar, Steven 55–58
Sullivan, Zack (Dodge, Echo, and/or Legion) 146–149
The Surrealist's Glass 176
Survivor 98–99, 115–121
"Sympathy for the Devil" 177

Tak (*The Regulators*) 143
The Talisman 16
Tan, Amy 75
Thinner 25
"Throttle" 16–19
"Thumbprint" 38–40
Tinker, Roger 78–81
Tony (*One on One*) 105–106
Tourneau, Lee 178–179
The Trap 85, 90–96, 98, 103, 113
The Tribe 17–19
Tweed, Gordy 91, 93, 95
20th Century Ghosts (collection) 13, 127–129, 131, 135, 140, 149–152, 180
"20th Century Ghost" (story) 154–155, 157
Twilight 45, 152
"Twittering from the Circus of the Dead" 3, 129, 139–140, 171
2000 Presidential Election 43, 53, 55–58

Under the Dome 94
Ur 142

Van Helsing, Abraham 170–171
Van Helsing, Maximillian "Max" 170–171
Van Helsing, Rudolph "Rudy" 170–171
Vietnam (war) 17, 92
Vincent, Bev 141
"Voluntary Committal" 165, 168–170, 182

Wayne ("My Second Wife") 66–68
Weiler, Nick 79, 81
We're All in this Together (collection) 45–46, 53–69
"We're All in this Together" (story) 35, 53–59, 76
Wertham, Frederic 37
Whedon, Elie 148
Whedon, Rufus 148
When I was a Loser 46
Who Can Save Us Now? 46, 69
"Who Made Who" 47
Wide Sargasso Sea 170
"The Widow's Breakfast" 161, 163–164
Williams, Merrin 178–179
Winston, Reverend George 26–27
The Wizard of Oz 96
Wolves of the Calla 20
"The Woman's Room" 182
"Wonders" 46, 59, 61–64, 67
"The Word Processor of the Gods" 149

"You Will Hear the Locust Sing" 156–158, 170
"Young Goodman Brown" 28

www.ingramcontent.com/pod-product-compliance
Ingram Content Group UK Ltd.
Pitfield, Milton Keynes, MK11 3LW, UK
UKHW021833140426
5217IPUK00021B/1431